When God Becomes History

Books by Bezalel Naor

Lights of Prophecy (1990)
Of Societies Perfect and Imperfect (1995)
Post-Sabbatian Sabbatianism (1999)
In the Desert a Vision (2000)
Kabbalah and the Holocaust (2001)
Bringing Down Dreams (2002)
Springtime of the World (2004)
From a Kabbalist's Diary (2005)
The Limit of Intellectual Freedom (2011)
The Kabbalah of Relation (2012)

When God Becomes History

Historical Essays of
Rabbi Abraham Isaac Hakohen Kook

Introduction, Translation, and Notes
by Bezalel Naor

Kodesh Press
5777/2016

When God Becomes History
Historical Essays of Rabbi Abraham Isaac Hakohen Kook
© Bezalel Naor 2016
978-1-947857-01-8
Hardcover edition

All rights reserved. Except for brief quotations in printed reviews, no part of this publication may be reproduced, stored in a retrieval system, or transmitted in any form or by any means (printed, written, photocopied, visual electronic, audio, or otherwise) without the prior permission of the publisher.

The Publisher extends its gratitude to Rabbi Yeshayahu Ginsburg for his help with this project.

This text has been slightly modified, including the addition of passages omitted from Rav Kook's letter to Aderet, on pp. 234-236 (April 2017), and an addendum concerning the relation of Rabbi Samson of Sens to Maimonides, on p. 233 (October 2017).

Published & Distributed by
Kodesh Press L.L.C.
New York, NY
www.KodeshPress.com
kodeshpress@gmail.com

Table of Contents

Introduction to the Second Edition (2016) 11
Introduction to the First Edition (2003) 17

The Lamentation in Jerusalem (*Ha-Misped bi-Yerushalayim*) . . 21
(Eulogy for Dr. Theodor Herzl, 1904) 38
Letter of Rav Kook to Rabbi Elijah David Rabinowitz-Te'omim . . 51
Death of a Messiah 57

The Way of Renascence (*"Derekh ha-Tehiyah," Ha-Nir,* 5669/1909) . 61
Letter of Rav Kook to Rabbi Dov Milstein 78
Letter of Rav Kook to Elhanan Kalmanson,
    Author of *Sinai and Golgotha* 81

To the Process of Ideas in Israel
    (*"Le-Mahalakh ha-Ide'ot be-Yisrael," Ha-'Ivri,* 5762/1912) . . 83
Eder ha-Yekar / 'Ikvei ha-Tson / Shabbat ha-Arets 113
Letter of Rabbi Zevi Yehudah Hakohen Kook 118

To the Two Houses of Israel (*"Li-Shnei Batei Yisrael,"*
    Mizrah u-Ma'arav, 5680/1920) 125

Address at the Opening of Hebrew
    University in Jerusalem (1925) 139
Letter of Rav Kook to Rabbi I. Kosovsky of Volkovisk, Lithuania . 146
Letter of Rav Kook to Rabbi Joseph Messas of Tlemcen, Algeria . 149
Letter of Rav Kook to Professor Abraham Fraenkel 151
Rabbi Ezekiel Sarna on Rav Kook 152
Letter of Rabbi Isaac Hutner to Rabbi Moses Zevi Neriyah . 153

Appendices
Maimonides on the Origins of Christianity 155
Rav Kook on Buddhism 157
Response to the Author of *Nitel u-Me'or'otav* 163

Notes 166

Passages Omitted from Rav Kook's Letter to Aderet 234

Bibliography 237
Index of Primary Sources 251
Index of Subjects 256
Index of Names 260

In Israel, God was revealed as the worker of history and its planter

— Rabbi Abraham Isaac Hakohen Kook,
'Ikvei ha-Tson, p. 147

Introduction to the Second Edition of *When God Becomes History*

The world order of Rav Kook's time was vastly different from our own. In Rav Kook's day, Christianity posed a threat to Judaism and Rav Kook did theological battle with the Church. Today, the Church is considerably less threatening, theologically and otherwise. In our present reality, the challenge to Judaism comes not from Christianity but from Islam. As opposed to the attention Rav Kook lavished on Christianity, his thoughts on Islam, by comparison, are few and far between.[1]

*

In the years since this collection of historical essays first appeared, the world of Kookian studies has been taken by surprise with the revelation of the full-length book *Li-Nevukhei ha-Dor* (*For the Perplexed of the Generation*),[2] Rav Kook's updated version of Maimonides' *Moreh Nevukhim* (*Guide of the Perplexed*). Written in Boisk (Bauska, Latvia), before his 'aliyah to Erets Israel in 1904, that work is optimistic and conciliatory toward the other faith communities in a way unseen in Rav Kook's later writings. The tone of the work is set by the following salvo:

> *There are others who hold that it is not possible for a person to have perfect faith in the Torah of Moses, unless one thinks that all the other faiths are vain and foolish, and of no benefit to their adherents. And this thing is without truth.*[3]

In *Li-Nevukhei ha-Dor*, it is apparent that Rav Kook is intent on establishing a common meeting ground with every other inhabitant of this planet, whether Christian, Muslim or pagan. And in order to start the conversation, Rav Kook is willing to concede points in a manner that may come to many of us as a shock. He knows how much leeway Judaism allows for these delicate negotiations and he pushes to the limits. If Christians are committed to Jesus as an exemplar of lovingkindness, then Judaism can abide that—as long as there results no deification of the man.[4] And if Muslims demand that Muhammad be recognized as a prophet, then based on Maimonides' hierarchy of prophecy, Jews can recognize Muhammad as fulfilling the requirements of the first of the eleven degrees of prophecy, "that an individual receives a divine help that moves and activates him to a great, righteous, and important action—such as the deliverance of a community of virtuous people from a community of wicked people, etc."[5] What is non-negotiable is supersessionist or replacement theology:

> *The opinion rooted in the literature of those religions—Christianity and Islam—that the value of Israel is already void, God forbid—must cease to exist.*[6]

As stated, this extremely conciliatory tone was not sounded again in the writings penned after Rav Kook's arrival in Erets Yisrael. The impact of *Li-Nevukhei ha-Dor* has left students of Rav Kook reeling from "cognitive dissonance." It is safe to assume that for many years hence, scholars will thrash out this question: Which work reflects the true(r) opinion of Rav Kook, the earlier or the later?[7]

*

Readers will no doubt welcome the additional essay, "To the Two Houses of Israel," an example of intellectual history, wherein Rav Kook explores the different receptions of the Talmud in the Sephardic and Ashkenazic communities, and how those respective methodologies produced mindsets that linger into the modern period.

*

I wish to thank Rabbi Alec Goldstein of Kodesh Press for shouldering the responsibility of re-issuing the collection, and for his patience and understanding throughout the process.

And thanks to Rabbi Ari D. Kahn for the "*tivvukh*."

Finally, it behooves me to thank a friend I shall refer to as "HaYehudi HaKadosh." He appeared to me as a beacon of light in a dark night. Without his constant inspiration, this book would not have happened.

BN
26th Day of the 'Omer, 5776

Notes to Introduction to Second Edition

1. See Karma Ben Johanan, "Wreaking Judgment on Mount Esau: Christianity in R. Kook's Thought," *Jewish Quarterly Review*, Vol. 106, No. 1 (Winter 2016), p. 95, n. 93.
2. Rabbi Avraham Yitshak Hakohen Kook, *Li-Nevukhei ha-Dor*, ed. Rabbi Shahar Rahmani (Tel-Aviv: Yedi'ot Aharonot, 2014). The book was given that title by the editor, not the author.
3. Ibid. beginning chap. 14a (p. 99).
4. "If [the pagans] attribute divinity to a man who so much wanted to benefit many people, and succeeded in some matters—such a brilliant light could not otherwise be received in the heart of peoples predisposed to idolatry. Only in this manner could the ethical goodness be of influence. But when [the pagans] evolve more, they will recognize that the glory of God is too exalted to be attributed to a man, even if he should be extremely desirous of the love of good" (*Li-Nevukhei ha-Dor*, chap. 39a [p. 197]).
5. Moses Maimonides, *The Guide of the Perplexed*, trans. Shlomo Pines (Chicago: University of Chicago Press, 1964), II, 45 (p. 396); *Li-Nevukhei ha-Dor*, chap. 39a (p. 197), and earlier chap. 8 (p. 56).
6 Ibid.
7. See Aryeh Sklar, "'Lovers of Humanity': Rav Kook, Christianity, and the Ongoing Censorship of His Writings," *Kol Hamevaser: The Jewish Thought Magazine of the Yeshiva University Student Body*, March 22, 2015.

I brought to the attention of the author, Aryeh Sklar that he misread a passage from my Introduction to *Orot*, creating the exact opposite effect. According to the article,

> Naor himself points out that the controversy surrounding Rav Kook's writings had such an effect on Rav Kook's son that in 1924, prior to the publishing of Rav Kook's *Orot HaTeshuvah*, R. Tzvi Yehudah Kook begged his father to be more careful in his writings. "For God's sake," he writes, "be exacting that nothing is issued which is not thoroughly explained."

What I actually wrote is the following:

> "In a practical vein, the lesson Rav Kook learned from the *Orot* incident was not to print ideas that were not fully elucidated. The publishing of his philosophic *oeuvre* would continue undaunted, but caution would not be thrown to the winds. Concerning the forthcoming publication of *Orot ha-Teshuvah* (1924), R. Zevi Yehudah was advised: 'For God's sake, be exacting that nothing is issued which is not thoroughly explained. Examine this with your straight intellect and consult with my intimate friend, the Gaon R. Ya'akov Moshe Harlap (may he live).'" (*Orot*, trans. Naor [Northvale, NJ: Jason Aronson, 1993], p. 60)

The passage occurs in a letter from Rav Kook to his family in Erets Yisrael. The letter is datelined: "Tuesday, 28 Adar Rishon, Trieste." That would have been in 1924, when Rav Kook was *en route* to New York for a fund-raising mission. The letter (#1225) was published in *Igrot ha-RAYaH*, vol. 4 (1984), p. 186.

Thus, it was not Rabbi Zevi Yehudah Kook who advised his father to be most exacting and precise in the process of publishing, but rather Rav Kook who demanded this of his son!

Introduction to the First Edition (2003)

Rabbi Abraham Isaac Hakohen Kook was, to use the rabbinic term, an *eshkol—ish she-hakol bo*, "a man who contained all." He excelled in diverse areas such as philosophy and poetry, law and mysticism. As is often the case when dealing with a polymath, one or more of the individual's strengths go unnoticed. The present collection comes to address a specific lacuna: Rav Kook as historian, or perhaps better said, as historiosoph.[1] (Rabbi Shim'on Starelitz, who was an eminent disciple of Rav Kook and who died an untimely death, coined the term *historiosofia di-mehemnuta*, "historiosophy of faith," to describe his master's philosophy of history.)[2] Men whom Rav Kook greatly admired—Rabbi Judah Löw (MaHaRaL) of Prague, Rabbi Moses Hayyim Luzzatto (RaMHaL), and Rabbi Zadok Hakohen of Lublin—have received the recognition they deserve in this realm. But Rav Kook has yet to receive his due in tracing the "hand of God" in history. Like the earlier anthology *Lights of Prophecy*, it is hoped that this collection too will be a step in that direction.

    A general word of introduction needs to be said about the essays contained herein. If Rav Kook takes the reader on a *tour de force* of recorded history, it is always to nudge him back to the present. And for Rav Kook, the present meant the challenge of Zionism and the State on its way. Throughout our history, our great leaders have always taken up the challenges of their time. For Maimonides, it was Aristotelian philosophy; for Rav Kook, it was Zionism. In essay after essay, he grapples with different dimensions of this new phenomenon. Sometimes his categories of thought seem to us outlandish: situating Herzl in the line of "Messiah son of Joseph," or placing the anathematic Jesus of Nazareth on the side of the famous or infamous charismatics of Jewish history, for example. But always Rav Kook is fresh and original. One may agree or disagree with his proclamations; one may question the wisdom of appearing at a memorial gathering for Theodor Herzl or at the opening of the campus of Hebrew University. Our differences with him, both philosophical and tactical, should not undermine our respect for him as a true *gaon* and *tsaddik*, genius and saint. Many of the points heatedly debated between the covers of this book will continue to be "hotpoints" for many years to come.

As for myself, perhaps the reader will be surprised to learn that during my years in Jerusalem I was befriended by men on both sides of the barricades. My earliest acquaintance was with Rabbi Zevi Yehudah Hakohen Kook zt"l, only son and spiritual heir of the Chief Rabbi. Later, I would make the acquaintance of Rabbi Barukh Naeh zt"l and—*yibadel le-hayyim tovim*—Rabbi Shelomo Fisher. The fathers of the latter two, Rabbis Abraham Hayyim Naeh zt"l and Aaron Fisher zt"l, were intimate associates of Rav Kook's antagonist, the saintly Rabbi Joseph Hayyim Sonnenfeld zt"l, rabbi of the secessionist *'Edah Haredit* of Jerusalem. If my first love was and continues to be Rav Kook, I am not impervious to the sparks of holiness and genius in the opposite camp. Rav Kook himself wrote of his critics:

> Those who stand back from, or oppose all the activities that bring about the revealed redemption—they too are deemed

meritorious. That is because through their demands, the content of the redemptive activity is clarified, becoming purer, more illuminating, more vital, more truly Israelite, drawing ever more from the source of pure life that wells up from the source of Israel, from the spring issuing from the House of the Lord.[3]

BN
Tishri, 5763

The Lamentation in Jerusalem

On the twentieth of Tammuz, 5664 (July 3, 1904), Dr. Theodor (Benjamin Ze'ev) Herzl, founder of the Zionist movement, died at the tragically young age of forty-four. Abraham Isaac Kook, the newly installed rabbi of the port city of Jaffa, was asked to participate in a memorial service to honor the departed leader. Rav Kook was placed in a difficult situation for which there was no totally satisfactory solution.

On the one hand, the Halakha is quite specific when it comes to those who have deviated from the norms of Torah:

> Whoever secedes from the way of the community, namely persons who throw off the yoke of commandments from upon their neck, and do not participate with the Jewish People in their observances, in honoring the festivals, and sitting in the synagogue and study house, but rather are free to themselves as the other nations, and so too the apostates and informers—for none of these persons does one mourn. Rather, their brothers and other relatives wear white [festive garments] and eat and drink, and make merry.[4]

However one might lionize Herzl, there was no getting away from the fact that his lifestyle was that of an assimilated Jew far from observance of traditional Judaism. If one were to adhere literally to the passage in *Shulhan 'Arukh*, the customary *hesped* or eulogy for the deceased would be out of the question.

On the other hand, Rav Kook knew his flock. If in Jaffa itself Rav Kook might find a few individuals capable of relating to the halakhic objection to memorializing a declaredly secular Jew, in Rehovot and the other outlying settler communities, Herzl, with his patriarchal beard and searing eyes, was regarded as nothing less than a modern-day "prophet." And Rav Kook had been engaged not only as rabbi of Jaffa, but of the recently established *moshavot* (colonies) as well.

The last thing Rav Kook wanted was renewed bickering, or what is worse, full-blown controversy. Rav Kook, who had arrived in Jaffa from Europe not quite two months earlier (on the twenty-eighth of Iyyar), was familiar with what had preceded him. Jaffa, not unlike the rest of Erets Israel, was a community with a history of controversy.

Undoubtedly, Rav Kook was not the only rabbinic leader sitting on the horns of a dilemma as to how to react to Herzl's untimely passing. Varied reactions to Herzl's death have come down to us in anecdote.

In Brisk (Brest-Litovsk), the renowned Rabbi Hayyim Halevi Soloveitchik ordered the doors of the great synagogue locked to prevent a memorial service for Herzl. Dov Ze'ev Begin (father of the future Prime Minister of Israel, Menachem Begin), an ardent Zionist and secretary of the *kehillah*, took an axe and broke down the door to hold a sparsely attended memorial service.[5]

In nearby Pruzany (today Belarus), a Jew stormed into the home of the rabbi, Elijah Halevi Feinstein, known as "Reb Elya Pruzhaner."[6] "Rabbi, something worse than the destruction of the Holy Temple has occurred!" Reb Elya was hard-pressed to imagine what might possibly cast a more somber shadow than that calamitous event. "Herzl has died!" Reb Elya, not known to be a friend of the Zionist movement, was taken aback. His sharp-witted daughter Pesha, who happened to be present at the time, remarked, "The fact that a Jew should think so, is truly more tragic than the destruction of the Holy Temple." She went on to chide her father and his fellow rabbinic luminaries for failing to assume leadership of the movement for return to Zion. Into the vacuum created by lack of responsible rabbinic leadership, so she claimed, stepped Herzl and his cronies.[7]

In Gur (Gora Kalwaria), Poland, the following exchange took place. A hasid walked into the studyhouse announcing Herzl's death. Another hasid shot back, "*M'zoll ihm begroben*" ("We should bury him").[8]

While Herzl yet lived, he met with mixed rabbinic response. At one end of the political spectrum, the venerable Rabbi Shelomo Hakohen, *dayyan* (chief justice) of Vilna (Vilnius), bestowed the priestly blessing on Herzl at a reception in honor of the visiting dignitary.[9] At the other end of the spectrum, the influential Rebbe of Lubavitch, Shalom Dov Baer Schneersohn, wrote a position paper in which he clinched that Zionism was a movement of unholy, satanic origin by the fact that Herzl publicly desecrated the Sabbath by traveling on that day in Jerusalem. This supposedly proved that Herzl's source of inspiration was from the Other Side, because even the most assimilated Jew would be seized with fear of God in the Holy City.[10] And then there were all the bands of the spectrum in between. Herzl himself, in his memoirs, recounts how he made overtures to two scions of the famed Ruzhin dynasty of Galicia, Rabbi Israel Friedmann of Sadagura (?-5667/1906) and his uncle Rabbi David

Moses Friedmann of Czortkow (5587/1827-5664/1903).[11] Herzl does not reveal what, if any, response he received.

The solution Rav Kook arrived at was the following. He would speak at the memorial gathering but at no time would he mention Dr. Herzl by name. Instead, he would speak in generalities. As it turned out, Rav Kook's non-eulogy for Herzl is without doubt one of the most inspired and profound *hespedim* ever! The address operates on many levels simultaneously—Biblical, Talmudic, kabbalistic—as well as responding to the contemporary maelstrom of Jewish life.

Unfortunately, as Rav Kook pointed out in one of his many halakhic decisions, whenever a rabbi grants a permission with a proviso, the proviso is soon forgotten, while the permission lingers for a long time. The same applies to Rav Kook's memorial address. The exact details he conveyed were soon forgotten (if ever they were properly understood), whereas the very fact that he spoke at the memorial gathering for Herzl would continue to haunt him to the end of his rabbinic career. Years later, Rabbi Isaac Jeruham Diskin of Jerusalem threw up to Samuel Kook that his older brother had eulogized Herzl.[12] (Not that Rabbi Diskin was living in Erets Israel in the year 1904; he arrived on the scene some years later.)[13]

The same holds true for Rav Kook's address at the opening of the Mount Scopus campus of Hebrew University in Jerusalem in 1925. Again, the content of Rav Kook's speech (in this case, a scathing critique of those elements in Jewry who are unselective in their intake of "Greek wisdom") was conveniently forgotten. What continues to this day to hang as a cloud over Rav Kook's reputation is the fact that he spoke at all on such an occasion!

The memorial gathering for Herzl took place a week after his passing, on the twenty-seventh of Tammuz. Two days later, on the twenty-ninth of Tammuz, we find Rav Kook justifying his behavior to his saintly father-in-law Elijah David Rabinowitz-Teomim (ADeReT), the assistant Ashkenazic Rabbi of Jerusalem (second to Rabbi Samuel Salant). We can only guess what prompted the reply. Evidently, Rabbi Rabinowitz had heard some disturbing things concerning the comportment of his recently arrived son-in-law.[14] (By the way, Rabbi Rabinowitz's behind-the-scene negotiations were instrumental in procuring the rabbinic position in Jaffa.)[15] His call for clarification was answered with a lengthy and eloquent response. In the letter, Rav Kook lays out his strategy for achieving rapprochement between the Old and New Yishuv as they were called, and his philosophy of outreach to alienated brethren. Certain remarks of Rav Kook are reminiscent of the Hasidic way in general and that of Braslav in particular. In his inimitable poetic style, Rabbi Nahman of Braslav, who has been referred to as the "genius of Hasidism," wrote:

> Even though rebuke is a great thing, and it is incumbent on every Jew to rebuke his friend when he sees that he is not acting properly, as it says, *You shall surely rebuke your companion*[16]—not all people are fit to offer rebuke. As Rabbi Akiva said, "I wonder if in this generation there is one capable of rebuking."[17] If Rabbi Akiva had doubts concerning his generation, how much more so the present generation! When the preacher is not worthy, not only will his admonition be of no avail, it will even bring out a "bad odor" from the souls of the listeners. Through his rebuke, he arouses the bad odor of the evil deeds and character traits of the people he reprimands. When a flask containing a malodorous substance is left inert, the bad odor is imperceptible. But when the flask is disturbed, the bad odor is perceived. By the same token, through the

rebuke of one who is unworthy, there is agitated and aroused the bad odor of the evil deeds and traits of the wrongdoers. In this way, he weakens their souls, cutting off the flow from all the worlds dependent on these souls.... Conversely, when the preacher is worthy, he enhances the good odor in the souls he ministers to.... This is the food of the soul.[18]

Though we might not be in total agreement with Rav Kook's attempted solution of the problem, at least we must credit him with consistency. Six years later, the Jaffa community would celebrate the fiftieth birthday of Herzl. Once again, Rav Kook advocated participation in the function. He explained to a questioning principal why the Tahkemoni School in Jaffa (under the auspices of the Orthodox Mizrachi movement) was dutybound to participate in the celebration.

With the help of God
Jaffa, Iyyar 5670/1910

Dear Mr. Schlesinger, Principal
Tahkemoni School

Shalom!
In reply to his respected query regarding participation in the celebration of Herzl's birthday, I must respectfully inform that it is impossible for us to increase schism, and it is imperative that our school participate as the others. Of course, they [the organizers] must inform us ahead of time of the program—and I ask that his honor forward it to us—so

that we can ascertain that it will not consist of anything in violation of holy Torah law.

With honor and holy blessing,
Abraham Isaac Hakohen Kook[19]

*

This leads to a broader question: What was Rav Kook's outlook on the Zionist movement in general? Today, it has become almost a byword that Rav Kook was politically naïve. Actually, we are now in possession of documents that show otherwise. The late Dr. Yitzhak Raphael published from the Archives of Religious Zionism at Yad Harav Maimon what was intended to be a circular to rabbis. For some unknown reason, Rav Kook decided at the last moment to "squash" the paper. The open letter to the "rabbis of Israel," preserved in Rav Kook's own hand, clearly outlines Rav Kook's thoughts concerning the Zionist movement. It goes on for several pages. Many of the statements will come as a shock to those who stereotype Rav Kook as a "Zionist."

> From the day Zionism began to resound in our camp, opinions concerning the movement have divided into three groups. (This applies also to the reception of Zionism among God-fearing Jews, observers of Torah and commandments.) We shall scan ever so briefly each of these approaches. There is no movement without its assets and liabilities, and Zionism is no exception to that rule. This ambiguity perforce produces mixed reviews. Those who focus on Zionism's strengths

become staunch admirers; those who focus on her foibles (whether inherent or coincidental) turn into sworn enemies. The economic and political advantages or disadvantages of Zionism are not our concern at the moment. Our remarks are limited to the results that Zionism has produced among our people—especially our youth who have become involved in the movement—as regards our Torah, our faith, which is our life. It is only for the sake of Torah that our fathers' blood was shed as water and that we yet survive in Exile.

Before we delve into the causes, let us examine the facts. True, Zionism influenced positively our national sentiment. If not for the awakening of Zionism, many of our children would have wandered far from their people. Put in the harshest terms, Jews who otherwise would have converted and assimilated among the nations have returned to us, taking up once again their Jewish identity. However, when it comes to the authentic Jewish spirit, to our faith and our religion, to practical observance of our Torah—which has kept us alive for so long and which will keep us alive in the future as well—what do we see from Zionism? It is incontrovertible that the vision is bitter and the causes deplorable.

One cause for this phenomenon is that the members of the organization who as a result of Zionism have recently reentered the Jewish camp, are men whose lifestyle is alien to Torah. Our children who join the movement learn from their ways. As a result, there is increasing "unyoking" from religion and Torah.

As a nationalist movement, Zionism produced literary talents. Who are these writers? Their education was corrupted long ago when negation of Torah and commandments was the vogue of the Haskalah movement. (Then too the writer might have arrived at these dangerous notions himself or through teachers and books that influenced him.) Those writers breathed into Zionism a spirit of delirium, tying the success of the Zionist enterprise to uprooting of Torah and her laws.

This in turn influenced the Zionist preachers. They take the material for their speeches from the Zionist literature. Their talks, which are specious, reflect their root. The branches add to the damage. By the time these ideas, which are the distillation of bad opinions and outright heresy, reach the ears of the masses, the result is readily discernible: desecration of all that is holy, corruption of the morals of the youth, and throwing off the yoke of Torah and commandments on a frightful scale.

The libraries established in our cities by the Zionist movement are mostly supplied with the new literature. A great portion of the books are written in a spirit pernicious to faith and holy sentiment. At risk are the morals of young readers who choose an extremely destructive path. The effect is insidious. In the opinion of the youth, these "evil waters" flow from the source of Zionism, because they are imbibed in a house of culture established by the movement. Is it any wonder then that destruction of faith and religion proceed in step with the spread of Zionism?

What is the cure for this malady? As we alluded to above, three schools of thought have emerged. One way is to muster the strength to eradicate Zionism. Many great [rabbis] hold that this is the simplest way to be spared the spiritual tragedy that time has proven results from the Zionist movement. If this approach were productive, many would rally to it. What good are all the advantages Zionism could conceivably produce if it will result in lessening the light of our life; if it will darken the sun of our souls? It is as if one tells a donkey, "Carry this *kur* [a measure] of barley, and we will cut off your head." Add to this the fact that the benefits promised by Zionism are considered by many doubtful and far off in the distant future, while the deleterious results, the extinguishing of the holy fire of faith, more precious than anything else, is tangible and immediate.

Unfortunately, we see that this approach [of the anti-Zionist rabbis] has not produced the desired effect, especially in the case of our youth, for whose spiritual survival we are obligated to sacrifice ourselves. In this age, nationalist aspiration is great in the world at large and specifically in our people. The reason for the latter is that truly nationalism is deeply rooted in the Jewish soul. Since Zionism pulls at these heartstrings, it is impossible to hold back the young generation that goes with the *Zeitgeist*. Since the force opposed to Zionism cannot hold back this current, it is inevitable that anti-Zionism too become destructive. It too contributed to the overall destruction. From the antagonism which did not appeal to the heart of the generation, came out the curse of *hutspah* (brazenness) that drags the honor of Torah through the mud and takes up the weapon of humiliating Torah scholars. This alone is enough to breed moral maladies, and to enlarge the territory of atheism.

The second approach is the opposite of the first. It claims that every God-fearing Jew who desires the betterment of our people and the upliftment of Torah and faith, must join the Zionist circle, widen and strengthen it. The thinking goes that when there will be many religious Zionists, Zionism itself will bestow only good on Torah and faith. These words do not fit the facts. At the present time, we see religious anarchy proliferating; to our chagrin, within Zionism no energy is expended to foster religious sentiment and faith, all the more so to regulate observance of Torah and commandments. Many of the leaders of the movement and their followers show by their lifestyle that they have no desire for religious observance. Effortlessly, by sheer example, Zionism weakens our religion and our faith. Zionist writers add misgivings. Zionist emissaries heap abuse upon religious life. The best of the lot accept this awful state of affairs with equanimity. So how can we strengthen a movement that visibly uproots and destroys the delight of our eyes? Can we rely on wishful thinking that in the future our position [within the movement] will be strengthened? Is it not more reasonable to fear that the very energies we contribute will be coopted by those intent on destroying religion? ...

The third approach finds succor in a division of tasks. They reason that our people are divided into orthodox and freethinkers. As long as their participation in the Zionist movement is mixed, the influence of the freethinkers pervades. Their solution? Setting up an orthodox society. Such thinking produced of late the "Mizrachi" movement. But neither is Mizrachi a comprehensive solution. In the long run, we are still adding to the strength of the central Zionist movement. We are still not impervious to the influence of the freethinkers. The writers and literature continue on their way. Now that the movement has been divided, most of the members will opt for the destruction of Torah and faith. Now that they encounter only people of similar dispositions, their demands will become even more outrageous. Seeing that the orthodox and the freethinkers are alike in their work for Zion, and that the unabashed religious renegade is counted as a "Zionist," what will save the children of the Mizrachists from the evil influence of a Zionism that is religiously anarchist? The Mizrachi approach did not succeed in softening the blow of Zionism any more than the previous approaches. In every city we see a terrible sight. Wherever Zionism established a chapter, religion is in shambles. Our eyes see and suffer.[20]

A man capable or painting in such vivid hues the devastation wrought by the burgeoning Zionist movement and its emissaries, can hardly be described as politically naïve! Again, one may disagree with Rav Kook's stance vis-à-vis Zionism, but labeling him "politically naive" will not do.

In his missive, Rav Kook advocates a fourth, radically new approach, namely revealing the root of Jewish nationalism in the divine soul of the Jew. Religion and Zionism cannot be pulled apart; they are inextricably bound. He spells out in no uncertain terms that the very thought of establishing a Jewish state without regard to religious observance constitutes a blatant denial of Torah:

If a Jew holds the opinion... that nevertheless it is possible to succeed in settling Erets Israel—is this not outright denial of the Torah? The *berit* [covenant] that governs our national and political success was made contingent on observance of the Torah.[21]

Rav Kook goes on to show that historically, throughout time, national renascence was always inextricably bound up with spiritual awakening:

> From the days of Moses and Joshua, David and Solomon... the days of Hezekiah, Ezra and Nehemiah, later the Maccabees.... Did not their courage and national fervor flow together with their personal sanctity and their fidelity to our religious faith? Throughout this exile, what gave us the strength to stand up to the waves of the sea that came pounding down on us, if not the force of our faith? How will we possibly survive without the strength of faith and the light of religion? We never attempted it. Never was there such a state of affairs; neither will there be in the future.[22]

The reader who knows Rav Kook only as "'the rabbi of the Zionists" will be equally surprised to learn that in an early essay published in the anti-Zionist journal *Ha-Peless*, Rav Kook was thoroughly understanding of (if not in agreement with) the antagonism to Zionism of many of his religious contemporaries:

> Because of the propaganda of the heretics, to the chagrin of all true patriots, it was forbidden to recite the Ten Commandments in public.[23] Woe! The Ten Commandments, our pride and glory in the eyes of the nations! But what could

we do? It was because of the propaganda of the heretics who claimed there is no Torah other than the Ten Commandments.

The greatest of the sages of Israel [Rabbi Eliezer] adjured, "Keep your children away from *higayon*."[24] And RaSHI explains, "Do not accustom them overly much to Bible." Woe, Bible! Bible, the breath of our nostrils, the words of the Living God. How is it possible to say *Enough!* to the source of good and light? But what could we do? We were left no choice on account of the propaganda of the sectarians who say there is no Torah but the Written Torah.

Because of the propaganda of the heretics, haters of Torah and commandments, who are far from understanding to what extent the power of Torah is the life force of our people, and who are unwilling to recognize that service of the Lord and prayer at the ruins of Jerusalem and Mount Zion, the focus of Israel's eyes and heart, are also considered national necessities—because of the propaganda of these freethinkers who ridicule her Sabbaths,[25] many lovers of Zion have refrained from being counted among the Hovevei Zion,[26] and the "love of Zion" has gone down from its glory in many hearts of the faithful of our people. Woe, Zion! Zion, my beautiful beloved! What shall I do for you? The propaganda of the heretics forces me to turn my eyes from you.

Because of the propaganda of the sectarians, the new Zionism becomes increasingly ugly. Because of the propaganda of those who are brazenfaced and haughtily declare the delight of Israel forever is finished; those who throw a shoe at Torah and faith, and the beauty of holiness—because of the propaganda of these, Zionism lost many fresh talents. The hearts pine, all long for Zion, for the awesome place,[27] for the place upon which our eyes and hearts are trained, for our cradle, our birthplace. But woe! A snake is curled about the ankle.[28] A dragon is wound about the barrel of honey.[29] Philosophies poison the hearts of our youth and stop up their moral sensibilities. These have already swallowed up the holy, and produced thorns and thistles in the furrows of the Zionist idea. So, "Stay away from Zionism!" A voice cries to us, "Keep clear of Zionism!"[30]

Rav Kook does not go along with this thinking, but the very understanding that he demonstrates for the religious anti-Zionist mindset should alert the reader to the fact that Rav Kook is a complex individual not readily pigeonholed in one of the conventional stereotypes.[31]

The Anti-Eulogy

Rav Kook's address pivots on a cryptic prophecy in Zechariah concerning a future lamentation that is likened to "the lamentation of Hadadrimmon in the valley of Megiddon." The Aramaic Targum of Jonathan ben Uzziel reveals that this is actually the conflation of two different events, the lamentation for King Ahab of the Northern Kingdom of Israel, killed by Hadadrimmon (in Ramot Gil'ad), and the lamentation for King Josiah of the Southern Kingdom of Judah killed (by Pharaoh Necho) in the valley of Megiddo.

Let us leave the similes aside for a moment. Whose death is Zechariah prophesying? The Talmud interprets it as the murder of Messiah son of Joseph. What has all this to do with the expiration of Dr. Theodor Herzl? Certainly Rav Kook did not entertain the notion that Herzl was Messiah son of Joseph.[32] To what was he alluding?

The notion of two Messiahs, Messiah son of Joseph followed by Messiah son of David, is very ancient. From a passing reference in the Talmud,[33] the theory assumes epic proportions in the Kabbalah.

The *Zohar* envisioned an especially somber outcome for Messiah son of Joseph. Not only would he be killed, but he would be desecrated and assimilated among the nations for the sin of Jeroboam son of Nebat, an earlier descendant of Joseph who worshiped idols. Due to Moses' intervention, Messiah son of Joseph would be spared this doubly tragic fate. Thus did the *Zohar* read the verse in Isaiah 53:5, "He was wounded [*mehullal*] for our transgressions." *Mehullal* was interpreted as meaning "desecrated" rather than "wounded."[34]

In Rabbi Moses Hayyim Luzzatto's understanding of the passage in *Zohar*, Jeroboam himself was destined to be Messiah son of Joseph. At the time of his sin, the holy soul which was within him departed from his midst. Luzzatto launches into an involved discussion of the subtle distinction between the soul of Messiah (which is to say Messiah *in potentia*) and the realized Messiah.[35] The writings of Luzzatto are full of references to the "two Messiahs" (*trein meshihin*).[36] The same goes for the writings of the Vilna Gaon.[37] In a work by a disciple of the Gaon, Rabbi Hillel Rivlin of Shklov, we find clearly enunciated the idea that Messiah son of Joseph is the power that holds up the material end, while Messiah son of David keeps up the spiritual end of Israel.[38]

There is another coordinate to Rav Kook's thought. This is the fact that *Zion* and *Joseph* share the same numerical value (156). According to some commentators, this is implicit in the sweeping statement of the *Midrash Tanhuma*, "Whatever befell Joseph, [later] befell Zion."[39] By a simple computation, "Zionism" is "Josephism." The founder of the Zionist movement might aptly be described as the ʿikva de-Mashiah ben Yosef (heel or footstep of Messiah son of Joseph). By situating Herzl within this Josephic tradition, Rav Kook was not declaring him Messiah son of Joseph, but rather a forerunner or predecessor (ʿikva in the sense of "footstep") or rather a downgraded version or a vestige (ʿikva in the sense of "heel")[40] of Messiah son of Joseph.

In the aftermath of World War One, Rav Kook would attempt—unsuccessfully—to launch a movement parallel to Zionism, which he called "Jerusalem," alternately *Histadrut Yerushalayim* (the Jerusalem Organization) and *Degel Yerushalayim* (Banner of Jerusalem).[41] In the literature of the abortive movement, Rav Kook would explain that "Zion" represents the material aspect of the redemption, while "Jerusalem" represents the spiritual side.[42] This is in keeping with the idea expressed in *The Lamentation in Jerusalem* that Zionism is within the tragic tradition of Messiah son of Joseph. The implication is that a parallel "Jerusalemite" movement will take up the work of Messiah son of David.

The Lamentation in Jerusalem

On the death of Dr. Theodor Herzl
The twentieth of Tammuz, 5664/1904

On that day the lamentation will be great in Jerusalem, like the lamentation of Hadadrimmon in the valley of Megiddon.[43]

The sages said that Jonathan ben Uzziel translated the Prophets into Aramaic and the Land of Israel trembled for an area of four hundred parasangs by four hundred parasangs.[44] The reason for the disturbance was that contained in the Prophets are things which are not explicit but veiled, namely this verse. As Rav Yosef said, "Were it not for its Aramaic translation, I would not know to what the verse refers."[45] The Sages report that Jonathan ben Uzziel stood up on his feet and declared: "It is I who revealed Your mysteries to men. He who said and the world came into being, knows full well that I did [this] neither for my honor nor for the honor of my father's house, but only that controversy not proliferate in Israel."[46]

We should inquire what was the veiled reference contained in this verse that was revealed by Jonathan's paraphrase, "Like the lamentation for Ahab son of ʻOmri who was killed by Hadadrimmon son of Tabrimmon in Ramot Gilʻad, and like the lamentation for Josiah son of Amon killed by Pharaoh Necho in the valley of Megiddo." Furthermore, how did revelation of this divine mystery prevent proliferation of controversy?

Now our sages said that this lamentation will be for Messiah son of Joseph who is killed.[47] The entire concept of two Messiahs, Messiah son of Joseph and Messiah son of David, requires explanation. Why the need for two Messiahs, when the goal is to have one man preside over the entire Jewish nation? As it says, "And David My servant shall be prince unto them forever."[48]

*

[The key to understanding this dichotomy lies in examining the individual human being.] God created in man a body and a soul, and corresponding to them, forces that strengthen and develop the body, as well as forces that strengthen and cultivate the soul. Ultimate wholeness is achieved when the body is strong and well developed, and the soul, vital and cultivated, leads all the faculties of the body in the service of the intellect, which is God's will in His world. So on the collective level of Israel, God ordained these two faculties: a faculty corresponding to the physical entity, that aspires to material improvement of the nation,[49] and a second facet devoted to the cultivation of spirituality. By virtue of the first aspect, Israel is comparable to all the nations of the world. It is by dint of the second aspect that Israel is unique, as it says: "The Lord leads it alone"[50]; "Behold a people that shall dwell alone and not be reckoned among the nations."[51] It is the Torah and unique sanctity of Israel that distinguish it from the nations.

Originally, these two faculties were assigned to the two tribes destined to rule Israel, Ephraim and Judah, which is another way of saying Joseph and Judah. "The deeds of the fathers are a sign to the sons."[52] Just as in the beginning, Joseph was the provider sent by God to save many from starvation[53]; who sustained Jacob and his sons materially when they came to Egypt looking for grain [so in future generations, the descendants of Joseph would develop the material side of Jewish national existence]. Joseph is paradigmatic in other ways as well: Joseph was swallowed up by the nations.[54] He was also fluent in seventy languages.[55] This last point symbolizes the contiguity between Israel and all the nations of the world.

Despite this, Joseph knew the power of his holiness. It is for this reason that "Esau succumbs only to the children of Rachel [i.e. Joseph]."[56] As the adage goes, "The ax handle that fells the forest is made of wood."[57]

Judah, on the other hand, symbolizes that which is distinctive about the Jewish People: "Judah became His sanctified one."[58] Whereas of Joseph the Psalmist says, "Shiloh, a tent pitched among men."[59]

*

The purpose of choosing the kingdom of David was that these two faculties be integrated, that they not cancel, but rather reinforce one another. We find an interesting comment of the Midrash regarding the person of David. David was "of ruddy complexion," just as Esau was "ruddy," the difference being that David had "beautiful eyes," symbolizing that he would execute only with the permission of the Sanhedrin [Supreme Court].[60] Written large, David's kingdom should have been the collection of the material powers necessary for a great and mighty kingdom, coupled with spiritual excellence. Unfortunately, sins brought about that Israel rejected the Davidic dynasty, whereby the nation was divided in two: The ten tribes that seceded were subsumed under Ephraim (which is in reality Joseph), and the two tribes that remained were subsumed under Judah. Were it not for this split, all would have been united under the "tree of Judah."[61] The Psalmist gave expression to this vision of unity: "He will subdue peoples under us, and nations under our feet. He will choose for us our inheritance, the excellence of Jacob which He loves. Selah."[62] By gathering together these two powers, both would benefit: The material would be rarefied and sanctified by its exposure to the unique sanctity of Israel, and the spiritual would be invigorated to enhance Israel. Eventually, the rays would light up the entire world. This will be the case in the future: "And it shall happen on that day, that the root of Jesse, who shall stand as an ensign of the peoples, to him shall nations inquire; and his resting place shall be glorious."[63] No longer shall there be war between two factions but rather complete peace. That is the greatest honor.

But it was not to last. Our sins brought about the division of the kingdom, and these two powers that should have been united, developed each in its own way, oblivious to its companion. Due to our many sins, both of the faculties were greatly damaged.

The kingdom of Ephraim [the Northern Kingdom] founded by Jeroboam, who was appointed by Solomon over the task force of Joseph in appreciation of his practical talent,[64] turned its back on Israel's unique sanctity. "And Me you have thrown behind your back."[65] This was the source of the sin of idolatry, that developed in time into Israel's ongoing aping of the nations' negative traits. At its nadir it was said, "Ephraim is assimilated among the peoples; Ephraim is a cake readily devoured."[66]

Judah, deprived of the material side that enlivens, was in need of a spiritual supplement to replace the missing material aspect. Unable to rise to the occasion, the spiritual power was also ruined. "Judah too shall stumble with them."[67] "For Jerusalem stumbled and Judah fell, because their tongue and their deeds are against the Lord, to provoke the eyes of His glory."[68]

Even after the separation, the wound might have healed, had the two sides realized that though each has its own propensity, they might benefit one another. Judah could receive from Ephraim ways to round the nation in terms material and universal; Ephraim could imbibe from Judah the ways of holiness unique to Israel, be they Torah, character development, or prophetic ability.

The political reality made no such allowance. Were this mutual cooperation to come about, the dominant side would have been the spiritual, for it is the soul that vivifies the body. This is precisely what Jeroboam did not wish to occur. Our wise men summed it up in anecdote:

> The Holy One grabbed Jeroboam by his garment and said to him, "Repent, and I and you and the son of Jesse will stroll together in the Garden of Eden."
> Jeroboam asked, "Who will lead?"
> The Holy One replied, "The son of Jesse will lead."
> Sniffed Jeroboam, "If so, I am not interested."[69]

God offered that together David and Jeroboam could bring the Jewish People to its goal of a nation consecrated to the Lord, God of Israel, while worthy of being a light to the nations. There would be room within the overall structure for the universalist dimension [represented by Jeroboam's kingdom]. But to the question—"Who is at the helm?"—

the answer must be, "The son of Jesse is at the helm." Without the recognition of the supremacy of the spiritual side—"For the portion of the Lord is His people; Jacob is the lot of His inheritance"[70] —heaven forfend, Israel's destiny would be lost. Israel is the smallest among the nations, and God forbid, the most likely to disappear. Jeroboam's ego stood in the way. "If so, I am not interested." This set into motion a long chain of calamities, culminating in Israel's exile until the End of Days.

*

So it came about that throughout the Exile there is a seesaw effect of these two opposing forces. At times, there is exhibited a drive toward material, worldly success that flows primarily from the foundation of Joseph and Ephraim; other times there is a stirring of the drive for observance of Torah and spiritual development; for awe and love of God.

"As when one cuts and chops wood upon the earth, our bones are scattered at the mouth of the grave."[71] [There is wanting] the power that could emcompass and unify the diverse workers into a single foundation, so that each might influence, and be influenced by, the other; the power to unify the leadership with accentuation of the spiritual side, to the point that it vivifies the body politic the way the soul enlivens the body.

Since it is impossible for our nation to attain its lofty destiny other than by actualizing these two components—the universalist symbolized by Joseph, and the particularist symbolized by Judah[72] —there arise in the nation proponents of each aspect. Those who would enhance spirituality, prepare the way for Messiah son of David, whose focus is the final destiny. Truly the focus of life is spiritual attainment, except that the spiritual can only develop properly if it is accompanied by all the material acquisitions of which a full-bodied nation is in need. Those who redress the material, general aspects of life, prepare the way for Messiah son of Joseph.[73]

When these two forces work at cross purposes as a result of the calamity of exile, shortsightedness and disarray, these are the "birthpangs of Messiah," or to be more exact, the "birthpangs of Messiahs" (plural). The Psalmist writes: "That Your enemies have defied, O Lord; that they have defied the footsteps of Your Messiahs."[74] Two footsteps of two Messiahs.

Now since the major achievement of Messiah son of Joseph, which is the general advancement of mankind, is accomplished by de-emphasis of the unique Jewish form, Messiah son of Joseph cannot endure, so he is destined to be killed.[75]

*

When this happens, all will recognize the perversity of the situation. They will realize that it was wrong not to subjugate the universal dimension to the spiritual aspect which is Israel's destiny; to the Messianism of the Messiah son of David.

They will lament him as one laments an only son, and grieve for him as one grieves for the firstborn son.[76] The lamentation for an only child is bereft of hope for future children. Elderly parents who have lost their only son are totally forlorn. If the verse were to end on that note, it would spell utter doom, but the bitterness is mitigated by intellect. Intellect perceives that the nation has produced the soul of the Messiahs. The nation is not as elderly parents who have lost their only child, but rather as young parents who have lost their firstborn child. Being inexperienced at raising children, they did not attend properly to the child in its state of illness, so the child succumbed.

By the same token, the nation comes to the realization that it did not know how to make proper use of this universalist dimension; did not understand how it could contribute to Israel's unique destiny. In that way, it could have survived. The nation labored under the illusion brought on by the divisiveness of exile that these two forces are truly at odds. The result is that whoever holds up the universal side of the nation becomes, unfortunately, an enemy of Torah and *mitsvot* (commandments). Contrariwise, whoever focuses on the uniquely Jewish, becomes an adversary of material wellbeing. In the first scenario, the fence of Torah is broken down; in the second, the result is weakness and morosity.

After this latest experience of Messiah son of Joseph's impermanence, let us deduce that truly the two forces are not mutually antagonistic. It is time to bring it all together and to organize the nation's ways. Let every universal perfection serve as a basis for perfecting the uniquely Israelite. Let both parties—those disposed to the material and universal, and those disposed to the spiritual and particular—come to the same conclusion.

Then the lamentation will be on both sides; both will recognize their mistake. These two forces were created to be united; once rent asunder, they were mutually injurious.

*

The quality of love of nation[77] was exemplified by Ahab. He had such love of Israel! He followed in the ways of his father 'Omri, who added a city to Israel.⁷⁸ Even when pierced through by an arrow [and mortally wounded, Ahab stood up in his chariot]. Ahab kept up the pretense, so that Israel not be demoralized [by the loss of their commander].⁷⁹ For this reason, he was assured the World to Come. "*Mine is Gilʻad*—This refers to Ahab who fell in Gilʻad."⁸⁰ Such courage comes from a wonderful love. Ahab even accorded respect to the Torah (because the honor of the nation depends upon it) at least when it came to external affairs, namely dealing with Ben-Hadad [King of Aram].⁸¹ Nevertheless, he did not recognize the value of Torah and its unique divine sanctity which is the advantage of Israel. Thus he followed in the ways of Izebel and the pagan rites practiced by the contemporary nations.

At the other end, Josiah strengthened the spiritual dimension. In this respect, he was unequaled among kings. "Before him there was no king who so returned to the Lord with all his heart, soul, and might."⁸² He would brook no linking of Israel to the nations. This reached an extreme in his refusal to accede to Jeremiah's prophetic demand that he allow the army of Egypt to enter Israel's territory.⁸³

Clearly, in Ahab and Josiah there found expression the two forces of Joseph and Judah, or put differently, Messiah son of Joseph and Messiah son of David. Once this distortion—whereby the nation failed to make proper use of the energies revealed in the gifted few—is removed, at the End of Days the realization is reached that it is possible to unite these two powers. So the lamentation is a double lamentation for both Ahab and Josiah together. As great as the distance separating them in actuality, so will be their closeness and interdependence. [The purpose of the lamentation is to learn from the mistakes of the past in order to rectify things] toward the future; to study how to integrate the powers into a unified system that contributes to the general welfare.

THE LAMENTATION IN JERUSALEM

*

Now the truth is, as long as the nation is fractured and incapable of uniting the powers, at times an attempt at unification will actually result in some theological or moral damage. This deep separation is the source of controversy in Israel. That to which the prophet Zechariah only alluded, Jonathan ben Uzziel paraphrased in Aramaic and made manifest, whereupon the Land of Israel shook for an area of four hundred square parasangs. In a generation unprepared for uniting these two tendencies, bringing them together produces a "short circuit." Undaunted, Jonathan ben Uzziel declared, "It is known to You that I did this neither for my glory nor for the glory of my father's house but only that controversy not proliferate in Israel." Through the door of intellect lies the way to unify these two resources, both of which are indispensable. Solutions must be found.

*

The Zionist vision manifest in our generation might best be symbolized as the "footstep of Messiah son of Joseph" (*'ikva de-Mashiah ben Yosef*). Zionism tends to universalism [as opposed to Jewish particularism]. It is unequipped to realize that the development of Israel's general aspect is but the foundation for Israel's singularity. The leadership of the Zionist movement must be greatly influenced by the gifted few of the generation, the righteous and the sages of Torah. On the other hand, the ideal of Israel's national renascence, including all the material accouterment—which is a proper thing when joined to the spiritual goal—to date has not succeeded, and the lack of success has brought on infighting, until finally, the leader of the movement has fallen, a victim of frustration.[84]

It behooves us to take to heart; to try to unify the "tree of Joseph" and the "tree of Judah"[85]; to rejoice in the desire for healthy material[86] life beating in the collective nation; and to know that this is not the end goal of Israel, but only a preparation. If this preparation will not submit to the spiritual aspect; if it will not aspire to it, then it is of no more value than the kingdom of Ephraim, "a cake readily devoured,"[87] because "they abandoned the source of living waters,"[88] and "Egypt did they call hither, to Assyria did they go."[89]

This is the benefit to be gained by remorse over one whom we might consider the "footstep of Messiah son of Joseph" (*'ikva de-Mashiah ben Yosef*), in view of his influence in revitalizing the nation materially and generally. This power should not be abandoned despite the wantonness and hatred of Torah that results in the expulsion of God-fearing Jews from the movement. We must develop the courage to seek that any power that is of itself good, be fortified, and if it is lacking spiritual perfection, let us strive to increase the light of knowledge and fear of the Lord such that it [i.e. the light] is capable of conquering a powerful life-force and of being built up through it. Then there will be fulfilled in us the prophecy, "I will grant unto Zion salvation, unto Israel My glory."[90]

Return (*teshuvah*) must be from our side. Return will be enduring only if all the powers presently found (and possible to be found) in the nation will be vigorous, and directed to good. Then we will be a vessel for the divine will, "a crown of ornament in the hand of the Lord, and a royal diadem in the palm of your God."[91]

*

Rav Yosef, who said that he penetrated the meaning of the verse [in Zechariah] only through its Aramaic translation, willingly accepted upon himself to witness the "birthpangs of Messiah." When other sages said, "Let him [Messiah] come, and may I not see him," it was Rav Yosef who said, "Let him come, and may I merit to sit in the shadow of the dung of his donkey!"[92]

The other sages were daunted by the intensity of the spiritual birthpangs that would perforce result from the pressing demands to fortify the material side that had been neglected in the course of the exile. Exile came primarily to preserve and enhance the spiritual, "to close up the transgression, and to make an end of sins."[93]

The shadow of the dung of his donkey. By a double entendre, the word *hamoreh* ("his donkey") refers to the material (*homer*). Customarily, devotion to the material affairs of the nation obscures and prevents spiritual ascent. Even so, if this movement would not be so audacious as to spread in a way unbecoming Israel, it would be easy to accept. But the "dung of the donkey" is difficult to accept.[94] Were it not for its extremism, the movement would not find oppressive the spirit of the Torah, and it would not attack the foundation of Torah, which is tantamount to "blinding the eye of the world."[95] But the *dung*, the gross tendencies that are loathsome to all peoples, produces a shadow that dims the pure intellectual lights flowing from the source of Torah.

Nonetheless, Rav Yosef was confident that eventually all these negative manifestations would surrender to the light of Torah and the knowledge of God. Rav Yosef will sit in the shadow of the dung of Messiah's donkey. In the very midst of the darkness, of the shadow, "rendering like night in the midst of the noonday,"[96] Rav Yosef will light the candle of the commandment and the light of Torah, and a little light dispels much darkness. The evil will be transformed into good, the curse into blessing.

This is the import of the cryptic passage in the *Zohar*:

> The Head of the Academy in the palace of Messiah said, "Whoever does not transform darkness to light and bitterness to sweetness, may not enter here."[97]

The prerequisite for the generation of Messiah is the ability to utilize all forces, even the most coarse, for the sake of good and the singular sanctity with which Israel were crowned.

(*Ma'amrei ha-RAYaH*, vol. 1 [Jerusalem, 5740/1980], pp. 94-99)

Letter of Rav Kook to Rabbi Elijah David Rabinowitz-Te'omim (ADeReT)

With the help of God
Jaffa, 29 Tammuz, 5664/1904

From between the straits lights shall shine.[98]

To my beloved teacher, my father-in-law, the Gaon, the glory of Israel, Rabbi Elijah David, may he live lengthy, good days, and all the dear members of his household, may they live, and my daughter Batya, may she live lengthy, good days.

Because of my burden leading the people of God, God bless them, I am not always able to satiate my thirst to write long, frequent letters to his honor, may he live, the joy of my heart and the treasure of my soul. In addition, these days I have been fatigued by events that have reinforced that which I knew beforehand: How difficult it is to go in the good and straight way of God purely for His name's sake and His love, especially in a place where there is a history of quarrels and various controversies that kindle anger, which is the case (due to our many sins) in the Holy Land in general, and in the holy city of Jerusalem specifically. Though I am aware of the severity of the situation, heaven forfend that I deviate from the way paved for us by our sages of blessed memory, the way of Torah: "Be of the disciples of Aaron, a lover of peace and a pursuer of peace, a lover of humanity and one who brings them closer to Torah."[99] This is the path I have chosen since youth, and thank God, through it I still see blessed results. May God grant me the merit to increase strength in days to come for good. I already expressed in *Ha-Peless* my opinion concerning the way to relate to the demands of the hour.[100] The honor of the divine name and the honor of Torah will be upheld not by shouts and quarrels, nor by banishment of whoever is found in the least blemished, but rather through words of pleasantness that appeal to reason, drawing them with ropes of love and cords of humanity.[101]

Now there came to me two gentlemen... and requested me... since they were planning to gather in the bank building here to honor the memory of Doctor Herzl and it was their finding that even those opposed to Zionism would not deny that there were in his heart thoughts concerning the betterment of Israel. Though unfortunately he did not find the straight path, nevertheless, "The Holy One does not withhold credit for even good talk."[102] It would be poor manners not to arrange a memorial in his honor in a public meeting place such as the Anglo-Palestine Bank here. Therefore I promised them I would attend.

Understandably, once I agreed to come, I did not want to refuse to speak there some words. I assessed that, God willing, benefit would derive from my words, inasmuch as the other speakers would not have the audacity to belittle God, His Torah, and the sages of Israel. Thank God, this assessment proved correct. Of course, I spoke pleasantly and politely, but I did reveal the fundamental failure of their [the Zionists'] entire enterprise, namely the fact that they do not place at the top of their list of priorities the sanctity of God and His great name, which is the power that enables Israel to survive. The sages employed the parable of a key and a long chain.[103] On the other hand, it is incumbent on the God-fearing to relate lovingly and peaceably to all who wish to do good for Israel, be it only in a material sense. One must draw such an individual to the good way of God, not by some vague remark intended to hinder him from his deed, but rather through some directed remark that demands coming closer to the name of God and His holy Torah. Then it is possible that all the powers presently being utilized for evil will be channeled for good. I humbly submit that this is one of the great mysteries alluded to in the *Zohar, Bereshit*, that the Head of the Academy in the palace of Messiah announced, "Whoever does not transform darkness to light and bitterness to sweetness, has no place here."[104] In other words, the redemption will be brought about only by attempting to transform the evil powers into good. We must not push the bad away. It is conceivable that they are evil because of extenuating circumstances. They have been influenced negatively and are not totally to blame. *How can we push a stone down after one who is falling?*[105]

Thank God, I see tangible results. When I came to Rehovot, due to our many sins, I found the youth there corrupted as far as their opinions, and one may assume the same goes for their deeds. I did not reject them but rather drew them close. I spoke before them words of wisdom and good reason from which they understood at least in a general way how the light of Torah dispels all the shadows of darkness and wickedness of evil opinions that in our many sins have proliferated in this day and age. The talk had a great effect on them in drawing them closer to the love of Torah. It was reported that the Sabbath following my stay they did not shave, though my talk contained not the slightest hint of practical reproach, but rather remained on a general level. I am confident that once the divine spark of love of God and His true awe has entered the heart, it will effect through a divine power much more than would be accomplished if we forced it in, using duress. Even more than is visible on the tangible level, there is a *tikkun* (fixing) of the emotion of the heart, which is the main thing.

Now if I would have turned my back on them [the residents of Jaffa who requested Rav Kook's presence at the memorial assembly for Dr. Herzl—BN], God forbid this would have brought about a situation in which the rabbinate would have absolutely no influence on the townspeople, the majority of whom are followers of Zionism. This is especially true of the inhabitants of the *moshavot* [colonies, such as nearby Rehovot]. How could I possibly desert many souls, the holy people in the Holy Land? Our eyes are turned to them to settle our holy soil. If I were to do so, the result would be, God forbid, that afterward admonishment or guidance would be of no avail. The main thing about guidance is that it hinges on the love relation between the guide and his protégés. And all of this I should do purely for imagined honor, so that persons unacquainted with my good thoughts for God and His Torah will not belittle me! Heaven forfend that I should entertain such an invalid option. I trust in God's lovingkindess. He knows my heart and my entire striving, and how bitter it is for me to befriend even for a moment empty people far from Torah and fear [of God]. But all of this and a lot more than this, we must bear and endure for the sake of the sanctity of His blessed name and for the love and glory of Israel—though it may mean inestimable spiritual torture.

God forbid that we conclude through "common sense" that any person whose deeds or opinions are tarnished is already outside the bounds of "brotherhood," and that therefore we are no longer responsible for his soul, or even more extreme, that we might turn on him as an enemy and attack him. This approach is absolutely wrong. We are not permitted to accept such reasoning from any man. In the case of something so exaggerated that it is beyond the realm of Halakha, our sages remarked, "Were Joshua son of Nun to tell it to me with his own mouth, I would not accept it."[106]

In this generation which is so confused and divided, if those Torah scholars who, thank God, have acquired fame, will not recognize their own impact, but rather will allow themselves to be deterred from seeking the welfare and improvement of Israel, by any hothead, God only knows where this will lead. Verily, one must deliberate how to lead on each occasion, but heaven forfend that one stand on one's own honor. Our only purpose should be the increase of heaven's honor (*kevod shamayim*), with an eye to Israel's return (*teshuvah*), which can be brought about only by the goodly ways of Torah scholars, by the "string of love" extended to them in the merit of the Torah.[107] Let not the slightest *tikkun* (fixing) be small in our eyes. A small beginning can end in great things. If we will do that which we are able, God will finish for us.

In summation, I could not have acted otherwise. All who truly fear God must give me the benefit of the doubt. If one has decided to transgress the positive commandment, "Judge justly your companion," we have no responsibility to pay heed to his words and dreams, being as he desires to block the way to peace in Israel and Torah outreach. Given that, I could not prevent a eulogy being held in the Talmud Torah. This too would have produced great controversy and eternal enmity.

In my remarks, I offered no homage to Dr. Herzl *per se*. What I did say was that such a thought of improving the situation of Israel in Erets Israel would be worthwhile if we would rise to the occasion. It would require return to God by observing and honoring the Torah, and a consensus that the foundation of all must be the power of Torah. Repenting of baseless hatred, and wholehearted peace-seeking as obligated [by Torah] would result in success because it would be close to God's will. We must make amends toward the future that the power of the sanctity of Torah be at the top of our list of priorities, that "the son of Jesse be at the lead."[108] If the will to improve materially will rest on Torah—then the Lord will shine His face upon us and crown our every deed with success. At first, the salvation will be gradual, as our holy rabbis remarked upon witnessing daybreak over the valley of Arbel,[109] but after it will gain momentum, appearing as a great and wondrous light, as in the days of our exodus from Egypt.[110]

After [the address], others came to me and reported that some read into my words ideas I never intended.... By using good reason and character traits, we will accomplish more than with shouting and curses, God forbid. What am I to do if there are some who consider such proper remarks as, God forbid, "justification of the wicked"? I trust in the Lord that all God-fearing people will recognize that the way of peace is the true way of God. It is in this way we will succeed. Especially at this time, we need to strengthen the way of peace. The Lord will show us salvation. His salvation is close to those who fear Him.

His son-in-law who loves him as his son,

Abraham Isaac Hakohen Kook

(***Ginzei RAYaH***, vol. 3 [n.p.: Makhon RZYH Kook, n.d.], pp. 16-18)

Death of a Messiah

This short piece is especially poignant in this so-called era of post-Zionism. Picking up where he left off in *The Lamentation in Jerusalem*, Rav Kook foresees a day when the nationalism symbolized by Messiah son of Joseph will be superseded by a new age of universalism ushered in by Messiah son of David. Humans will evolve beyond the provincial concerns of the nation to embrace the family of man. Even an ego as large as an entire people will still be considered narrow by Messianic standards. However, the center of David's Messianic map will be Jerusalem, just as the center of Joseph's Messianic map was Zion. This centerpoint is not exclusive of the world but rather an ideal focal point to surrounding humanity.

Perhaps the most eloquent statement of Rav Kook's universalism is his famous *Quatrain (Shir Meruba')*:

I

There is one who sings the Song of the Soul, and in his soul he finds all, full spiritual satisfaction.

II

And there is one who sings the Song of the Nation. He goes out of the circle of his individual soul, which he finds lacking breadth.... He aspires to mighty heights and cleaves to the totality of K'nesset Israel. He sings with her her song, shares in her suffering, delights in her hopes, contemplates her past and future, and investigates lovingly the inner content of her spirit.

III

And there is one whose soul broadens so that it extends beyond the border of Israel, to sing the Song of Man. His spirit encompasses the totality of man and his majestic image. He aspires to mankind's collective destiny and longs for its perfection. From this living source, he draws his thoughts and research, his ambitions and visions.

IV

And there is one who broadens even beyond that, until he unites with all existence, with all creations, with all worlds. With all of them he utters song.

And there is one who ascends with all these songs together in one bond. They all lift their voices and harmonize. The Song of the Soul, the Song of the Nation, the Song of Man, and the Song of the World, all combine in his midst constantly.[111]

THE LAMENTATION IN JERUSALEM

*

In Messiah son of Joseph there manifests the quality of Israel's nationalism per se. However, the final goal is not nationalism itself, but rather the aspiration to unite all the inhabitants of the world in one family, "that they may all call on the name of the Lord."[112] This too requires a special center, nevertheless the purpose is not the center but its effect on broad humanity. When the time comes for the world to pass from the stage of nationalism to universalism, concomitantly there results a sort of destruction of elements rooted in narrow nationalism, which carries with it the fault of egoism. Therefore in the future, Messiah son of Joseph will be killed; a lasting, enduring kingdom will be [that of] Messiah son of David. When the amount of longing for the general welfare reaches the point of abolishment of particular nationalism, it will be just one more step before evil is eradicated from the lives of individuals.

What we find is that the eradication of the evil impulse and the murder of Messiah son of Joseph are conceptually related. Therefore, our sages were divided concerning the verse in Zechariah, *They will look to Me for the one whom they have thrust through*, whether it refers to Messiah son of Joseph who is killed, or to the Evil Inclination that is "killed."[113]

(*Orot* [Jerusalem: Mossad Harav Kook, 5710/1950], p. 160; *Kevatsim mi-Khetav Yad Kodsho*, ed. Boaz Ofen, vol. 1 [Jerusalem, 2006], *Pinkas Aharon be-Boisk*, par. 5 [p. 37])

The Way of Renascence

Like the other essays in this collection, this piece too touches on some aspect of Zionism. Zionism came with a certain allure. It unleashed psychic energies that had long lain dormant. During its collective exile, the Jewish nation focused on Torah study to the exclusion of other dimensions of humanity. In the past, outbursts of repressed psychic energy were associated with false Messiahs: Jesus, Shabbetai Zevi, Jacob Frank, to name the most notorious. The Gaon of Vilna, Rabbi Elijah, feared that Hasidism was but one more pseudo-Messianic episode. According to one chronicler, Rabbi Menahem Mendel Schneersohn of Lubavitch, author of *Zemah Zedek*, is said to have been grateful to the Gaon for reining in the antinomian elements within the nascent hasidic movement.[114] The question underlying Rav Kook's essay is: Will Zionism too, with the enormous psychic energies it tapped, prove but the latest in a series of bouts of pseudo-Messianism? Or will Zionism be able to make its peace with the cerebral aspect of Judaism, with the forces of Torah and Halakha? The verdict is not in yet.

This is without doubt one of Rav Kook's most brilliant essays. With masterful strokes, he paints a picture of Jewish history oscillating back and forth between the two antipodes of reason and charisma. The spirit of man forever wavers between these two poles, producing a historical dialectic.

The essay briefly touches upon such distinguished charismatics as Rabbi Akiva and the Ba'al Shem Tov, and a few dredged from the rogue's gallery of Judaism: Jesus, Shabbetai Zevi, and Jacob Frank. The opposition of the Vilna Gaon to the Hasidism of the Ba'al Shem Tov is famous. But Rav Kook finds in Simon the Amsonite's disagreement with Rabbi Akiva a hint of reservations concerning this earlier charismatic approach. By the same token, Rav Kook might have cited Rabbi Yohanan son of Tortha's chiding of Rabbi Akiva when confronted with the latter's endorsement of Bar Kokhba as Messiah: "Akiva, grass will grow in your cheeks before the Messiah will arrive!"[115]

Rav Kook's brief remarks concerning Jesus were taken out of context by his enemies.[116] In a subsequent letter to Rabbi Dov Milstein, Rav Kook clarifies that it was not his intention to laud *oto ha-ish* ("that man"). Actually, it seems that Rav Kook's portrayal of Jesus as a charismatic lacking formal learning occurs already in a medieval polemical work, *Kelimat ha-Goyim* by Profiat Duran.[117] Unfortunately, to this day, the ugly lie that Rav Kook harbored some positive affect for Christianity continues to circulate in certain circles. (See Appendix C.) It is poignant that many years after he penned these ill-fated words, Rav Kook shared with Elhanan Kalmanson, author of the book *Sinai and Golgotha*, his disapproval of some modern Jewish writers who write positively of Jesus.

THE WAY OF RENASCENCE

*

It is impossible to recognize spiritual existence per se through research and investigation. Knowledge, rational inquiry, philosophy note only the outer signs of life. Even when they delve into the inwardness of life, they see only the shadow of life, not what lies within. The strength of rational demonstration is only in paving a way for the spirit to approach the outer vestibule—of sensing spiritual existence. However, as long as man is sunk in his senses and their narrow confines, he will never know spiritual existence, only gossamer shadows. And if he treats the shadows as if they are the true reality, then those shadows will become so burdensome to him, diminishing both his material and spiritual power, that he will seek to flee them as one flees from harm. Yet as much as man will flee from the shadow, the shadow will pursue him. There is but one recipe for being rid of the shadow and that is—shedding light.

The illumination can come about only by gaining access to the interior, the essence of spiritual existence, but there is no psychic means to accomplish this other than the "deepest height"[118] of the sense of divine faith. This is the knowledge beyond knowledge, the intuition beyond intuition that connects the spiritual existence of man, grounded in fact, with the supernal spiritual existence, and mixes man's life with life that is beyond borders and removed of all physical infirmity.

The concrete psychology of the individual, with its currents, mixes with the general psyche through its channels—the spiritual heroes and treasures of the collective psyche—and leaves an imprint on groups, families, peoples, species, worlds, eternities, and existence. The beauty and pleasure seep down from the loveliness of spiritual existence to the most minute particles—that are separated from the universe only by subjective filters that evaporate as morning clouds with the appearance of the strong sun of universal objectivity—engulfing every cell of spirit and soul.

The psyche of existence is revealed in the rare sight of the giants of history, who through their personalities revolutionized whole worlds, erased lines that were written in stone, and carved in their place other lines, stronger and more beautiful. These giants changed the face of humanity, or of portions of humanity, who then impacted on the totality.

The existential psyche that is found in fact and releases a plethora of energy—not the silhouette, the shadow image captured by superficial science or even in-depth study—is revealed only in the titans of the world, girded round with the might of God, who have learned to navigate the great sea of the life of faith.

However, scientific culture, based on tangible knowledge and the senses, and the rational ethics that follow from them, prepare mankind to absorb the flow of light of the general spiritual psyche. When that happens, the cultural direction of the intellect, the senses, and material ethics, receives much strength and a divine arrangement that is both penetrating and enduring. If on the other hand, the flow of light arrives without the prior preparation of intellectual culture and ordinary morality, this light will produce only darkness.

The result of the spiritual existential light bursting upon unprepared soil was the murky aspect of paganism, which in turn, brought illusions and very evil inclinations. To this day, mankind has not purified itself of these sour grapes. Even today, civilization has not reached the point where the divine sympathy of pure good may rest in the depths of the soul of the collective organs. Therefore, the divine connection that is in their midst is a strange god, a foreign god, a caricature possessing bizarre qualities. Up to the very present, we witness in these collectives signs of wickedness and despotism, while the essence of morality gradually departs from their heart.

Despite this, there is salvation for mankind in *K'nesset Israel* (Ecclesia Israel), in whose inner orbit is found the divine sympathy. Feeling attests and understanding clarifies that the one and only God of the Universe is pure good, life, light, exalted above all, better than all good, good to all and His mercy is upon all His works, vivifying all and safeguarding all, and raising salvation for all. The general sympathy penetrates not only the individuals of the [Israelite] nation but especially its totality. If at times the nation forgot its soul, the source of its life, the gift of prophecy reminded her, and descent into exile straightened her out, until eventually, the divine sympathy of absolute good will win out.

It would be a fundamental error to abjure our superiority, to repudiate our chosenness by God. Not only are we different from all peoples, set apart by our historical experience which is unique in the annals of nations, but we are better and greater than other peoples. If we know our greatness, then we know ourselves; if we forget our greatness, we forget ourselves, and a people that forgets itself is certainly small and lowly.

Our way—the life of the nation and its interaction with broad humanity—is very long. Our life is long and therefore our way is long. We are great and great are our errors, and therefore great are our misfortunes, but equally great are our consolations!

K'nesset Israel (Ecclesia Israel) longs to influence through its psyche, to bring closer the great day when the influence of existential spirituality—which in the past sowed its seeds on untilled soil and gave rise to thorns and thistles that cause pain—will find a plowed furrow, "And many peoples and mighty nations shall come seeking the Lord of Hosts in Jerusalem... and they shall take hold of the skirt of a Judean man, saying: We will go with you for we have heard that God is with you."[119]

Then mankind will no longer be satisfied with dry grains of human investigations and mortal computations whose axioms are weak and misleading, but rather will provide space for a mighty psychic influence, the spirit of the Living God. "Righteousness and justice are the foundation of His throne; kindness and truth precede His presence."[120]

When there is a tradition or heritage of moral and intellectual refinement, it is possible for psychic illumination from the world above—from the essential spiritual existence—to penetrate the individual or community; it is possible for it to be ensconced in a governmental infrastructure that is the epitome of social morality. The result of this illumination will far surpass synthetic civilizations produced by the stirrings of mortal hearts and the ephemera of the mind.

Refinement is crucial when it comes to this illumination. Just one wild ray mixing with the existential light can confuse an entire world and cause considerable damage for many generations. Even if humor, satire, criticism, drama, art, and philosophy should try their utmost, emptying all their pointed arrows, they will fail to sober a society that has been touched by one wild ray of the existential psyche. The latter, flowing from the essence of existential spirituality, has the ability to subjugate all the souls that have come under its influence. Though individuals might imagine that they have already extricated themselves from its influence, and they might pursue free, rational ways directly opposite the psychic influence that pervades their circle—this freedom is superficial and peripheral. In their innermost existence, they have never left its web. At any given time, their thoughts would betray to the eye of an investigator their true color.

The only thing capable of removing from the world a maverick ray of alien spiritual explosion—which was subverted by the barrenness of the field in which it grew—is the influence of a higher, more absolute existential light that would encompass all the moral and intellectual dimensions that make up free, logical, critical culture.

This higher existential light comes through pure awe of God, powerful faith in God, that is implanted only in *K'nesset Israel* (Ecclesia Israel), in a psychic domain upon whose history the moral and intellectual refinement effected by the experience of the fathers and the suffering of Egypt exerted a profound influence. Only after the patriarchs and Egypt seasoned her, was Israel prepared to receive into her the absolute divine influence as a pervasive force in the life of the collective and its norms, in its aspirations and hopes. That divine influence would be deeply rooted in Israel, in both individuals and the collective, for eternity. The moral and intellectual refinement that preceded the invasion of the supernal spirit provided that the tendency to natural culture, the desire for free, rational inquiry, for clear, intellectual ethics, would remain Israel's heritage, manifesting in every generation, collectively and individually.

The temporal strengthening of the nation depends on the strength of the soulful existence of the nation, and that depends on existential spiritual illumination, on the cosmic psyche. At the end of days the spirit of man and the spirit of the world will harmoniously unite in the cosmic psyche.

Through the divine psychic illumination that fills heaven and earth, that encompasses all lifecycles and strengthens all the nation's assets—history, language, geography, lifestyle—all fills with ecstasy and pleasure, strength and wealth.

The preparation of the soul of the nation to be united with the cosmic psyche comes about through the highest ethical Torah, which is a divine revelation to the nation, embodied in paths of ethics and wisdom, and in commandments designed to refine human character. This is not a superficial ethic, quick to spoil through the churning of the psychic sea and its silt, but a shining forth of the original spirituality—the essential Godly good—found in general existence and reaching the most specific unit. The direction of divine good sticks out of every nook of this eternal Torah.

If the assets of the nation are distant from the divine flow, they absorb rivulets of an unrefined psyche that clouds the splendor of the absolute morality, removing from the assets the divine strength that beats within them.

The symptoms of this malady are an inner coldness coupled with an outer passion for external assets. Those outer assets, which are devoid of the holy fire of perfect faith, gradually weaken and freeze, bringing anger at dashed hopes, at meaningless life.

Then the nation will longingly remember the days of her marriage. Beyond all sophistication, she will soar to the divine world she left behind. The divine psyche hidden in her soul will awaken; the spirit of wisdom and ethics poured into her will come back to life. Then all her external assets will be illuminated by a supernal light, and a divine charm will permeate them. In every heart there will begin to penetrate an inner, secure love.

With that, the divine psychic movement, the movement of worlds, will be revealed in vision, and in the song of every ripe soul. Its sounds will send waves throughout the collective, first the Israelite collective, followed immediately by the human collectivity. All that was erased will once again be engraved; all that was forgotten will be recalled. The joy of heaven and earth will return to its original state.

*

The soulful illumination of full spiritual existence manifests in a society, in an organic collective, in direct relation to the collective's preparation for the divine ideology with its eye to the general good, the absolute good that encompasses the many states of being. Just as the movements of subatomic particles are geared to intergalactic movements, so every spiritual movement of society is geared to the movement toward cosmic good that organizes through its general laws the ethics and justice of existence. Understandably, our eyes are dazzled by this cosmic framework, and therefore we are unable to delineate it.

The soulful illumination sends mighty waves through individuals who are spiritually strong. This strength is perfected when their collective root, their national soul, is healthy. The opposite is true as well: Any defect in the national soul impairs their strength.

When the psychic current of substantive spirituality—which surpasses academic spirituality—shows up in lives of individuals who are the points of enlightenment of a nation at the apex of its flourishing, it reveals in their midst the brightest spark of the whole light of the nation, and pronounces through them its supernal direction. This was the character of Israelite *prophecy*.

The national psyche was healthy throughout the lengthy period from Israel's entry into the Land up until the destruction of the First Temple—of course with breaks and slight interruptions. The spiritual illumination filled the spirit of nationalism, injecting it with divine longing that required processing through talent and wisdom. The spiritual illumination brought prophecy to the hearts of the chosen few of the nation. The enormous personality of the prophet dominated the nation, not so much academically, but in terms of psyche which is the actual current running through the spiritual experience.

This current running through the nation was clouded by the admixture of foreign currents, they too being more psychic than academic. The psychic flow was diverted to the evil of paganism, and the Israelite soul, rooted in the Living God, the holy God, was sullied. The nation's collective movements, such as her politics and the like, were fed by a strange psyche, whose effect was to poison the nation.

The impoverishment of the nation brought on by her exile from the Land interrupted the soulful current which hitherto was at its peak. Broken in body and spirit, the nation returned to her land after brief Babylonian captivity. She sought to reestablish herself, but she no longer possessed the full strength of the psychic current. As a replacement for the soulful current, there was new emphasis on book learning, which would establish in her a cultural dimension tailored to her origin and existential needs.[121] In this way, she would be prepared to receive the soulful illumination of the spiritual experience. The writing was changed [in the days of Ezra from "Hebrew script" to "Assyrian script"] after the original script failed her.[122]

The hankering for idolatry was stopped, but not totally vanquished. Its voice was muffled in a "lead pot,"[123] but in dark places it continued to exist and influence. It was necessary that it endure until which time as it would be vanquished by the power of the nation,[124] meaning that great spiritual current would remove its darkness in a mighty sublimation of all the energy found in the wild nature of paganism.[125]

In this period of the Second Temple, there arose sects that absorbed the outer shell of nationalism and its dregs. The disdain for human beings that is peculiar to nationalism grew stronger. Though one would think this hatred is directed to foreigners and spares members of the nation, with time it becomes an internal curse. Infighting took all the good out of the nation.[126] Individuals yet made use of the "holy spirit," viewing through a speculum of holiness the soulful current running through the nation—but these were but individuals. Pedagogy was no match for the demands of life, so control of everyday life, especially politics, was taken over by people far removed from the ideal divine soul that is Israel's source.

At times, there was felt within the nation longing for the soulful illumination of days gone by. At times, there awoke persons possessing a great soulful current who attempted to rejuvenate the nation through the impact of the personal psyche and bring the nation to a state whereby learning would be based on direct experience of the spiritual—but the time was not ripe for this.

While the nation was in such a weakened state, there arrived Christianity, which created fault lines in the nation. Its founder possessed a wonderful personal power, his soulful current was great, but he was not spared the deficiency of paganism, which is the strengthening of the soulful current without ethical and academic education.[127] The founder was so taken with his soul current, and captivated thereby his followers, that eventually they lost the Israelite character and were alienated in deed and spirit from their source.

Nonetheless, a diet restricted to the academic alone weakens the nation. It was inevitable that there would once again be ignited personal charisma as an influence over the nation. That is when Rabbi Akiva taught: "*You shall fear the Lord your God*—to include sages."[128]

This bold declaration provided for personal charisma within Judaism, though the nation was not fully prepared for it. The trepidation of Simon the Amsonite, who gave up hermeneutics rather than draw this inference [of Rabbi Akiva], resided within the soul of the entire *K'nesset Israel* (Ecclesia Israel).

Many generations passed. The power of the soul aided the power of learning. The *tsaddikim* (saints) and holy sages displayed exceptional personality which adorned their academic and practical side. But the many troubles, the impoverishment of life, at times caused the feeling of the soulful current to be forgotten, leaving the academic portion detached and dry. Immediately cracks were visible: There arose unrefined personalities, clouded by hallucinations and wicked drives, who set themselves up as visionaries. They filled a vacuum, smiting the nation with astonishment. We are referring to the various false messiahs who confused the world and caused untold suffering.

Despite all the bad in them, there was not lost the minute good that was contained in them. This arousal to psychic renascence—versus total reliance on the foundation of pedantic education—conjured up the memory of the healthy state of the nation in its early youth, when the candle of God yet shone within her and her prophets found vision from the Lord.[129]

Hasidism too came out of the demand of the soulful current that lay dormant. After the unsuccessful attempt of the latest false Messiah, Shabbetai Zevi, who reduced the psychic current to a level of mental instability and wicked intoxication, culminating later in the apostasy of the semi-official pseudo-Messiah Frank and his followers—after all these episodes, there was great apprehension lest the nation totally revile any vestige remaining to it of the hidden power of living soul currents, and revert to repetition of the letters and observance of the commandments and customs with a bent back and a broken heart. [If that were the case] eventually, the nation, lacking freshness and upliftment of the soul, would cease to exist.

This danger was sensed by the great personalities who were the founders of Hasidism, in whom the divine soul current was alive. Yet this current was not sufficiently academic. It did not lend itself to gradual education which would have fenced it in and provided a "railing" so that the expanding light not fall out.[130]

Though there was within Hasidism one safeguard to protect this current from becoming what became of the abnormal movements that preceded her—and that was wonderful nostalgic love of the nation.[131] The love of Israel as a whole and of individual Jews stood as powerful pillars not to be toppled by any wind. Even that was insufficient. Coming generations might have perverted this living good, had it not been purified by the conflagration of the opposition, the so-called *Mitnagdim*. At the helm of the opposition was the shining light of the Israelite soul in terms of learning and practical education. (Though he combined learning with the living current, he held the latter to be secondary in importance.) This was the Torah psyche of the Gaon Rabbi Elijah that stood opposed to the expansion of the divine soul current of the Ba'al Shem Tov's psyche, for it was not sufficiently based on learning. There were grounds to fear that with the passage of time, Hasidism would become alienated.[132]

Precisely through the tension between the two sides, this "controversy for the sake of heaven"[133] built a beautiful cupola over the great square of *K'nesset Israel* (Ecclesia Israel) in exile. It is only through the existence of these heavens that there may be established a practical foundation for Israel in the land of our fathers. All the practical movements that come to our aid today are but a preparation for the divine psychic movement.

The national psyche is beginning to make waves. Initially, it is interested in the external aspects without joining the divine inner soul. At the outset, the nation is satisfied with the rebirth of the language, the land, knowledge of history, and confused nostalgia. But as long as they are devoid of the light of God, the soul is filled with anguish: Where is the love of truth? Where is the love of Zion and Jerusalem, which was so fresh in the hearts of the fathers despite the weakness of soul brought on by the wanderings of exile? This great question posed at the right time will remind the living nation, her sons and builders, to return to the psychic source, the source of vision and of prophecy that is absorbed only through mighty faith in God, that comes after every manner of logical exploration, after every undefined form, after experimentation with various free and exciting lifestyles.

With mighty hands and muscles strong as iron, with upright stature and a soul full of vigor, the young Israelite of the future will approach the revival of his people and his land. With a raised flag, he will speak in the name of the Holy Land, and he will glory in the God of Israel out of the midst of a deep living stream. Then the dew of life will descend from the currents of spiritual existence upon bones desiccated by the heat of dry logic, bloodless metaphysics and rotten skepticism.

> They shall come and sing on the height of Zion and shall stream to the goodness of the Lord, for wheat and for wine and for oil, and for the young of the flocks and of the herds, and their soul shall be as moist as a garden, and they shall not grieve any more.[134]

And the spirit of God hidden in the young Israelite's midst will blow upon him with all its might, in a paved way, in a way that contains strength, wisdom, piety, and redemptive glory, that composes a new song and gives his people "a new name which the mouth of the Lord shall pronounce."[135]

*

When the current of existential spirituality—which is able to produce more on the practical level than methodical learning—is purged of the outer dregs, of deceptive rays of light that make for hallucinations, of a wicked will, "of an evil eye, a stout soul, and an arrogant spirit,"[136] it returns the nation's honor inasmuch as it restores the patriarchal honor of the "princes of Israel," who are blessed with a lofty personal spirituality.

The belief in *tsaddikim* (saints)—with the psychic bonding that comes about through souls connecting in reality—uplifts the spiritual value of the nation and mixes the inner light at work in the psychology of the higher man, the truly godly man, with the rest of the souls who cleave to him in love and faith. A great ethical personality flows with divine currents of longing that the greater good spread in the world and that God's full love appear in every living soul. Light rays of spiritual existence envelop the souls of persons who are spiritually weak, who are driven by the small winds blowing in their narrow heart. This mixing gives psychic strength, straightens the crooked, and brings to merit, and there appears a light of forgiveness even for sinners living under the oppression of their vulgar nature, of their animalistic materialism.

Such charisma requires watching, but great indeed is the general boon it provides. The collective will never appreciate the spiritual advantage if it measures it in academic terms. Quite the contrary, measured this way, spirituality will turn into a weak form of assistance. The rabbinate will be valued only for the bureaucratic role it plays. Rabbinic ruling will be valued in terms of the beasts and birds, the pots and spoons, and all the petty needs that have been judged kosher. Only this does practical common sense find palatable. Eventually, all these values will fall if there does not arise a strong spiritual hand to strengthen them all with their source. Thereby, all these spiritual needs will be uplifted. The only thing capable of uplifting in this way is the personal influence nourished by full spiritual existence, which in turn derives from the residue of the gift of prophecy.

In exile, even these relics are weakened because the nation is weakened there. The nation longs to set down roots in her land and to return to her ancient strength. Since the nation is preparing for something great, she must find on her own a mighty spiritual current that will flow into all the areas of her life; she must discover great personalities of her chosen ones close to the source of her soul, full of vision and holy song, and anticipating light and salvation[137] with all the strength of their souls.

Alone, the revealed Torah, whose focus is practical life, will not produce this personality that is so essential to the renascence of the nation and the land. The soulful current will come out of the hidden mysteries [of Torah], from immersion in the world of light that is gradually revealed to strong-willed humble people who await salvation, who are brimming with the currents of divine life in the living soul of *K'nesset Israel* (Ecclesia Israel). These mighty men of God will comprise all the currents, general and specific, necessary for the renascence; all the currents of life and action; all the currents of feeling and thought. They will dispense gifts to every spirit, after resurrecting all with the waters of the Living God; after they will be crowned with the supernal love that appears on the existential soul of the living people, in whose soul is revealed the soul of God.

The mixing of areas and "courts" of different souls will invigorate all the souls.[138] The defects brought on by sins will be erased, and a supernal light of "streaming to the Lord and to His goodness"[139] will penetrate with its rays all that have gathered for the rebirth of the holy people on its soil.

When literary creation clothes itself in the spirit of the reborn nation, it will find new treasures it never dreamed of seeing. This literature will engage the finest souls throughout the world in the new vision of a divine psychology coursing through this nation that has begun anew to be immersed in its native land; that is destined to revive through the spirit of God in its midst, the spirit of all the peoples, who are weary of a coarse life that oppresses mercilessly.

> For there is yet a vision for the appointed time, and it speaks of the end, and it will not deceive; though it tarry, wait for it, because it will surely come, it will not be delayed.[140]

> Behold, disturbed, not at rest is the soul [of the wicked] in him; but the righteous lives by his faith.[141]

(*Ha-Nir*, Year One, Number One, 5669/1909; reprinted in *Ma'amrei ha-RAYaH*, vol. 1 [Jerusalem, 5740/1980], pp. 1-9)

Letter of Rav Kook to Rabbi Dov Milstein

With the help of God
19 Menahem Av, 5671/1911

Peace and blessing from the Holy [Land] to the friend of my soul, a leader in Torah and fear [of God], Rabbi Dov Milstein,

... Regarding his question concerning what I wrote in the journal *Ha-Nir* regarding "that man" [i.e., Jesus of Nazareth—BN], that he possessed a wonderful personal power and soul current. There were some people that were astonished at this and suspected me of, God forbid, praising that "sinner of Israel," whom the gentiles idolized. My friend should know that this is not so. Whoever reads that deep article of mine with the attention worthy of such lofty matters cannot possibly entertain the thought that there is a strain of praise. These are my words: The essence of personal power and soul current is a natural force that depends on preparation. If it is prepared by supernal holiness, it is uplifted; if it is left as is, and people submit to it the way it is, they will fall into the depths of the pollution of idolatry.

One who has tasted of the *Tree of Life* will know and recognize that this is the mystery of Inwardness and Outwardness.[142] When

Inwardness vivifies Outwardness, it is transformed into holiness; and when Outwardness turns away, refusing to receive from Inwardness, all reverts back to chaos and impurity. I explained the source of the impurity of that "sinner of Israel," and whence derives his power: from the power of chaos[143] to which he was attracted. Those children of Israel who were attracted to him, he drew to the abyss of the pollution of idolatry.

At this time, when due to our many sins, there is much missionary activity to convert Jews, I deemed it a holy obligation to explain these things. This has always been the way of the sages of Israel: not to minimize the personal worth of the classic villains, but rather to demonstrate their great power and to explain that with all their greatness, they were corrupted by sinking into impurity. Thus it was said of Bil'am: "In Israel there did not arise [another such as Moses], but among the nations of the world there did arise, and that was—Bil'am."[144] This is a reference to the greatness of his worth, but it was on the negative, opposite side.

My works evoked criticism from the small of intellect, but thank God, true scholars, great in Torah, initiates in the secret of the Lord, distinguish the truth and utility of those words. They are truly eternal mysteries. Because it is "a time to do for the Lord,"[145] I agreed to reveal them. The time calls for it.

Men greater and better than me were slandered for such matters. Their pure spirit pressed them, for the *tikkun* (fixing) of the generation, to enunciate new ideas and to reveal the hidden. The common mind was not accustomed to them and therefore many complained about them. Eventually their righteousness "went out as a bolt of lightning,"[146] "and the holy one was vindicated."[147]

If time would allow, it would be worthwhile to expand on these lofty matters, but for now the brief explanation above will suffice.

Whoever gives me the benefit of the doubt shall be judged accordingly by heaven....

His faithful friend who constantly inquires into his welfare with great love,

Abraham Isaac Hakohen Kook
(*Igrot ha-RAYaH*, vol. 2 [Jerusalem: Mossad Harav Kook, 5722/1961], Letter 375, pp. 33-35)

Letter of Rav Kook to Elhanan Kalmanson, author of *Sinai and Golgotha*

20 Tevet 5[685]/1925

To a writer wise of heart and straight of opinion,
Mr. Elhanan Kalmanson,

Shalom.

I gratefully acknowledge receipt of his pamphlet *Sinai and Golgotha*.[148] I enjoyed many flashes I found there that are a blessing and that illumine the truth of Eternal Israel.

Concerning the [positive] attitude of a segment of our modern literature to that oppressor who left our fold and became our enemy—I think it appropriate to share with his honor my response to one of the learned Christians: If a man would fashion an idol of gold, we would always invoke in this regard *Shakets teshaktsenu* (Abomination!),[149] until the idolater would nullify the idol, at which time we would once again appreciate the value of the metal. Being as the new paganism made a man into an idol, and we suffered so much as a result, we stand resolute in our eternal opposition to this idolatry. We will not substitute our cry of *Shakets teshaktsenu* (Abomination!) with any other concept until which time as this segment of humanity will nullify this idolatry and publicly acknowledge our great truth. Only then at that fortunate time will our writers be able to say something positive concerning this personality—but only then, not now.

His friend who honors and blesses him from the holy place,

Abraham Isaac Hakohen Kook
(*Igrot ha-RAYaH*, vol. 4 [Jerusalem: Makhon RZYH Kook, 5744/1984], Letter 1276, pp. 216-217)

To the Process of Ideas in Israel

This essay first appeared in Rabbi Meir Berlin's (Bar llan's) journal, *Ha-'Ivri* (5672/1912).[150] Subsequently, it was included in the first edition of *Igrot ha-RAYaH* (*Letters of Rabbi Abraham Isaac Hakohen Kook*) (5683/1923).[151] Though it was not part of the original edition of *Orot* (5680/1920), starting in 5710/1950 it has been appended to that volume.[152]

In a broad sweep of history—general world history and specific Jewish history—Rav Kook shows that three ideas are forever vying with one another for the consciousness of man: the divine idea (*ha-idea ha-elohit*), the national idea (*ha-idea ha-le'umit*), and the religious idea (*ha-idea ha-datit*).

It is important to know to what stimulus Rav Kook is responding in this essay, in order to appreciate the boldness and revolutionary character of the author's thought. Secular Zionism, founded by Theodor Herzl, posed a grave threat to traditional Judaism in terms of the "transvaluation" it sought to achieve. It set out to replace the religious ideal of Judaism with a national ideal. Jews were told that they need not bother themselves with practical observance of the commandments; they would be contributing more to Judaism by political activism on behalf of a Jewish state. On the other hand, an

Orthodox Jew who failed to rally to the banner of Zionism would be considered remiss in fulfilling his duty to his nation. The battle was fought especially over the hearts and minds of the youth. Rabbis attempted to keep young Jews in the traditionalist camp; Zionist leaders swayed them to join the burgeoning movement. This *Kulturkampf* continues to rage in Erets Israel to this day.

There were those Zionist ideologists who went so far as to suggest that the *mitsvot*, the commandments of the Torah, were designed primarily to preserve Jewish identity in the Exile; with the nation's return to its land these observances would be rendered supererogatory![153]

How was a rabbi writing in 1912 to respond to the challenge of Zionism? There were a few alternatives. One might counter, as did some, that what makes Jews a people is not the Land of Israel but the Torah of Israel. They might cite Saʿadyah Gaon, "Our nation is a nation only by virtue of its Torah."[154] One might point out that Israel was already a nation in the Sinai Wilderness before it ever entered the Land.[155] It could also be argued that nationalism per se was a recent European invention. In a couple of years time Serbian nationalism would act as the powder keg igniting all Europe in the conflagration that has come to be known as World War One.[156] These are undoubtedly legitimate moves. Rav Kook chose none of the above.

What Rav Kook does is take the discussion up to a higher level, by exposing the roots of both phenomena, nation and religion, in a higher plane—Godliness. His source for this bold assertion (which remains unnamed throughout the essay) is the *Kuzari* of Judah Halevi.[157] Halevi made the claim that what distinguishes the Jewish race from other races is what he termed in Arabic, *al-ʾamr al-ilahi*, translated into Tibbonide Hebrew as *ha-ʿinyan ha-elohi*, which we might translate into English as "the divine phenomenon," or even "the God thing."[158]

Rav Kook goes on to paint the First Temple Period (sometimes referred to as the First Commonwealth) as the glorious time of the "national idea," and to portray the Second Temple (or Second Commonwealth) as the period when the "religious idea" took hold of the Jewish People. But again, both the national and religious ideas were but expressions of the divine idea. Rav Kook envisioned *Bayit Shelishi*, the Third Commonwealth, in the process of formation, as the synthesis of all these elements.[159]

The First Commonwealth was the golden age of Judaism. Geopolitically, it witnessed the extended borders of David and Solomon's kingdom. Spiritually, it experienced the splendor of Solomon's Temple in which the *Shekhinah* (the divine indwelling) was present. In terms of literature, it produced the Song of Songs, a romantic expression of the love relationship between God and Israel.

The Second Commonwealth represented a reduction, not only geopolitically, with the loss of full sovereignty and diminished territory,[160] but more significant, spiritually, with the Temple but a semblance of its former self, lacking the essential Ark of the Covenant and other symbols of the divine presence.[161] These differentials between First and Second Temples are common knowledge.

Rav Kook engages in some speculative historiosophy. (Perhaps psychohistory would be a more felicitous term.) He is convinced that the Second Temple was an age of individualism, which is to say, the roots of individual religious consciousness lie in the Second Temple Period.[162] This is Rav Kook's explanation for the fact that the TaNaKh or Bible is reticent regarding a personal afterlife, while the Mishnah waxes eloquent on the subject of the World to Come.

The denizen of early Israel basked in the radiance of the nation; he looked for fulfillment, spiritual and otherwise, in the success of the nation. He lived his life through the life of his people; he saw eternity in the eternity of Israel. There was no need to trace for First Temple man his soul's journey after death. The process of individuation initiated in the Second Temple entailed a morbid fascination with the afterlife. People needed assurance that they would survive eternally as individuals, not merely subsumed within the collective entity of Israel.

This new focus on individual ethics made Judaism exportable. Thus Paul, apostle of the new Nazarene religion, was able, once he stripped Judaism of its practical commandments, such as circumcision, to sell gentiles on a refracted Judaic morality.

A word of caution is in order here. From the fact that Rav Kook relegated individual morality and discussion of the afterlife to the Second Temple, one might receive the mistaken impression that Rav Kook introjected the Zionist critique of Jewish history.[163] While there are certainly similarities in their presentations, there are subtle but crucial differences. Rav Kook spells out where he differs with the Zionist reading of history in a personal letter to Samuel Aleksandrov of Bobroisk, dated 29 Shevat 5668/1908:

> Regarding his honor's comment concerning the difference between the collective and the individual. Certainly, our nationalists are wont to theorize that through the weakening of the national spirit in the later periods there arose the study of individuality. There is some truth in this, but not as they formulate it. They are of the opinion that personal immortality is a new doctrine engendered by attenuated nationalism. The

truth is that in most ancient times, when the national spirit flourished, it was already said, *The soul of my master will be bound in the bond of life.*[164] The woman of Teko'a's words were, *God does not lift away the soul but devises thoughts so that the banished one may not remain banished from Him.*[165] Finally, a recurrent phrase was "being gathered to the fathers."[166] The medieval authorities who dealt with these matters already commented on these expressions.[167] These are eternal truths. The principle of individuality can never be totally elided from the mighty collective spirit. Rather [an accurate description is] when collectivism is strong, the individual principle is not discernible or pronounced, because it serves as a centerpoint to the great circle. When [on the other hand] collectivism is weakened, the centerpoint becomes discernible. [This point of individuality] fills with many maxims and sermons, and assumes a prominent place in the lives of individuals oblivious to the life of the collective. So when the sun of the national spirit set, there were established studies concerning the individual unit, the individual personality. These studies were expanded and publicized; this in turn forced the disclosure of several inner mysteries from the spiritual past concerning absolute existence [i.e. the afterlife]. Out of the darkness of this decline issued a great light: the worldwide dissemination of spiritual information, which greatly refined personal character.[168]

The claim that personal immortality is an invention of the Second Temple Period constitutes heresy. The concept of "resurrection of the dead" was always inherent in the Torah.[169] Rather, it is a matter of focus and emphasis. Whereas First Temple man could be satisfied with a few elliptical remarks concerning the afterlife, Second Temple man, who suffered all the insecurity of individual identity, needed the reassurance of lengthy discourses on the subject. There was also the matter of making public "mysteries of the Torah." What previously had been recondite knowledge reserved for an elite, came into the public domain for the first time.

*

It would be very convenient to pigeonhole Rav Kook as advocating national-religion. It is not hard to imagine why he has been embraced as an ideologist by the National Religious Party (NRP) in Israel today. (For some reason, in English translation National comes before Religious, while in the Hebrew original it is the opposite: Religious National Party [*miflagah datit-le'umit*].) But then Rav Kook would not be Rav Kook. He would not be the mystic, the soul at once drenched by and thirsting for God, that he was. He would not be the visionary, longing for Israel to once again be a nation of prophets; longing for Erets Israel, whose "air is the life of souls" (Judah Halevi); longing for the "divine idea."

To the Process of Ideas in Israel

I. The Divine Idea and the National Idea in Mankind

The lifestyle and style of thought of man that sum up his entire essence are pronounced in the social idea and the spiritual idea, which are the treasuries of the national form and the faith form of human collectives. When these styles are clarified and their strokes are painted by the artistry of history, then we find the two basic ideas of mankind that recur at every turn of life, whether it be individual or societal, spiritual or pragmatic: the national idea and the divine idea. The first determines the lifestyle of society; the second determines the style of spiritual thought. If we would be more precise in our use of terminology, we might speak of the national sentiment and the divine opinion. Sometimes, these positions are reversed. Then we have national opinion and divine sentiment. The ups and downs that are required for this role reversal are first evidenced in the life of society as a whole; their influence penetrates to the depths of the individual's innermost life.

The preparation for the divine idea is found, whether openly or covertly, directly or indirectly, in the hearts of all mankind, in all its many branches, families, and nations. This preparation establishes various religions and sentiments of faith, orders, and laws.[170] They in turn set in motion a multitude of mighty actions in the life of nation and individual, in the arrangements of society and in the political processes. They weave a web of awesome events in the spirit of man and in the features of his life. These are all stages in the movement toward perfection of the divine idea and its clarification, and the soaring to life lived to its fullest, its most vital, in the present and in eternity.

As this preparation advanced vertically, it gave birth to various national institutions corresponding to its state in every human collective and geographical location. It always found some natural resource sufficient to act as a basis for nationality; through its lofty inspiration the breath of life was breathed into that natural resource. Will, energy, art, imagination, reason, and all the inclinations of the spirit came together to form a national body. There arose social and national collectives which betray to the discerning eye all the mighty causes that shape their existence: They all pour forth from the interpenetration of the divine idea and the collective national form. However, after the latter is concretized, it sometimes tries its luck at detaching itself from the divine idea. Human history has never shown any success in this direction. [On the contrary] we see that the divine idea in man, even in its most degraded, reduced form—when it is "fainting and nullified, but not yet dead"[171]—gives the most innermost strength to all life's urges.

It sometimes occurs that the practical life is perfected, the social, ethical, and material aspects have all come together in a well organized, cohesive bond—yet the divine light as reflected in society is so distant as to be dim. With all its perfection, its wide resources and cultural opportunities, should society pursue this dim light, it will find only obscurity and upheaval. Then nationalism does an about-face and attempts to barricade itself in its isolated concept; no longer shall it turn to the source of its fundamental existence, namely the divine idea. Eventually this will catch up with it. Isolated nationalism experiences aging and infirmity; the mechanical energy will continue to push for some time the collective machinery, but the lifesap will wither away. When spiritual ascent loses its value, the collective automatically disintegrates. The needs of the individual and his private demands will surpass the value of harmony; the territory of individuals will assume ever greater proportions. The result will be utter caprice, accompanied by existential nausea[172] and bouleversement of the entire logical order. "There is no truth, nor kindness, nor knowledge of God in the land."[173] The collective national idea will be brought low and will no longer be able to maintain its vitality; its army will falter, and its throne will be toppled.

> The earth reels to and fro like a drunkard, and shakes like a booth. Its sin rests heavy upon it; it shall fall, and not rise again. And on that day, the Lord will visit punishment on the host of heaven in heaven, and on the kings of the earth upon the earth.[174]

When society wanders down this narrow path, having concluded that it must divest itself of the source of its vitality [i.e. the divine idea], it will quickly feel the repercussions. To an ailing society, suffering from loss of purpose, meaning, and content, materialism will offer supposed solutions: Various economic theories whose bases are shaky; psychological impulses devoid of purity of heart.[175] All these will recoup their remaining strength to nourish heart and mind, the centers of life of individuals, in an attempt to raise from these fragments a technical foundation for the life of society and humanity. But for nought! Their toil will produce nothing. Death, black, still, and cold, cannot give life. Only from the source of life can life pour forth.

> Woe! He says to the wood: Wake up! To an inert stone: Get up! He gives instruction? It is overlaid with gold and silver; there is no breath in it.[176]

II. The Divine Idea and the National Idea in Israel

Propelled by the preparation for the divine idea, the intense longing of the human spirit in general to base itself on the divine idea and find there its refuge, the inner attraction to the light and serenity, the loftiness and strength of the divine idea—the spirit of man contorts itself to find its goal by various means, by visions opposed to one another, by a confusion of shadows of death and sparks of brightness, until the living expression of the divine idea comes harmoniously clothed in the national style—in Israel.

From the very inception of this people—which knew to call on the name of the distinct divine idea at a time when savage paganism held sway—there was manifested the aspiration to establish a great human collective that would "keep the way of the Lord to do righteousness and justice."[177] This aspiration flows from a powerful recognition and a lofty ethical demand that mankind be freed of the terrible bondage of spirit and matter, and brought to a life of freedom in the light of the divine idea. All of mankind must know this success. In order that this goal be accomplished, this human collective must be in possession of a socio-political state, a sovereign state at the peak of human civilization: "A wise and discerning people is this great nation."[178] In this state, the divine idea will reign supreme and vitalize people and land with its energy. Such a nation will make a statement that not only an elite, not only pietists and anchorites may live in the light of the divine idea, but entire peoples with all that society has to offer in the way of "creature comforts"; entire peoples, encompassing all the socio-economic strata, from the intelligentsia all the way down to the proletariat.

Once the light of the divine idea has been purified in such a people, and has put its stamp upon its national life, it then goes to work on the entire world, incorporating the specific talents of each people wherever they may be, seeing that all are illumined by this light. This action brings to the realization that the socio-political dimensions of life will find true value only if they are nurtured by the life-giving dew of the absolute divine idea, that is capable of taking all of existence—an existence that surpasses the limitations of our consciousness and its categories—to its open-ended goal.

Israel was predisposed to the divine idea by its psychology, its heredity, and its geography. All of these helped the Jewish People. *K'nesset Israel* (Ecclesia Israel) in days of yore, at the zenith of her flourishing, in the days of her romance with God,[179] soared with her spirit to the source of the supernal light. With all the fire of her love, with all the thunder of her might, and the lightning flashes of her intellect, she rooted her national identity in the depths of the lucid divine idea. In the treasury of her national idea was hidden the divine idea. Israel possessed the talent to light up the entire world.

It is true that once the national dimension became a tangible reality, in Ancient Israel too it acquired the right to exist based on diverse factors as well. Once it descended from the abstract level of

Godliness to the earthly level, it learned the ways of the world that ramify from the complexities of ordinary life; that encompass the material and spiritual needs of man and of the beast within. But in all of its descents, there was never erased from the national dimension the signature of her source. In the innermost hidden recess of her being it is forever nourished by the divine idea.

III. The State of Rupture between the Ideas

Those two luminaries "wore one crown"[180] in Israel; the national idea was on equal standing with the divine idea that vivifies all and lends all life's activities a heavenly scent. Alas, there arose the "accusation" of the practical dimension which had encountered the murky ways of secular life, individual and collective. Despite that, the elevated status the nation once enjoyed prepared spiritual reserves for the days of descent, for the days when the national idea would be forced to descend from the source of the divine idea "as a bird wanders from its nest"[181] to the practical arena, gross and material as it is. The air of the world was so polluted by bestial, savage paganism that it choked the life-breath of the aspiration for Godliness in the nation. The *Shekhinah*, the divine indwelling in the nation, was brought low. In direct proportion to the loss of divine inspiration, was the loss of national strength.

Even after the light of the wondrous generation of the Exodus receded, there arose redeemers and saviors to prop up the falling nation. At times there appeared mighty men of God who almost succeeded in raising up the nation; they would once again bind her to the source of her vitality, the idea of God. The nation will never forget the golden age of Solomon's rule, of which the crowning achievement was the building of the First Temple. The latter gave expression to harmonious interpenetration of the divine and national ideas. "The moon existed in a state of fullness."[182] At that period, short in duration but long in quality, the national idea was suffused with vitality; its light came from the pure divine idea. The national wealth and honor enhanced the divine idea; the thought of God in its Israelite form bestowed upon the entire nation a life of joy and honor. The nation waxed poetic, singing of God and nation, and love.

> The world was never so worthwhile as the day the Song of Songs was given to Israel, for all the Writings are holy, and the Song of Songs is holy of holies.[183]

However, during those good days of historical ascent it was only vis-à-vis the collective that the national spirit was uplifted and discovered its source in the divine idea. Individual morality did not reach this level; the lifestyle of the individual was incompatible with this higher harmony. There grew "thorns surrounding the supernal rose."[184] The idolatrous kingdoms beckoned with all of the allure of pagan culture; in the frenzy, unbridled lust and base emotions were awakened. The beast in man erupted; there developed apathy toward all that is high and holy; toward all that transcends the material senses and the common imagination that depends on them. These stood as heavy clouds keeping out the divine light that had begun to shine into the innermost depth of the national soul. Within a short time, the bright light of the national idea as it relates to the influence of the divine idea, was removed. From that point on, the mighty throne of David, the throne of the Lord,[185] began to shake. The national idea started to be weaned from the breasts of the divine idea.

Humanity as a whole had not yet totally sundered the branch of nationalism from its natural root [in the divine idea]; in many peoples the national and divine elements were thrown together in a hodgepodge. But for broad humanity what was the character of this tendency? A savage, evil, base tendency, vivified by a thin sliver of light masked by waves of impurity. *K'nesset Israel* (Ecclesia Israel) is connected by known arteries to the body of mankind. As long as Israel does not rise to the occasion of charting a distinct Godly path for herself—by which she will be in a position to influence positively the organism of humanity, rather than be influenced negatively—she will suffer the pains of all mankind. When Israel strayed from its original way in life, it was no longer able to sustain itself with a dry nationalism separated from its source in the drive for divinity. Such a proposition would run counter to the entire historical process. Seeking to "moisten" its materialism, Israel too was enchanted by the minute divinity wrapped in illusions capable of seducing a human collective. That was the spiritual vogue at the time. This restricted spiritual diet was sufficient for the puerile soul of the contemporary nations whose natural demand for spiritual light was weak. It would suffice for their limited lifespan, for their brief appearance on the stage of history. This dim spiritual light could not satisfy the needs of a great nation, whose surging vitality matches its longevity and global influence. Its soul had even outgrown the light showered upon it in its youth. So the nation then went into a deep slumb. The source of the divine idea—which nourished the national idea—dried up; the fount of morality stopped pumping. Israel's nobility was eclipsed, and her national idea ceased bearing fruit. "A sterile vine is Israel."[186]

Our forefathers' sins took *K'nesset Israel* (Ecclesia Israel) down from her plateau of strength and holiness. The community's sin was so extensive that the floodwaters of corruption reached to the neck. The national idea became so distant from the divine idea that no mortal eye could make out the imprint of the divine idea upon this nation grown unruly and impoverished. A feeling of desperation gave birth in the heart of the prophet to the frightful thought that God "had exchanged Israel for another people."[187] A bitter reproach was let out:

> Contend with your mother, contend! She is not my wife, and I am not her husband.[188]

But in the depths of the nation's soul, in a place no eye can see, not even that of a prophet, there yet burns brightly the final divine spark. The appointed time must come. After the artificial tendencies, foreign to Israel's true nature, will have exhausted themselves, the divine dimension will wake up from its long slumber.

> On that day, says the Lord, you will call *My husband*; no longer shall you call *My Ba'al*. I will remove the names of the Be'alim from her mouth, and they shall no longer be mentioned by name. I shall establish for them a covenant on that day with the beast of the field and with the bird of the sky, and the reptile of the earth; I will break the bow and the sword and war from the earth, and I will cause them to lie down in safety. And I shall betroth you forever, and I shall betroth you with righteousness and with justice, with love and with compassion. And I shall betroth you with faith, and you shall know the Lord.[189]

IV. The Situation in Exile

When the spirit of God departed from the nation, when her nationhood was sundered from its life-source, exile was a necessity. Communal life which was corrupt to the core, had to be repressed. Iniquitous individuals had learned to manipulate the legal system.[190] Exile—internal destruction and external dispersion—smashed the already shriveled idea of a nation that had drifted away from her God. Detached from the root of her life, she was polluted by pagan culture and all its charms. The pride and glory of Israel fell from heaven to earth.[190*]

However, the divine idea and the Israelite national idea are so intertwined that each always contains the germ of the other. Ultimately, the national idea bears within it the divine idea, and the latter cannot but influence that nation of Israel which is God's resting place in the expanse of history. So even at Israel's nadir, the divine idea vivifies in some form the national sentiment.

Throughout the exile, when there was no longer opportunity for the divine idea to influence the national idea—because most of the latter's resources had been defiled and turned to "sour grapes,"[191] and afterward destroyed to the foundation—the divine idea squeezed into the small, fragile nest of the "minor sanctuary," the synagogue and the studyhouse; into pure family life; into the residue of religious observance and Torah. These have value as signposts in exile.[192] They are relics of something that was once whole and alive, and which will one day come back to life, when the Lord restores the captivity of His people.[193]

Certainly the mighty vision of the two ideas united could not be revealed in a nation bruised and broken; in bones fractured and splintered; in a people prone to oppression and held up to ridicule.

That strength was something of the past, when the people dwelt securely in its land. "A throne of glory exalted from the beginning is the place of our temple."[194] The remarkable thing is that because of its loftiness, because of the power of its vitality, the divine idea is able to breathe life into dry bones. It was only the divine idea that preserved "the innermost point of Zion,"[195] the foundation of *K'nesset Israel* (Ecclesia Israel), including her national dimension. This was preserved to thaw out at the appointed time.

How painful and fragile is the Israelite national idea at the present time! Its glory and might are revealed only when the divine idea is resplendent in its midst. Subjected to humiliating servitude, deprived of oxygen and sustenance, the national idea grew faint. Scattered individuals stopped living the life of a people, and national life with all its powerful sentiments was forgotten, as a dead man is forgotten. Only in a very condensed form were those [national] sentiments captured in the "minor sanctuary," in a life of observing commandments and studying Torah. This came about by virtue of the fact that the hidden aspect of the national idea is absorbed in the divine idea. What survived was the ethical and organizational side of the national idea. The national sentiments persisted to the degree that the reduced vitality of the nation could accommodate them. They inspired pride in the past and hope toward the future, for the time when "the Lord would comfort His people, redeem Jacob, and return him to his habitation."[196]

Only the pure of soul estimate the depth of this pain, the all-encompassing *Weltschmerz* (world pain) that penetrates to the most minute details of an unfortunate life full of the wrath of the Lord—that results from the sundering of interdependent ideas and the lessening of lights.

Deprived of space within the Israelite national idea since the exile of the people and the destruction of the Temple, the divine idea transcended the borders of any specific nation, reaching the heights of the quest for moral justice, scientific analysis, pure reason, and abstract wisdom. From those heights, the divine idea projects slender rays of light, the majority (qualitatively if not quantitatively) of which penetrate the tents of Jacob through the vestigial light of the surviving Torah scholars and the leftovers of prophetic inspiration. In addition, the divine idea throws scattered lights here and there on individuals seeking God, on champions of truth and justice among every people and tongue.

In this way, the divine idea created the vision of the "Israelite destiny"[197] that was able to overcome all opposition to its basic fundamental. Eventually, it succeeded in purifying millions of hearts, breathing a new spirit in peoples, and mitigating the evil of paganism. But the divine idea cannot rest back on this accomplishment. Of what value is the weak expression of ethics, when it lacks official standing in the life of people and in government, when it no longer manifests in the national idea? The thick shadows that bring wickedness and impurity attach themselves to the lights of the divine idea scattered among the nations. The tear between the divine idea and the national idea—which is the cause of all the confusion and disturbances in the world of society and politics—can be mended only in the place of their natural union: Israel. That union awaits the complete rejuvenation of Israel in its land, the return of the Kingdom of Shaddai to its fastness.

V. The First and Second Temples • The Religious Idea • The Israelite Condition and its Relation to Mankind

Since the souls of the individuals were not yet equipped to receive the strong light of the divine idea; to conduct their lives in consonance with the collective, therefore, the exalted state of the nation during the First Temple Period had to be fragmented. The Second Commonwealth was not adequate to restore the full might of the nation. What appeared in the Second Temple was not a collective power, but rather a power of individuals "who separated themselves from the iniquity of the nations."[198] Through these individuals, the Lord perpetuated Israel. The mighty collective power had not yet been refined; its character was still raw, chock full of the impurities it accumulated in the days of plenty when the people was corrupted. It was at this time of the Second Temple that the personal, individual influence of divinity became ensconced in nation and land.

Now during the Second Temple Period, with the receding of the great universal light, the divine idea began to take on features of individuality. Individual observance of Torah and the minutiae of the commandments, opinions regarding a personal afterlife, which previously were subsumed "as a candle is outshone by broad daylight"[199] in the divine idea, in the collective soul of the nation, are now prominent. Now the mighty divine idea is replaced with its derivative: the religious idea.[200]

The religious idea will never forget its source in the divine idea specific to Israel by virtue of its national soul. Individual morality, concern for personal immortality, and scrutiny of each individual action were well established in this "religious idea," which was not but a reduction, an individualization of the divine manifestation. The position of prominence assigned individual observance endowed the nation with a fortitude she could carry with her even in the days of exile and wandering. It also paved the way for her to reach gradually, through a tortuous, circuitous route, the highest goal, namely that the divine idea might once again appear in her midst in all its might. But first the people would have to long for it, for days of yore and years gone by. This is the long arduous process of education that comes through embellishment of religious observance, through "the minutiae of Torah and the minutiae of scribes," "new and also old"[201] —aided and abetted by concern for personal immortality.

Inasmuch as the divine idea is the soul of the nation, it proceeds from the collective to the individual. Its revelation is the foundation of the collective; from the wealth of the divine light flowing through the collective—generating an organic spirituality—the individual is filled. The individual is fulfilled inasmuch as he is part and parcel of the collective. This general light travels on high clouds; it has no need to speak of the reward awaiting individuals. The lives of individuals are complete only insofar as they find fulfillment in the life of the collective. The great inclusive statement, "I will walk in your midst, and I will be to you a God, and you shall be to Me a people,"[202] that invigorates the soul more than truth acquired by logic, is the foundation of all. Everything else that involves individuation is but a derivative of this thought.

When the lofty divine soul vivifies the nation, the latter transcends all the individual differences that divide life; in that lofty state, the thought never occurs to divide this world from the World to Come. In the depths of every soul is ingrained the knowledge that before the divine light there are no borders or blocks; that divine life never ceases, whether in this world or in the World to Come. The thought never occurs to picture the exact character of that eternal life of which we have but the vaguest notion. By the same token, we have no conception of the divine light other than the fact that we sense its existence and enjoy its splendor to the depths of our soul. Not only that, but the inner certitude and general arousal are so potent and pleasant that the general thought never gets sidetracked to a discussion that must perforce restrict itself to the worry of the individual. The divine light is so strident that there is no need to think in terms of "mine and yours." That divine might that rests upon the nation as a whole—that expresses itself in the sentiments of her heart and by geopolitical self-assertion—reaches on its own more in the way of inner morality than the egocentric thought of a personal afterlife could ever yield. The eye and the other senses, "the means of gathering information,"[203] do not operate there [in life after death]; they are powerless to chart clearly the afterlife. There is no way the thought of an afterlife could provide a light comparable to the divine light felt in the life of the nation, in all the tangible and spiritual assets. *Light does not need to be described; it just shines.* This general light of the nation reaches eternity through God. It transcends every border, time, or place, by the power of the life of worlds, and by the flow of wholeness, and inestimable capability. Through this general light there shine also the specific truths hidden in esoteric wisdom.

It was the darkness of night that turned man's attention to the heavens, to the expanses of infinite space. And it was the destruction of the First Temple and the departure of the *Shekhinah*, the divine idea, which is to say its ceasing to manifest in the actual life of the nation, that turned the nation's focus to the distance, and to spell out that which hitherto had been submerged in the light of the collective. Investigations concerning the World to Come and the Resurrection of the Dead—so far removed from the ordinary senses—that had previously been reserved for the elite, now came into general possession of the nation.[204] These esoteric studies conveyed the divine light in an eternal sense that allows thought to transcend the sensate reality.

No sooner had individuality asserted itself and the divine idea been interpreted in terms of spiritual concern for the individual, than the outside world was able to relate for the first time to Israelite spirituality, to the ethics of the Torah and to the sentiment of belief in God.[205] The secular spirit of humanity that had no truck with the *divine idea*—was able to relate to the *religious idea*. This is something needed not only by the Israelite nation who live in the light of the divine idea, but by any heart seeking eternity; by sensitive, ethical individuals such as can be found throughout the world.

From this [religious idea] arose the mismatch represented by the contemporary religions of civilized peoples: distorted fragments of the divine light of Judaism grafted onto a base of paganism fraught with barbarism. This state of affairs was brought about by [Jewish] apostles who were alienated from their spiritual home,[206] and by the recipients, the peoples themselves whose national and social sentiment is closer to paganism. Not them but us did the Lord lift on eagles' wings to be to Him an eternal nation.[207] "A match of grape berries and briar berries does not go well."[208]

The divine pleasantness that is displayed in *K'nesset Israel* (Ecclesia Israel) in its simplicity and naturalness—in light of the divine idea implanted in her—makes for an agreeable, delicate, sweet life. Such life is not in question; not only will it continue to exist, but will even be renewed and replenished. This is the source of an inner *joie de vivre* that bonds with all the ideals of man's higher soul. The strong natural energies do not incite any moral protestation or opposition; these energies are viewed from the perspective of a higher science of eternal peace and divine joy.

This divine pleasantness that is imbibed with every draught of life enables one to view life and existence with a goodly eye and the joy of the righteous, to recognize that "all God made is very good."[209] At the other extreme, the pagan world that lacks this divine pleasantness—from the source of light of the divine idea innate in Israel—is unable to relate to the joy of life. Its dim view uncovers only misfortune; it becomes frustrated with itself, with its existence, with everything. It finds itself in opposition to its very self. As the pain increases, paganism finds a temporary relief (before it disappears from the earth) in a lifestyle that offers no resistance to all the barbaric elements. But it is impossible to stop up the spirit; the spiritual beauty of man and his inner morality demand their due. They are not to be pacified, especially after maturation of the worldview that inspects life inside and out. Therefore, paganism comes to the hiding place of Buddhism, which finds peace in nothingness and absolute negation. The cup of wrath—anger with life and its bitterness—is full to the brim; all the talents of intellect and emotion, faith and imagination are summed up by a singular will: to self-annihilate.[210]

Out of this strange hybrid of two sources, Judaism and paganism—on the heels of the separation of the Israelite national idea from the divine idea, the source of its life and light of its salvation[211]—came contemporary world "religion," from which God has departed. The separation of ideas in Israel brought about this general flaw. To this very day mankind, despite all its sophistication, is unable to enunciate clearly the divine idea, in order to imbue with it the social idea. Since then, mankind has been limping along on a "falsehood that has no legs,"[212] on a moral foundation that is nourished by the religious idea. But the national idea is diametrically opposed to the religious idea! Though the national idea needs the religious idea for the lifesap hidden in its depth, the two ideas are at each other's throats.

Instead of clear concepts that may be readily delineated, comes the artificial conception of religion of contemporary civilization. It attempts to lump us [the Jewish People] together with the nations by virtue of that which separates us: the distinction between the holy and the profane. The study of comparative religion includes the Jewish "religion."[213] The truth is, the sparks of Judaism in this contemporary religion, taken out of context, have turned into a catastrophe, a morbid morality preoccupied with graves. As consciousness evolves, it surpasses the dark sentiments of gross fanaticism. These are replaced by despair and pessimism, which weave a "spiderweb" over all the palaces of literature and art, depressing every spirit.

The "religious sentiment" that replaced the divine idea lowered considerably the ideal strength of man's soul. Erased were the inner joy, the spiritual power that makes man's gait light as a gazelle's, that leads him with music and strident song. These were supplanted by the approach of some of the ancient Pharisees who would say, "What is my duty that I may dispense it?"[214] This approach smacks of petty servitude. On a par with the descent of the divine light in both communal and individual life, was the downfall of the national idea. From a mighty, charming ideal it became a "political idea," a sort of "trade that extends over many souls." "The state is a great corporation." This double descent—of the *divine idea* to the *religious dimension*, and concomitantly, the descent of *nation* to *state*—took the splendor of life from the world. The appearance of great souls became rare indeed. Gone are the powerful giants. In their place have proliferated cowardly, weak businessmen, wallowing in the mud of small ideas, material and spiritual merchandise.

The attempts that were made during this time of spiritual failure were themselves doomed to failure. That is because mankind did not and cannot create a national center in which the divine idea would be revealed as national aspiration. Only this people [the Jewish People] feel that this spice—the divine idea—needs no further spice, that it is sufficient to move all the wheels of life, of national aspiration and renascence. Only Israel is prepared for this role by the nature of its unique creation. "This people I have formed for Me; they will recount My praise."[215] The religious disposition—that departed from the idea resting in Israelite nationalism, and whose only standing in the world of spirit is the individual morality it turns out—is unable to survive when civilization comes of age. When that happens, individuals who are ready for ethical awareness will demand a morality purer and more natural than that offered by religion in the way of worrying about personal immortality. The very general spiritual need that activated these murky pieces and introduced them into life, will remove them from the world once they have served their function. Consciousness gradually rises to higher, purer levels of morality. Only then will the quest for Godliness be exposed in its mighty purity.

And for the duration of history, as long as humanity is divided into nations, the religious idea will persist as a reflection of the divine-national idea alive in the source of Israel. Then the religious idea will ascend to its source, taking with it all the spiritual baggage it acquired remarkably in those days of darkness.

And the Lord alone shall be exalted on that day. And the idols He will utterly abolish.[216]

He will utterly abolish all the idolatrous kingdoms;
Your strength is eternal,
For generation upon generation your nazirites.[217]

VI. The Reunification of the Ideas in *K'nesset Israel* (Ecclesia Israel) with Her Rebirth in Her Land

The degree to which the national spirit of *K'nesset Israel* (Ecclesia Israel) is prepared to spring back to life, depends on her capacity for receiving into her as the breath of life the supernal divine light. Fortunately, time worked its effect and the darkness of exile also contributed. The scattering of *K'nesset Israel* (Ecclesia Israel) throughout the world improved greatly the general process of the world. The destruction of the national center put an end to the mistaken notion that God-consciousness is limited to a specific geographic location or specific kingdom. "Your eyes will see, and you will say, 'The Lord is magnified beyond the border of Israel.'"[218] Though this conceptual breakthrough might seem an isolated thought, it played a major part in clarifying early ideas in general.

This improvement that *K'nesset Israel* (Ecclesia Israel) worked upon the world at large, especially in Israel's state of dispersion, is a branch of the nation's own self-improvement, which in turn arouses to national renascence. A sinner wallows in guilt as long as the sin remains unexpiated. Should he brazenly overcome his consciousness of guilt, the respite will be temporary. Soon enough his soul will once more be consumed by guilt. Only after he has expiated his sin, will he feel anew his purity and his self. Only then will his vitality, strength of spirit and courage return to him.

Throughout the days of exile, *K'nesset Israel* (Ecclesia Israel) knew her sin and felt her spiritual pain. Hers was a weakness resulting from internal shame. None of the famous persons throughout the generations of exile were able to change this state of affairs. Though on the personal level—despite the depressing atmosphere of exile and debasement—they rose to become persons of holiness, most exalted holy ones, none were able to inject in the nation *as a whole* a spirit of strength, a visible, pronounced courage. This was because the collective soul of the nation had to undergo a process of purification. Exile with all its fears and dreadful pains was the refinery of this catharsis. The Second Temple Period served as a good preparation for the oncoming exile. The long cessation of statecraft and its quarrels allowed the collective spirit of *K'nesset Israel* (Ecclesia Israel) respite to take stock of her world. Now, after the passage of so much time, during which Jerusalem "took from the hand of the Lord double for all her sins,"[219] the nation as a whole begins to feel her purity, innocence, and righteousness—and simultaneously, her will to be reborn. Her national sentiments come home to roost in her, and the desire to return to her nest, to her place and her land, waxes within her. She still does not know her own mind, whence comes this spirit, nor does she know its value and its power—and in the hidden recess of the heart she seeks her Beloved, she longs for the divine light, that it be revealed to her in its splendor as in days of yore and bygone years.

Now the ideas—divine and national—make waves toward the process of their natural reunification within the context of national renascence. The lights of both Temples, First and Second, are presently fused in the return to Erets Israel. Not only the divine light in the form it assumed in other peoples, not only the religious idea in the form it took on in Exile, not only the detached national idea—but all of these together we prepare to receive. In our state of destruction these ideas manifested separately in different parties. But eventually, the banner of peace must be lifted; in the land of rebirth these ideas and their bearers will meet, and each will find in his opposite number the completion of what his soul is lacking. From the early period will shine the divine might; from the late period—the shaping of the individual style; and life lived in its natural habitat will add new, ever expanding acquisitions.

"With weeping they shall come."[220] A certain dark sorrow yet fills the hearts of those returning from captivity to the eternal inheritance. This melancholy stems from the wedge exile drove between the divine influx and vigorous national life on the one hand, and the religious influence that originated when Jews became distanced from the eternal light of the nation as a whole. However, as soon as a spark of redemption is fanned—once the light of the divine-national idea, which is demanded even by the individual Israelite soul, becomes manifest through all the religious currents—immediately, a new song breaks out, a new sound is heard:

> The redeemed of the Lord shall return, and come to Zion with song, and eternal happiness on their head. They shall obtain joy and happiness, and sorrow and sighing shall flee.[221]

When the mind will be filled with the harmonious combination of these ideas, and will be at peace, its light will be reflected in all the ways of "the Mosaic-Judaic religion" (*dat moshe vi-yehudit*).[222] The commandments of the Torah and their minutiae will be observed with heartfelt respect. Especially in those commandments that do not directly relate to general humanitarian ethics, those commandments that universal perfection does not warrant, and may even reject on occasion—the so-called non-rational commandments (*mitsvot shim'iyot*)—is revealed the divine light.[223]

After the total spiritual organism, with all its sentiments, soulful and bodily, connects to this general influence, intellect is able to perceive clearly that each individual contributes to the collective as a whole, and that every specific action of the individual contributes to shaping his overall lifestyle and character. Then there dawns awareness that the sum of the parts is sealed with a divine sign. What we find is that the divine light reflects on every individual through each of his actions, and after the commandments and all the minutiae of "the Mosaic-Judaic religion" disappear in the spiritual storehouse of *K'nesset Israel* (Ecclesia Israel), they bounce back and shine with divine light in the soul of every individual Jew. These prosaic acts provide the staple diet of *K'nesset Israel* (Ecclesia Israel); the best of our people always felt the inner nutritional value hidden therein. [Many would recite this *yihud* (mystical intention) before performing a commandment:] "To unite the name of the Holy One, blessed be He, and His *Shekhinah* [divine indwelling] through that which is hidden, in the name of all Israel."[224] When that is the case, all the most lovely, invigorating thoughts find their basis in this natural, practical "food" that provides energy for the nation's soul and healing for her flesh.

Out of this approach, the longing to connect with Erets Israel—the physical place which is the eternal repository of the nation's vital energy—grows ever stronger and comes to fruition in holiness. All those who abandoned the light of the Lord and were abandoned by it, because they left the basic diet through which it lives and exists, namely practical observance of and esteem for Judaism in its highest, divine sense, whereby God is revealed in our midst precisely through this material support—all those will return to us, to restore to Israel practical Judaism in its full glory. This will come about through the divine illumination garbed in Jewish nationalism. The spiritual character of the nation ascends, becoming more glorious from one generation to the next. May the Lord's pleasantness be upon us[225] and His beauty upon our children.

WHEN GOD BECOMES HISTORY

*

Hidden away in the inner recesses of *K'nesset Israel* (Ecclesia Israel), in a place where the hand of destruction did not reach, the lovers—these ideas of *K'nesset Israel* (Ecclesia lsrael)—are yet wrapped in a loving embrace, just as they were when the soul-of-souls was first bestowed. So long as practical life was not prepared for this beautiful unity, all these rarefied concepts and their ramifications were considered to be in the realm of "mysteries of Torah" (*sitrei torah*) transmissible only to persons capable of totally transcending ordinary life—and even then, only in a whisper. But now that the world has improved, and *K'nesset Israel* (Ecclesia Israel) has begun to feel within, her righteousness and innocence, and to look disdainfully on the Exile, the inner demand for unifying the ideas is stepped up. Now all those recondite opinions must come forward, to rejuvenate the nation from its source, until the light of renascence shines upon all the dispersed of Israel. The national spirit, which penetrates broken hearts here and there, will be reinvigorated by the scent of the divine soul, and the national soul will accommodate the divine light that comes to illumine the dark places of the earth through Israel's strength and their resurgence.

This is where the wisdom of Israel and her true literature can come to our people's salvation, to revive Israel with the dew of resurrection.

> This shall be written down for the latest generation, and a people created shall praise the Lord."[226]

(*Ha-'Ivri*, 5672/1912, nos. 9-12; reprinted in *Orot* [Jerusalem: Mossad Harav Kook, 5710/1950], pp. 102-118)

Eder ha-Yekar /
'Ikvei ha-Tson / Shabbat ha-Arets

One of the themes that Rav Kook treats in his essay "To the Process of Ideas in Israel" is that Israel is capable of assuming its rightful role as a spiritual teacher to the world only when the nation itself is whole, full-dimensioned, and balanced. Thus does Rav Kook interpret the *halakha*, "The law of *ger toshav* [resident alien] applies only when the Jubilee is in effect."[227] The results of Israel impacting the world at a time of spiritual and physical impairment are horrendous. The living proof of this, according to Rav Kook, is Israel's so-called "daughter religion," Christianity. The reasoning goes that Christianity has such a skewed outlook on life because it imbibed teachings from Judaism when the latter was really in no position to teach. At one point, Rav Kook goes so far as to lay the blame for Spinozism at the door of Christianity, a conclusion that will no doubt surprise many readers because Benedictus (Barukh) Spinoza was a Jew! The following pieces, which precede in time "To the Process of Ideas in Israel," probe this issue from a few angles.

*

If the religious influence of Israel would have come to the world at a time when the nation was brimming with life, then the religious dimension of those nations among which most of our people dwell [i.e. Christendom—BN] would not have received that somber, morose form that causes life to shrivel and the soul to shrink. By the same token, there would not have been the reciprocal influence on Israel's dimension at the time of the exile and dispersion. Religion would not have excited all the negative traits that are aroused by melancholy and depression, especially when it is cloaked in holiness and divinity. And finally, there would not have been triggered the general revolt against religious sentiments and the power of faith—which essentially is the power of healthy life. And then Israel, imitating the nations of the world, would not have been negatively influenced.

[But the historic reality was otherwise.] The religious influence vis-à-vis the nations of the world commenced at a time when Israel had already nullified the desire for idolatry,[228] and the command, *You shall love the Lord your God with all your heart*[229]—"with both your inclinations," as our sages interpreted it[230]—could not be fulfilled in its fullest sense. The Second Temple was not a fully endowed, enduring structure. "*Ve-ekavda[h]* [and I will be glorified] is missing the letter *hé*." The Second Temple lacked the *Shekhinah* (divine presence) and the holy spirit.[231] The fire from above was not in full force; it did not appear as a "crouching lion."[232]

Since the foundation, the source was bereft of vitality—*In dark places he sat me down, like the dead of olden times*[233]—it was not a time to give birth to "daughter religions." Reflecting on the inner state of the nation, Beruriah, the wife of Rabbi Meir, told a *min* [heretic, possibly Christian—BN]:

Rejoice, O barren woman, that you have not given birth.[234] Rejoice *K'nesset Israel* [Ecclesia Israel] who is as a barren woman that has not given birth to children destined for Hell, the likes of you![235]

However, it was brought about by the Lord; the Holy One, blessed be He, assisted those who sprang to force the End; to make *K'nesset Israel* against her will into a "student who is unfit to teach but teaches anyway," concerning whom it is said, *many corpses she fell*,[236] the result being that in many peoples the general religion assumed the trembling, weak form—incapable of mixing with life, and confined to dark monasticism—that is less capable of confronting life than any idolatry.

(*Eder ha-Yekar* [Jerusalem, 5666/1906; reprinted Jerusalem: Mossad Harav Kook, 5745/1985], p. 31)

*

This nation, in which a treasure of eternal life is hidden, knows full well that in truth, cultural enlightenment has already erased a good portion of the idolatrous beliefs—through her influence. This assistance was not granted wholeheartedly on her part, because she did not find herself worthy yet of influencing others; neither did she find the recipients worthy of this lofty influence. Nevertheless, wherever the light penetrated, paganism fell—because the inferior civilization always vacates its place to the superior civilization.

(*'Ikvei ha-Tson, "Avodat Elohim"* [Jerusalem, 5666/1906; reprinted Jerusalem: Mossad Harav Kook, 5745/1985], p. 149)

*

When the ideal knowledge that is unique to Israel was missing—because of the setting of the nation's light—it left the feeling of longing for the divine essence in a state of desertion and desolation. In the very midst of that terrible darkness, there could emerge at the end of the Second Temple Period a system of unity [of God] covered with paganism, in which antisemitism is latent. Through that system [i.e. Christianity—BN], much later, Spinozist heresy could emerge in its dark form, as a prime mover of several antisemitic theories.[237] Most of the world came to understand Israel in a lowly fashion and to be influenced thereby—unable to behold the lofty life that flows from the source of Israel. This life lights up the ends of the earth; it amounts to the broadening of the divine ideals through human government and the orders of existence in general. Only the stopping up of the heart and the personal effacement brought about by the reduced vitality of the Middle Ages, especially by pontifical influence—whose imprint is discernible even in the modern age, on individuals afflicted by that dark malady—only this caused the feeling of freedom to be silenced. Even rationalist philosophy, which must spring from life itself, lost its vigor and thunder; it was unable to forcefully present the demand of the healthy spirit, a cry all humanity utters with one mouth: How could this man [i.e. Spinoza—BN] deny the existence of general divine freedom, when freedom—internal and external—is the choicest of His ideals? "*Engraved (harut) upon the tablets. Do not read harut (engraved) but herut (liberty)!*"[238] It is only through the influence of a foolish people,[239] a humanity sunk in ignorance and illusion, that appropriated the unity of God and His service from

Holy Scripture in a superficial sense, and converted it into a pagan monstrosity. Only this influence could give birth to, and afterward accept, a dark, hellish teaching from which life, its splendor and hope, are missing.

(*'Ikvei ha-Tson*, "*'Avodat Elohim*," p. 153)

*

Only when the nation experiences such *elan vital*, does it rise to a level whereby it might fasten its life to the life of mankind as a whole through the mediation of individuals—*gerim toshavim* (resident aliens)—who while standing in the midst of broad humanity, feel a special affinity for the refreshing spiritual aspirations of the [Jewish] nation. Only then does the nation possess the inner fortitude to repress its impurities, so that the general light may shine brightly "The law of *ger toshav* applies only when the Jubilee is in effect" (*'Arakhin* 29a).

(***Introduction to Shabbat ha-Arets*** [Jerusalem, 5670/1910; reprinted Jerusalem: Mossad Harav Kook, 5745/1985], p. 10)

Letter of Rabbi Zevi Yehudah Hakohen Kook

The following letter of Rav Kook's only son, Zevi Yehudah, to an unnamed correspondent, expands on many of the themes contained in "To the Process of Ideas in Israel." The writer reveals his familiarity with the philosophy of Nietzsche ("Friedrich Nietzsche and his war against *Sklavenmoral* [slave morality], which is truly the main significance of his personality").[240] The idea put forth by Rabbi Zevi Yehudah that the appearance of Christianity on the stage of history represents a divergence from the divine plan, seems to be at loggerheads with what Maimonides wrote at the end of his code:

> Man is powerless to understand the thoughts of the Creator of the universe. Our ways are not His ways, and our thoughts are not His thoughts. All these matters of Jesus of Nazareth and of this Ishmaelite [i.e., Muhammad] who arose after him, are only to clear the way for King Messiah, and to fix the entire world to serve the Lord in unison, as it says, "Then I shall change unto peoples a pure language, that they may all call on the name of the Lord to serve Him with one accord" [Zephaniah 3:9]. How so?

Already the world has been filled with the concepts of Messiah, of Torah, and of the commandments. These concepts spread to distant isles and to many pagan peoples. They debate these concepts and the commandments of the Torah. Some say, "These commandments were once true but they are nullified by this time, for they were not intended for posterity." And some say, "They contain esoteric ideas; they are not to be taken literally, and the 'Messiah' has already revealed their hidden meaning."

And when the true Messiah will arise, and succeed, and be exalted, immediately they will be taken aback and realize that "their fathers inherited falsehood" [Jeremiah 16:19], and their prophets and forefathers deceived them.[241]

*

St. Gallen [Switzerland]
Third Day of Hanukkah
27 Kislev [5679/1919]

Shalom.[242]

This is the continuation of our conversation on the night of the fourteenth [of Kislev]. Forgive the delay because of various preoccupations.

What is the inner relation and the direct connection between Judaism and Jews, and the general spiritual movements of mankind, ancient and modern?

Beforehand, let me mention this: In our previous conversation I emitted the words, "Christianity placed *stumbling blocks* in the way of the historical process of man's spiritual evolution." Then "X" contradicted this by praising Christianity and the great benefit it brought to humanity's conception of religion, culture, and morality. As the discussion expanded, I forgot to explain what I meant. When I said "placed stumbling blocks, etc." I did not touch at all on this question whether the benefit of Christianity outweighs its detriment, or vice versa, in terms of its specific historic value in generations past, present, and future. Rather, I had in mind the universal, eternal history which encountered on its way stumbling blocks and delays due to Christianity. Again, I am not referring to specific, overt influences that Christianity brought to the world, but rather to the "historical mistake" of its creation.

The overall view of human history and Israelite history brings to an awareness of the great universal value of Israel. This value lies primarily not in the generosity or spirituality of individual Jews, be they sages, prophets, or mighty warriors; be they a small number or even millions, but rather in the character of the nation qua nation, in the "collective psychology," the national soul, "a kingdom of priests and a holy nation,"[243] "the people of the Lord." We already discussed this on a few occasions. This is to say that the blessing the nations receive through Israel, Israel's influence upon human civilization, consists not of sermons by Jewish leaders or their exemplary lifestyle, neither in "humanism," nor in an abstract, illusionary "Judaism," but only in an indivisible Jews-and-Judaism, in the existence of the *nation itself*, through which the light of God is manifested in the world.[244] Through this nation, humanity comes into possession of the light of God. It is not an influence external to mankind; it does not consist in reducing the strength of life or its joy "for the sake of heaven." Rather, this is the revelation of the light of God in mankind's very midst;

it addresses human beings in their normal state, fortifying strength and joy, and advancing their development—through the currents that flow to them from the living people of Israel, its prophecy, priesthood, wisdom, temple and kingdom, including all aspects of society, whether they be economy or politics, etc. Israel influences all automatically (*von selbst*).

So this should have been the program, the historical process of man's spiritual evolution: The natural, vigorous life of early pagan man, complete with culture, should have developed unhindered, paralleled by the natural holistic life of the Israelite people in its land, with its statecraft, language and civilization, with the spirit of the Lord its God resting upon it and vivifying all its ideals and deeds. From the Israelite people, from their essence, the light of the Lord would appear and permeate the entire earth, all nations and kingdoms. Then all of the promises of the prophets—cosmopolitical and cosmological—would have found concrete fulfillment. Out of the very flower of life, the holy life of a living people, the people of the Lord—man and the world would have become sanctified and purified in a normal evolution true to character.

But the confluence of many circumstances, culminating at last in the historical appearance of Christianity, arrested the natural process of this divine historic program. There set in delay and reaction. There was established the way of the "historic mistake," "the program of the anti-program": A spiritual, ethical influence, a global "calling by the name of the Lord" that did not arise from the divine program, from the general creative process, but rather from human thoughts, aspirations and imaginings of the name of the Lord. This program does not come to encompass *all of life*, to exalt and strengthen life in the light of the Lord, but only to impose upon life spirit and morality, to cower and repress life. This is not a natural penetration of light and holiness flowing from the *elan vital* of the Godly people, corresponding to the general evolution of human civilization, but rather a superimposition of moral influence—based on the Torah of Israel *sans* Israel's living spirit—on early mankind in its primitive state of spirituality. It was a heavyhanded influence that necessarily involved bending the stature of man and robbing him of his creativity, his natural strength, material and spiritual. This massive counterfeit influence interfaces with a pessimistic, monastic, Essene regime, with alienation of human psychology and civilization from man's natural surroundings, with weakening the divine unity and fusing it with fetishism, with the infamous abolishment of the values of the Jewish nation and commandments of God, and finally, with wicked antisemitism. The historic process of this [Christian] influence is connected to the length of our exile.

Yet certainly there is no forgetfulness before the Holy One[245]; no counterfeit, no error before His Throne of Glory. From all the downfalls and obscurities themselves there are always revealed mighty upliftments and important illuminations. The meanderings of history and all the contributions to man's culture, spiritual refinement, and moral guidance that they brought to the world, certainly add to the total picture, just as all the benefits—material and spiritual—that derive from our exile. But the "counsel of the Lord is eternal"[246]; understandably, the divine historic program can never be cancelled by human diversions even if they be multiplied a thousandfold—only delayed. Despite all these delays, eventually history will revert back to its original program. In an evolution of hundreds or thousands of years, the human spirit seeks its destiny. The biblical influence that was thrust upon the nations of the world against their will and their nature, to their detriment, is evaporating through various currents, scientific and popular. Wittingly or unwittingly, the nations are freeing themselves of its yoke. They vomit the superficial sustenance that they derived from Holy Writ in order to arrive at their natural state. (This is discussed in the writings of our rabbi. Of what we read together, there is a relevant discussion in "To the Process of Ideas in Israel," published in *Ha-'Ivri*.) ....

(*Zemah Zevi: Letters of Rabbi Zevi Yehudah Hakohen Kook*, vol. 1 [Jerusalem, 5751/1991], pp. 179-181)

To the Two Houses of Israel

The claim that by and large Sephardic Jewry excelled in codification, in breadth, and Ashkenazic Jewry in dialectic, in depth, has been made time and time again by various historians of Halakha.[247] It was even given poetic expression by Abraham Joshua Heschel in his essay *The Earth Is the Lord's*.[248] Rav Kook's "soul friend," Rabbi Pinhas Hakohen Lintop, applied the theory to the realm of Kabbalah, writing that the orderly presentation of Rabbi Moses Cordovero is attributable to the enduring Sephardic legacy, while Rabbi Isaac Luria's rather disorderly teaching derives from his Ashkenazic heritage.[249] The fact that a theory is repeated numerous times does not necessarily make it true.

Rav Kook contends that if we find an Ashkenazic authority who exhibits codificatory ability, or a Sephardic sage who displays dialectic ability, that should be chalked up to the influence of the opposite community, or to exceptional endowment of soul.[250] Yet, if we find enough exceptions to the rule, then the rule itself is in jeopardy. If we poke enough holes in the walls, the entire edifice will collapse.

Let us examine this theory dispassionately without prejudice and preconceived notions. Are there great Ashkenazic codifiers? Are there great Sephardic dialecticians?

The showpiece of Sephardic Jewry is Maimonides' code of *Mishneh Torah*, a monumental work unsurpassed both before and after. The "poster child" of Ashkenazic Jewry is *Tosafot*, in actuality a compilatory, collective work; a polyphony of many voices—the most strident being those of Rabbi Isaac of Dampierre (Ri) and Rabbi Jacob of Ramerupt (Rabbenu Tam)—which in our popular imagination have morphed into a single personality. These two exemplars would have stood out foremost in Rav Kook's mind as he wrote this essay.

But, you counter, is the comparison fair? Comparing code to commentary is like the proverbial comparison of apples and oranges. Halakhic codes and Talmudic commentaries are two different genres; scholars laboring on codes and those producing commentaries are employed in two different industries.[251]

Printed in the margin of the "standard" page of the Talmud (the "Vilna Shas"), under the heading "*Eyn Mishpat, Ner Mitsvah*," are notes that refer the reader to the classic codes of Halakha: Maimonides, *Sefer Mitsvot Gadol* (Semag), *Tur*, and *Shulhan 'Arukh*.[252] These codes are equally distributed between Sepharadim and Ashkenazim. Maimonides and Rabbi Joseph Karo, author of the *Shulhan 'Arukh*, were both Sepharadim, while Rabbi Moses of Coucy, author *Sefer Mitsvot Gadol*, was a French Jew, and Rabbi Jacob ben Asher, author *Arba'ah Turim*, a German Jew by birth (although he later settled in Toledo, Spain).[253]

One might counter-argue (as did, in effect, Rav Kook) that these Ashkenazic codes, though their contribution to the development of Halakha is immeasurably great, were inspired by the lead of Maimonides the Sepharadi. Rabbi Moses of Coucy and Rabbi Jacob "*Ba'al ha-Turim*" were in a sense "copycats." (In the case of

Rabbi Jacob, though born in Ashkenaz, the majority of his life was spent in Spain, and therefore it is fair to assume that he came under Sephardic influence.)[254]

But for the sake of "devil's advocate," the argument can run in the opposite direction as well. The Sephardic *Shulhan 'Arukh* of Rabbi Joseph Karo, which has dominated Jewish life ever since its publication, was poured into the template of the Ashkenazic *Tur*.[255] And if that is so, then we have whittled down supposed Sephardic codificatory competence to a single stellar example: *Mishneh Torah*.

Not so fast. There preceded Maimonides' *Mishneh Torah*, the *Halakhot* of Rabbi Isaac Alfasi, whom for all intents and purposes we may consider a pillar of Sephardic Jewry. (Whether Al-Fasi originated in Fez, Morocco, as his surname indicates, is not to the point. What is relevant, is that his career burgeoned in Lucena, Spain, where he headed the Talmudic academy and trained Rabbi Joseph Migash, teacher of Maimon, father of Maimonides.) While not a code in the strict sense, but rather abstracts of the Talmudic *sugyot* or discussions, the *Halakhot* of Alfasi certainly paved the way for later codification inasmuch as they streamlined the discussion to halakhic decision and stripped out the extraneous *Agadah*. It seems totally justified to say that the *Halakhot* of Alfasi together with the *Mishneh Torah* of Maimonides set their stamp upon the intellectual identity of Sephardic Jewry.[256]

But, you ask, what of the splendid genre of *Hiddushim* (Novellae) produced by Spanish Jewry: *Hiddushei Ramban*, *Hiddushei Rashba*, *Hiddushei Ritba*? Certainly these are dazzling in depth! Rav Kook is ready with the response. Nahmanides, who founded this school, introjected the conceptual method of the Sages of France. We now know that both of Ramban's major teachers reached northern France and sat with Ri and Ritsba. (Ramban's cousin and townsman Rabbenu

Jonah Gerondi travelled to France to study in the Tosafist academy of Evreux.) Thus, the Sephardic *Hiddushim* were inseminated by the Ashkenazic *Tosafot*.[257] Rabbi Solomon ben Abraham ibn Adret (Rashba) was Nahmanides' disciple, and Rabbi Yom Tov ben Abraham Al-Sevilli (Ritba), ibn Adret's disciple. Through the Rashba and Ritba as well, the impact of the Tosafists is great.[258]

(Haym Soloveitchik has recently observed that while the texts of the *Tosafot* made their way southward to Spain, where they exerted considerable influence upon the development of Spanish Talmudic studies, the opposite scenario did not occur. The *Hiddushim* of Ramban and Rashba did not travel northward, and evidently, held no attraction for Ashkenazic Jewry. The intellectual baggage travelled in one direction only. Even the majestic *Mishneh Torah* with few exceptions did not grab the attention of Franco-German Jewry.)[259]

One imagines Rav Kook would deal in the same manner with the more recent development of the much vaunted "Tunisian analysis" (*"Ha-'Iyyun ha-Tunisa'i"*). In the modern era, there arose among Tunisian Jewry the phenomenon of a dialectic method of studying Talmud. Here we have not an individual but an entire Sephardic intellectual community devoted to dialectic. Again, Rav Kook's response would be that the Tunisians adopted the Ashkenazic methodology of the Tosafists.[260]

And then we come to the Vilna Gaon, Rav Kook's other example of a "hybrid" who crossed the great divide between Ashkenaz and Sepharad to create a fusion of the two.[261] To what aspect of Elijah Gaon's intellectual endeavor is Rav Kook referring?

First and foremost, the Vilna Gaon stressed *peshat*, the simple meaning of texts. The search for the simple, uncluttered meaning pervades both his Biblical and Rabbinic commentaries.[262]

Then there is the fact that the Gaon recommended for himself and his students the daily study of Alfasi's *Halakhot*, a practice that was continued by Rabbi Naftali Zevi Yehudah Berlin (NeZIV), *Rosh Yeshivah* of Volozhin, and his disciple—Rav Kook![263] This ties in with the Gaon's insistence on a global command of the Talmud; mastery of Alfasi's *Halakhot* was designed to provide the desired breadth.[264]

There is also the testimony of the Gaon's sons that he aspired to write a new *Shulhan 'Arukh* but was prevented by Heaven from doing so.[265] (Hasidim will tell you that Heaven assigned that coveted honor to the Vilna Gaon's opposite number, Rabbi Shneur Zalman of Liozhna and later Liadi, who did succeed in producing a *Shulhan 'Arukh*.)

Short of a *Shulhan 'Arukh*, the Gaon of Vilna (Gra) did bequeath to us his *Be'ur* to Rabbi Joseph Karo's *Shulhan 'Arukh*. In the *Be'ur ha-Gra* we do see some of the predilection for magisterial decision-making worthy of a Sephardic grandee. (Though as Rabbi Abraham Isaiah Karelitz [*Hazon Ish*] pointed out, these notes of the Gaon are so cryptic that oftentimes one is hard-pressed to say on which side of an issue the Gaon has ruled.)[266] Rav Kook was so taken with the *Be'ur ha-Gra* that he applied himself to penning a commentary thereto: *Be'er Eliyahu*.[267] (In private conversation, Rav Kook would confide that while writing *Be'er Eliyahu* he saw himself as a *shamosh* or assistant in Vilna handing the Gaon the many texts he summoned.)[268]

In the later period of the *"Aharonim,"* the Sephardic sages excelled as encyclopedists. There developed a typically Sephardic genre of halakhic literature whereby entries are arranged in alphabetical order. For example (and examples abound), several of the halakhic works of Rabbi Hayyim Palache of Izmir are alphabetical in their arrangement.[269]

In closing, we note with interest that Rav Kook commended to his son-in-law, an aspiring student of Talmud, the "way of the Sephardic summarists" ("*ha-me'assefim ha-Sefaradim*").[270]

*

Rav Kook's suggestion that the Ashkenazic propensity for in-depth analysis may have been what prevented Ashkenazic Jews of the Middle Ages from engaging in the study of Philosophy, whereas the Sephardic predilection for breadth and encyclopedic knowledge predisposed them to the pursuit of general Philosophy—simply does not stand up to historic scrutiny.[271]

The facts are that the Franco-German intellectual climate was vastly different from the Hispanic climate. In both Muslim *al-Andalus* in the South of Spain,[272] and later in Christian Castile in the North, there flourished enlightened rulers who invited to their courts wise men of the three faiths—Christians, Jews and Muslims—to share knowledge and ideas. This was the case in Cordoba of 'Abd al-Rahman III, and later in Toledo of Alfonso X (known as *"El Sabio,"* "the Wise"). In such an open society (Americo Castro coined the term *"convivencia,"* or "coexistence"), it was only natural that the Jews take advantage of the rich opportunities offered, which resulted in an intellectual cross-pollination. In France and Germany, where Jews were barred from participating in the general intellectual foment, such opportunities for a healthy exchange of ideas, simply did not exist. Philosophy, *tout court*, was not an option for a Jewish sage.[273] (The suggestion raised by some scholars that the Tosafists were influenced by Abelard has received a thorough thrashing in the recent literature.)[274]

We might very well argue that Rav Kook actually reversed cause and effect when it came to Sephardic Jewry's fondness for Philosophy. Rather than deriving the attraction to Philosophy from Sephardic Jewry's orderly, encyclopedic approach to the study of Talmud, it makes more sense to assume that the ability to produce magnificently organized codes of Halakha, may ultimately be traced to Greek influence. Perhaps Maimonides received his taxonomical ability from reading works of Aristotle. We know that he consciously styled his

Mishneh Torah after Rabbi Judah the Prince's *Mishnah*.²⁷⁵ And as is famous, Rabbi Judah the Prince and the Roman ruler Antoninus were fast friends. Perhaps future scholars will be able to determine exactly to what degree the *Mishnah*, a logical, orderly, systematic presentation of Halakha, is indebted to Greco-Roman literary influence present in *Erets Yisrael* at the time of its composition.²⁷⁶ Rav Kook viewed Sephardic codification as the continuation of the Geonic enterprise. He does not articulate specific titles of Geonica. Here too, scholars are beginning to explore general Islamic influence upon the manner of presentation of the various Halakhic treatises issued during the Geonic era.²⁷⁷ (For example, recently David E. Sklare has limned the influence of Islamic jurisprudence upon the presentation of Rabbi Samuel ben Hofni Gaon, the last great Gaon of Sura, who in turn, so it is hypothesized, may have influenced Maimonides.)²⁷⁸

*

Despite the many valid criticisms we have raised, there is still much food for thought in Rav Kook's essay. Rav Kook was of the opinion that the relation between any given community and the literature it produces is reciprocal. In ways subtle or not so subtle, literature has a way of influencing people's thought patterns. Consider this *pensée*:

> Every language in its totality is one specific illumination, possessing an entire worldview that contains *in potentia* all the literature that it will bear for the entire length of its existence, from the beginning of its development until it shall pass from the world (*Shemonah Kevatsim* 2:357).

*

The phrase "to the two houses of Israel" first occurs in Isaiah 8:14 where its meaning is ambiguous.

To the Two Houses of Israel

Our national renascence which is taking place before our eyes in *Erets Yisrael*, must encompass in their entirety all the values of our life. There can be no true renascence as long as it applies only to special sectors and specific values. It must encompass all our sectors and the totality of our life-values.

For this reason, we come to appreciate the two main plans of the sacred and the secular. As much as we might tend to the right or the left, we cannot divest ourselves of the view that in our national life we are dealing with two life-values: the sacred and the secular.

The present national renascence bases itself more on the secular value of our national life. This is not an essential lack in the national renascence in its [present] condition, but there can be no doubt that as long as the value of the sacred content of our national life does not manifest in the movement of renascence in all its power—we have no characteristic renascence; no complete renascence.

And since we are certainly summoned to a total renascence of the people, we must stir the renascence of the sacred by [utilizing] the very ways that the national renascence is aroused and arranged; exactly by the means in which the movement of our secular renascence develops.

As we are about to arouse a national renascence of the sacred, we come to appreciate more the two great Houses of Israel, whose lives are so typical, so well-defined here in our Holy Land: the Ashkenazim and the Sepharadim. From the perspective of the secular renascence, there is practically no difference of character; we are brothers, sons of one people, and the national affairs that pertain to the building of the nation in its land, are equally close to all our hearts. Inasmuch as they must be equally close to Sepharadim and Askenazim, there exists the possibility of formulating all the movements of our national life in a manner equal to both these Houses of Israel. But as soon as we come to arouse the national renascence from the perspective of it sacred value, we become involved in deep psychologies that took root over long periods of time in forms and characters so diverse that we are left wondering at this spectacle, and the question before us—"In what manner shall we realize the process of national renascence in *Erets Yisrael* in its sacred value?"—must interest every sensitive heart and every thinking brain among us.

Just as those who tend to the left forever err in making light of the value of the national renascence on its foundation of the sacred, so err those who think that by lip service and mere convention we can at once "disappear" all the different styles of the sacred life of our people, differences which are most pronounced in these two great Houses of Israel: the Ashkenazim and the Sepharadim.

These present not just technical, legal obstacles. Worlds full of life, full of the majesty of holiness are at stake; by rubbing out one of these characteristic forms, we stand to lose great wealth, great value which we are incapable of ignoring.

These differences in ways of life, in worldview, that trickle down in specific laws and customs—interlock organically with the life of the soul conducted thereby. We must pay attention to the source [of the soul] until there open before us the pathways of a general national renascence that encompasses the entire House of Israel from the vantage of the values of the sacred life.

Without engaging in historical speculation which puts off those seeking solid, clear facts, we may [nonetheless] come close to grasping the recent manifestations of the spirit whose imprint is yet discernible in our lives, or at least, we can grasp them through the literature of the not so distant past. Through them [i.e., the manifestations of the spirit] we can come to outline to a degree the unique characteristics of our two great Houses, of our brothers the Sepharadim and the Ashkenazim. And through such views we can also come somewhat closer to the solution to the question: How might the general renascence encompass the value of the sacred in our national life?

*

From the time that the Talmud—more specifically the Babylonian Talmud—was sealed, and particularly from the time that it was publicized in Israel as the unique book in which the life of the Nation (both collective and individual) is elucidated and shaped, it became apparent that the Nation's reception of the Talmud—as the book bearing responsibility for the integrity of national life—lent itself to two alternate forms. We see that with time, Ashkenazic Jewry adapted to one form, and Sephardic Jewry to the other. We must assign to these forms the names "Critical Form" (*tsurah bikoratit*) and "Dialectic Form" (*tsurah pilpulit*). The Talmud can serve the Nation of Israel as a practical guide in all the ways of her life, by either of these two forms. But the shape that life takes differs between these two forms, and as a result, many details differ according to these two forms of Talmudic influence.

The Talmud as a book comprising a great wealth of Halakhic and Aggadic material; a book full of differences of opinion regarding all life's values, requires a method of arriving at conclusions, at a general consensus. Toward this end, it is possible to employ either of these two faculties, either the critical or the dialectic. Each of the two faculties necessitates much labor and prodigious talent to achieve its perfection. The critical faculty necessitates great diligence, incisive familiarity with the material, broad intellect, straightforward simplicity, and steady organization. The critical faculty is not hard pressed to resolve contradictory passages. [When it comes to] a book such as the Talmud, which comprises so many differing opinions, the critical faculty is not grieved if after study there remain differing opinions. The main concern is to determine which view of the Halakha or the Aggadah is the more fundamental. And this, the critical faculty clarifies by [the use of] time-honored principles (*kelalim*). For example, something stated upon a single, solitary occasion will be rejected when faced with something stated on numerous occasions; likewise, something stated in passing or tentatively, must give way to an outright halakhic decision, *et cetera*.

But not always is criticism correct in its judgment. Not all that appears contradictory is truly contradictory; by delving deeply into the content of the matter, its reason and logic, there is room for reconciling the opinions. Thus, there was born the dialectic method. By virtue of the depth of its logic, dialectic is not pressured by contradictions. Seeming contradictions are resolved by the power of its understanding and by the appearance of the novel explanation. For this reason, it makes more use of in-depth reasoning and sharpness of intellect than does criticism. On the other hand, dialectic does not require as much the organizational ability that is the primary instrument of criticism.

When we observe the work of the early Ge'onim in relation to the Talmud, we find the critical side predominating and the prints of *Pilpul* relatively indiscernible. However by the time we arrive at the generation of the Tosafists, we find *Pilpul* on a high niveau, even as criticism and organization fall into disuse.

From the earliest generations in which there is recognizable the divergence of Ashkenazim and Sepharadim, we witness that the Sepharadim adapted to organization and criticism, and to the lifestyle that derives therefrom. There rested upon them the spirit of the early Ge'onim, and the dialectic faculty that was fortified by the sages of *Tsarfat* (France) and *Ashkenaz* (Germany), never became mainline in their sacred life. For the Ashkenazim, their opposite numbers, the glint of *Pilpul* shone brightly. Sharpness of intellect and in-depth understanding of the Talmudic opinions developed to the point that they became the signature of their lives. The spirit of the Tosafists rested upon them, and in direct proportion, their involvement in criticism and organization decreased.

This difference of style, whose origin lies in the fundamental understanding of the depths of Talmud, impacted upon culture and general worldview.

In truth, each of these two methods is in need of the other. It is impossible for criticism and organization to achieve perfection unaided by the dialectic faculty that analyzes each matter in depth, and penetrates every contradiction to assess whether it is founded or not. On the other hand, the dialectic method is in need of organization and criticism to light up its horizon, so that it might discern the [objective] value of a novelty born of the attempt to reconcile contradictions.

It is understood that the tendency to dialectic encouraged depth, while the tendency to criticism encouraged breadth.

The dialectical method caused the Ashkenazim to develop a sharpness whereby there were revealed to them with great clarity the cracks and contradictions in contemporary philosophies vis-à-vis Judaism. This was also the reason that the Ashkenazim distanced outside, foreign influences from Judaic studies.

The method of criticism and organization which was absorbed more by the Sepharadim, gave rise to the inclusion of general studies and ways of life within the overall system of Judaic consciousness; at times, these enriched their spirit and left behind a trail of stellar success—after those general studies were purified in the crucible of our exemplary great men.

We must not deconstruct this overview based on the fact that we witness isolated incidences of in-depth dialectic and novelty (*hiddush*) among the Sephardic sages, and by the same token, appearances of organization and criticism among the Ashkenazic sages. All this comes about because of the influence that each community received from the other, or due to exceptional character traits. But at the foundation, it is clear that the abiding tendency to organization and criticism is a Sephardic characteristic, just as the tendency to depth, sharpness and novelty, is an Ashkenazic characteristic. Of those greats who strove to combine criticism with dialectic in regard to Talmudic logic (whose effects crossed over to general outlook), Nahmanides is distinguished in the period of the *Rishonim* among the Sephardic sages, and the Gaon of Vilna is distinguished in the period of the *Aharonim* among the Ashkenazic sages.

Each sector of the nation must perfect its talent. In addition, our obligation is greater now than at any other time, to have each sector influencing, and influenced by, the other. Then there will be perfected within us these two talents, and all the branches, manifold and great, that ramify from them in all aspects of life, practical and cultural.

From the constant desire growing mighty within us to penetrate the depth of one's own spirit, and to contemplate—to the best of one's ability—the spirit that is different from one's own, so that one might thereby supply that which is lacking in oneself, the mutual influence [of Sepharad and Ashkenaz] will progressively increase, in order to build the nation in its fullness, and in order that the spirit of the nation be perfected in its totality—until Sepharad and Ashkenaz exert upon one another a living, full influence. In the course of time, these two disparate talents will be equalized, and the inner spirit of life which is truly a unified spirit pounding in these two Houses of Israel, will be revealed in all its majesty and beauty, to build together the House of Israel with the value of national renascence that is founded upon the sacred, into a structure so perfect that no talent, no advantage, no good quality, no good idea, present in either of these two Houses, will be lost to us. The essence of life derived from these two faculties—incisive understanding (*pilpul*) and critical enlightenment (*bikoret*)—will yield its fruit to the pride and glory of the House of Israel, about to be built into "one nation in the Land."[279]

We hope that the hand of the Lord wrought this to gather these two Houses of Israel into the Land of Israel in a manner in which their different characters are discernible, in order that they should be ready to exert upon one another a good influence that allows each its role in the collective life of the nation. Out of the preservation of the distinct character and the deepening of the specific gifts, will proceed the complete national content in all its beauty, which will then be a force acting to enrich all general avenues of life. Thereby Israel will be built, becoming "one nation in the Land," by the light of the Holy One of Israel and its Redeemer.

(*Mizrah u-Ma'arav* 1 [1920]; reprinted in *Ma'amrei ha-Rayah*, vol. 1[Jerusalem, 1980], pp. 45-48)

Address at the Opening of Hebrew University in Jerusalem

On April 1, 1925 (7 Nissan, 5685), the Mount Scopus campus of Hebrew University in Jerusalem was officially opened amid much pomp and circumstance.[280] In attendance was Lord James Balfour, famous for the Balfour Declaration, the British document that promised the Jews a homeland in Palestine. Seated at the dais were the Sephardic Chief Rabbi, Ya'akov Meir; the Ashkenazic Chief Rabbi, Abraham Isaac Kook; Lord Allenby (who as General Allenby liberated Jerusalem from the Turks in 1918); the British High Commissioner, Sir Herbert Samuel; Dr. Chaim Weizmann; and the British Chief Rabbi, Dr. Joseph H. Hertz.[281] For the occasion, delegates arrived from throughout the Diaspora. By all reckoning, this was truly a momentous event in the life of the Yishuv. Zionism could count the opening of the university in Jerusalem as a milestone on the road to realization of its goals.

Of all the many addresses delivered that spring day, the remarks of one man continue—three quarters of a century later—to arouse controversy. Did the full-bearded, otherworldly ascetic with fur *spodek* atop his head, utter the words *For out of Zion shall go forth Torah*[282] from the podium of Hebrew University?

Those interested in besmirching Rav Kook's good name, forever cite the fact that at the opening of an institution dedicated to secular learning, the Chief Rabbi cited this prophecy.[283] Unfortunately, the rabbi's remarks were lifted out of context. Rav Kook took advantage of the occasion to plea the cause of the *yeshivot* in Jerusalem,[284] especially the Central Yeshivah he was working so hard to establish. Indeed, throughout the early 1920s, Rav Kook lanced appeals to world Jewry to establish a "universal central yeshivah" in Jerusalem. It was in reference to the holy *yeshivot*, the traditional bastions of Torah learning, that Rav Kook invoked the verse in Isaiah, *For out of Zion shall go forth Torah, and the word of the Lord from Jerusalem.*

Rav Kook's tactics had not changed since he first set foot on the holy soil a generation ago. Unlike some other rabbis, he would not boycott the event organized by the secular Zionist establishment. He would make his appearance, and make his voice heard. As at the memorial gathering for Herzl, Rav Kook would use this golden opportunity to impart to his listeners an alternate vision of reality, a vision of holiness.

In his outline of history, Rav Kook dwelled on the troubled relations between Judaism and Greco-Roman civilization, starting with the translation of the Hebrew Bible into Greek. While the hellenized Jews of Alexandria greeted this highly symbolic event with hearty enthusiasm, the Jews of Erets Israel viewed it as cause for mourning. Rav Kook cited the *Scroll of Fasts* (*Megillat Ta'anit*) to the effect that "darkness descended on the world for three days." Rav Kook made the astute observation that the Jews participating in the present event in Jerusalem were all descendants of the Jews of Erets Israel, not those of Alexandria.[285] The hint was obvious. Unselective intake of foreign culture would spell doom for the people dwelling in Zion.

ADDRESS AT THE OPENING OF HEBREW UNIVERSITY

Rav Kook alluded to the fact that over eons of time, Israel both exported and imported culture. The thesis is tantalizing. If only he had more time to develop his theme. A sustained effort buttressed by many more concrete examples would have produced a major contribution to Jewish history. As it is, Rav Kook leaves us wanting more Rav Kook....

*

The prophet of consolation said:

> Lift up your eyes round about and see, they have all gathered, they come to you, your sons are coming from afar, and your daughters are brought along in arms. Then you will see and be filled with light, and your heart will dread and be enlarged, because unto you will be turned the abundance of the sea, the riches of nations will come unto you.[286]

The great event of this day, the opening of the Mount Scopus campus of Hebrew University in Jerusalem, in a ceremony so beautiful, in a celebration so full of light, in a gathering of tens of thousands of our sons and daughters from throughout Erets Israel and the Diaspora—displays for us the holy vision of this prophecy as if it had come to life in miniature.

Though to date not all have gathered and the beginning of the ingathering of exiles is still miniscule, nevertheless, this gathering is great assurance that the time is nigh and the gates of redemption are opening before us. Our hope is strengthened that the great day, when all will be gathered to us and the redeemed will go up to Zion, will not tarry.

At the beginning of our process today we recognize what the prophet meant when he said: "Then you will see." With our own eyes we see the wonders of the Redeemer of Israel, who has done for us this great thing, to raise up His people's horn among the nations, to give us a rule in Judah, and the strength and inspiration to begin to establish the life of our people upon the sacred soil as in ancient days. We recognize too the expression, "You will be filled with light." This is brought to life by the thousands of faces shining from joy, from the distinguished presence of our guests: the man chosen by heaven to issue the declaration, Lord Balfour; the high commissioner, our brother, Sir Herbert Samuel; Lord Allenby; and the great rabbis and sages who grace this splendid celebration. Their attendance illumines the souls of all those gathered here, and the tens of thousands of our brethren abroad whose soul is attentive to the nation's honor on this day.

But where does the "dread" arise? Why did the prophet preface the "enlargement of the heart" with "dread"? However, when we scan the distance, the many generations past and the various spiritual movements at work in our people, we are prepared to agree that "dread" is the appropriate concomitant to "enlargement of our hearts."

There are two roads the spirit of Israel takes. One road is inner-directed. It is pure holiness; it serves to deepen the spirit and to illumine the Torah within. This was always the purpose of the Torah institutions, Israel's citadels of the soul, the *yeshivot* of the past, of the present, and of the future. Their goal is to enhance and strengthen Torah in the fullest sense of this holy longing throughout the generations. This spiritual path is certain. "Great peace have they who love Your Torah, and for them there is no stumbling block."[287] And despite all that certainty, Rabbi Nehunyah ben Hakanah would

ADDRESS AT THE OPENING OF HEBREW UNIVERSITY

pray upon entering the house of study that no grievous error come about through him.[288]

The second spiritual road of the nation serves not only to deepen the Torah within us, but also provides a path to export Judaic concepts from our private domain to the public domain of the entire world. It is in this role that we serve as a light to the nations. At the same time, by this route, general sciences are imported from broad humanity. The best of these sciences are fit to the purity of our lives. Even this "importing" serves in the long run the goal of exporting from our world to the world at large, because in this way we are able to effectively communicate with the outside world. It is in this capacity that the university can serve as a great and lofty vessel. And here, my friends, is where the "dread" enters in.

In bygone days we were tested, when an effort was made to export from our domain to the public domain our most cherished and holy concepts. I am referring to the event of translating the Torah to Greek.[289] At that time there arose in Judaism two reactions to this enterprise. The Judaism of Erets Israel was seized with *dread*, and its world became dark.[290] Simultaneously, Hellenistic Judaism experienced a *broadening of the heart*, and received the event with great joy.

We have also experienced *importing*. Currents of various cultures—Greek wisdom and the other cultures of the peoples of the world whom we encountered in different epochs of our history—penetrated our interior. This process of importing was also greeted with mixed reactions: *Dread* in some circles, and *broadening of the heart* in others.

When we take reckoning, in retrospect we see that the dread was not groundless; neither was the "broadening of the heart" without grounds. We gained much from those currents in certain respects, but we also lost considerably.

One thing is clear to us. Of those circles who received both trends, importing and exporting, without dread, with banal optimism and unmitigated "breadth of heart"—not many descendants are partners with us in the holy work of building our land and resurrecting our people. Most of the descendants have been assimilated among the peoples, swept away by the waves of the sea of nations who invaded us.

All the creative energies at work in our great enterprise, the great bloc of the people faithful to its identity—are descended either from those Jews who dwelt securely in our inner fastnesses, in the "tents of Torah," or from those Jews who, while engaged in exporting and importing values and concepts between Israel and the nations, viewed the process with ambivalence. Their "enlargement of the heart," their joy at the great vision of a sea of nations, was accompanied by "dread."

On this account, the Prophet [Isaiah] predicted: "Then you will see and be filled with light, and your heart will dread and be enlarged, because unto you will be turned the abundance of the sea, the riches of nations will come unto you."

How does one quiet the fear? How does one brace the nation against this great flood? Gentlemen, I stand here on this august platform as the representative of the community to transmit to you the cogitations of the heart of faithful Judaism, of some of its most distinguished elements.

We need to know that the university alone will not exhaust all the demands of our life as a people. First and foremost, we must have great, mighty *yeshivot*, those that are already and those destined to be formed, including the Central Yeshivah that we are attempting with God's help to establish in Jerusalem. Such a *yeshivah* will illumine

Israel with Torah in all its departments: *Halakha* and *Aggadah*, practical rabbinics and philosophy. We need *yeshivot* that will, as in days past, establish securely the spirit of the nation.

At the same time, the university must stand on a level such that the name of heaven and the name of Israel and Erets Israel will be sanctified thereby. The name of heaven must be desecrated neither by the administrators nor by the instructors and students. Especially, the teachers of Jewish studies, starting with the book of books, the Bible—the light of our life—proceeding through Talmud and Jewish history, must be men who with all their scientific ability, are also whole in their Jewish belief, sentiment, and lifestyle. This is also a sign of broadmindedness and scientific method.

In this way, our dread, together with our great vision at today's awesome spectacle, and the light kindled in our spirit by the many and varied currents passing over us will bring about the desired *broadening of heart* that is a source of blessing.

We aspire that this institution adorned today with the glory of Israel, from a sea of nations that have come to us, will assume such a state, and may there be fulfilled in us the prayer of Rabbi Nehunyah ben Hakanah, "that no grievous error come about through me."

"And my people will abide in peaceful dwellings, and secure abodes, and in undisturbed resting places."[291] May we merit to see the joy of our nation, and the rebuilding of our holy Temple, to which all the nations will stream, to learn "Torah from Zion and the word of the Lord from Jerusalem."[292] Amen.

(*Ma'amrei ha-RAYaH*, vol. 2 [Jerusalem, 5744/1984], pp. 306-308)

Letter of Rav Kook to Rabbi Isaac Kosovsky of Volkovisk, Lithuania

In the town of Volkovisk, over the protests of the rabbi and the community, some Zionist enthusiasts hung on the wall of the synagogue a poster comparing the opening of Hebrew University to the establishment of the Third Temple. Rabbi Kosovsky appealed to Rav Kook to intervene. There follows Rav Kook's response, in which he sides with the rabbi in demanding the poster's removal.

*

9 Adar 5687/1927

Peace and blessing from the Holy [Land] to his honor, the outstanding *gaon* (genius), a Sinai and an uprooter of mountains,[293] treasury of Torah and pure fear [of the Lord], Rabbi I. Kosovsky, *Av Beit Din* (head of rabbinic court) of Volkovisk, may he live long, good days,[294]

After inquiring into his welfare with great love.

His dear letter reached me. I was very pained concerning the goings on. To what degree the moral condition of the generation has deteriorated that in synagogal affairs, which all agree are the jurisdiction of the rabbi, in an important community such as theirs, there are found elements who would dare disobey a *gaon* such as he, of whom Israel could use more!

I strongly hope that soon they will realize this way is not to the greater glory of the national awakening and all our striving to build the Land. I see fit to enclose for his honor my speech at the celebration of the University, which was well received by the organizers, who published it in Hebrew and a faithful English translation in the special album they issued on the occasion. I expressed the contents to Lord Balfour who was present, and he agreed with me wholeheartedly that the University could provide only the secular component necessary for building the Land, whereas the main foundation is the holy idea, the hope of generations for the Messiah and the rebuilding of the Temple. And the way to that lies in strengthening Torah throughout the Land, but especially in the Holy City of Jerusalem. God forbid that we should confer on secular studies, which is the primary purpose of the University, the prophecy, *For out of Zion shall go forth Torah, and the word of the Lord from Jerusalem!* Therefore, I am confident that with the help of God, the best of our children who truly cherish Zion, who are members of his holy community, will put into proper perspective the honor due any national enterprise, and will not exaggerate in such a way that the honor turns to dishonor. Let them ascribe this verse of the Prophet to the event it was truly intended for: the Final Redemption, when "our eyes will behold a proper palace and a handsome king."[295] The steps along the way to this final goal should be assessed each on its own merits without the exaggeration that breaks down the borders dividing the holy from the profane. Let them listen to the voice of their teacher and rabbi, and the voice of one from Zion and Jerusalem connected with all his heart and soul to the salvation of the people of God, and take down the poster.

Perhaps it was a fitting poetic gesture on the day of the occasion, but it should no longer be affixed in the synagogue, where it causes strife between brothers and mars the highest, most holy values of the nation, when it ascribes a saying that is holy-of-holies to a prosaic secular event (though it is worthy of honor within proportion).

I hope that my few words will be pleasing to all those who are straight of heart in his respected congregation. May He who chose Zion, who preserves truth forever, quicken the redemption of His people and His inheritance. May He build mightily His Temple, and may all the ends of the earth see that the name of the Lord is called upon His people and His inheritance. He will show us wonders as in ancient days, granting from Zion salvation for Israel His glory.

This is my greeting of peace and blessing as is his honor's desire and the desire of his faithful friend who inquires into his welfare with great love from the holy mountain, from Jerusalem.

Abraham Isaac Hakohen Kook

(Rabbi Moshe Yehiel Zuriel, *Otserot ha-RAYaH*, vol. 2 [Tel-Aviv, 5748/ 1988], pp. 1117-1118)

Letter of Rav Kook to Rabbi Joseph Messas of Tlemcen, Algeria

13 Adar, 5688/1928

Peace and blessing from the Holy Place to the great luminary in Torah and fear [of Heaven], the righteous and just Rabbi Joseph Messas, chief justice of the community of Tlemcen, may he live long, good years,

His holy letter of 27 Kislev reached me. I saw there evidence of his pure, gentle spirit. I was very upset that the smear sheet called *Beit Va'ad le-Hakhamim* had such impact that it caused pain to a great person such as himself. Does his honor not know that in our many sins there abound Epicureans who make trouble for rabbis,[296] and slanderers? The straight of heart pay them no heed and do not bother with their fabrications....

Regarding the University, God forbid that I should say regarding the secular, *For out of Zion shall go forth Torah!* Quite the contrary, I told them outright that I fear lest a disaster result from neglecting Torah and fear [of the Lord] and restricting their diet to foreign philosophies.[297] I brought them examples from past events when in our many sins, there departed from our midst parties that turned from the Lord and abandoned the source of living waters.[298] [I explained that they will survive] only if the instructors and students safeguard the sanctity of Israel, and do not depart from the Torah and the commandments to stray after strange ideas. Even then, Torah will not come out from secular wisdom, but only by strengthening the holy *yeshivot* (Talmudic academies) consecrated purely to Torah, and uplifting the power of the righteous and God-fearing giants of Torah, and provided the Central Yeshivah in our Holy City we are working to establish, will stand in all its glory. In regard to the holy *yeshivot*, I said that there will be fulfilled the prophecy, *For out of Zion shall go forth Torah*. This was the explicit content of my talk delivered before all the lords who attended the celebration, and a great crowd of thousands assembled from all over the Holy Land and the Diaspora. How can malicious people pervert words of the Living God in such a wicked way?

(Rabbi Moshe Elharar, *Li-Khevodah shel Torah* [Jerusalem, 5748/1988], pp. 41-47; reprinted in Rabbi Moshe Yehiel Zuriel, *Otserot ha-RAYaH*, vol. 4 [Ashdod: Ha-Menorah, 5753/1993], pp. 189-190)

Letter of Rav Kook to Prof. Abraham Fraenkel

With the help of God
30 Sivan, 5688/1928

To my friend, the glorious wise man,
Professor Fraenkel, may his light shine,

Peace and blessing!

Surely he has already received my telegraphic response that I agree to his accepting the position at the University.

Despite the many limitations of the University, we cannot ignore our responsibility to fight to conquer in its midst a position that benefits faithful Judaism and broadens its influence. And there is no other way to do this than by adding professors who are truly Jewish.

I hope that his honor's influence will be great over the general atmosphere of the University, and that through his good behavior and his lifestyle faithful to the Torah and commandments, he will serve as an example to the other professors.

I sign with blessing as is his desire and the desire of one who greatly esteems him. With great love from the holy mountain, from Jerusalem,

Abraham Isaac Hakohen Kook

(Rabbi Moshe Yehiel Zuriel, *Otserot ha-RAYaH*, vol. 4 [Ashdod: Ha-Menorah, 5753/1993], p. 190)

Rabbi Ezekiel Sarna on Rav Kook

The *Rosh Yeshivah* of Hebron, the Gaon Rabbi Ezekiel Sarna zt"l, was one of the great admirers of the Rav [Kook], and more than once, he lavished upon him praise as a *gaon* and *tsaddik*. Once, he especially noted the Rav's desire to influence and to bring close to true Judaism. Reb Chatzkel (as he was referred to affectionately) told the following story:

I once went with some request to the Rav. As I was ascending the stairs to his home, I encountered two distinguished gentlemen leaving the Rav's residence. Their dress told me that they were not affiliated with the religious community. Approaching, I was able to observe them up close. I noted on their faces a look of deep emotion.

Once inside the Rav's abode, before I had a chance to open my mouth, the Rav addressed me: "Certainly his honor has come about some pressing matter, but first I would like to relate what just took place. Two professors from the university paid me a visit to discuss a certain topic. However, I seized the opportunity and began discussing with them matters of belief. The discussion dragged on, and at its conclusion, I had the feeling that I aroused in them thoughts of *teshuvah* (return) and that I brought them to the way of faith."

(Rabbi Moshe Zevi Neriyah, *Likkutei ha-RAYaH* (Kefar ha-Ro'eh: Hai Ro'i, 5750/1990], p. 110)

Letter of Rabbi Isaac Hutner to Rabbi Moshe Zevi Neriyah

Isaac Hutner
Brooklyn, NY

With the help of God
28 Ellul, 5722/1962

My dearly beloved friend,

... I will tell you exactly what transpired: I first arrived in Erets Israel a few days before the opening of the Mount Scopus campus of the University. This was when I first became acquainted with our teacher *zekher tsaddik ve-kadosh li-verakha* (the memory of the righteous and holy for blessing).

In those days, he spoke with me extensively of his decision to be present at the ceremony. He clarified his decision by weaving from world to world, from celestial palace to celestial palace, as was his wont. The speech would pour forth.

One of the pillars of his talks was the promise given him that there would be no chair in this university for Bible criticism.

A long time passed, and I happened to be present in our teacher's room, may he rest in peace, when someone walked in and reported the content of Professor Torczyner's lecture at the University the evening before.[299] Of course, the whole lecture was full of Bible criticism of the worst sort.

Our holy master gazed at me with a look of disappointment, bitterness, frustration, and piercing pain, such that to this day I feel this look like the prick of a hundred needles at once.[300] I was astonished by this look. Then, without meaning [to offend] my lips pronounced the words: "Evidently, in addition to knowing the *soul*, one must know the *body*." I saw fit to transmit to you this anecdote.

A good inscription [for the New Year].

Ascend yourself and raise others with you as you are accustomed.

With love,
Isaac Hutner

(Moshe Zevi Neriyah, *Bi-Sdeh ha-RAYaH* [Kefar ha-Ro'eh, 5751/1991], pp. 435-436)

Appendix A

Maimonides on the Origins of Christianity

Maimonides' assessment of the historical facts was that antinomianism or anti-halakhism originated with Jesus. (*Par contre*, there are historians today, such as Hyam Maccoby, who would argue that Jesus himself had a basic respect for Halakha, and that the antinomian element in later Christianity was the innovation of Paul [Saul of Tarsus].) But Jesus certainly had no intention of founding a new religion. Christianity *per se* is a Roman invention.

*

The first one who adopted this approach was Jesus of Nazareth, blasted be his bones. He was a Jew, for his mother was a Jewess, though his father was a gentile.[301] The halakhic principle is: "If a gentile or slave has relations with a daughter of Israel, the child is kosher."[302] The reason we refer to him as a *mamzer* (bastard) is to increase his shame. [In other words, Jesus was not halakhically a *mamzer* (bastard), but is only referred to so colloquially—BN.] He brought people to think that he was a messenger of God to explain the doubts in Torah, and that he was the Messiah promised by all the prophets. He interpreted the Torah in a way that would nullify the Torah and all its commandments, and relax all the prohibitions. The sages, of blessed memory, grasped his intention before his fame spread among the nation, and did to him that which he deserved. God already forewarned us through Daniel that a renegade of Israel would attempt to destroy the Torah by boasting of prophecy and arrogating to himself the claim of Messiah. It was prophesied that God would foil his attempt, as happened. This is Daniel's statement: "The rebellious sons of your people will lift themselves up to establish vision, but they will stumble."[303]

A long time after him [i.e. Jesus], a religion issued from the children of Esau [i.e. the Romans] which they attributed to him.[304] But this [i.e. establishing a new religion, Christianity—BN] was not the intention he aspired to. His [i.e. Jesus's] action did not harm Israel. Neither as a group nor as individuals did they entertain doubts concerning him; the contradiction of his words was made apparent to them through his defeat and downfall at our hands, his end being what it was.

(Maimonides, *Epistle to Yemen*, in *Igrot ha-RaMBaM*, ed. Shilat, vol. 1 [Jerusalem: Ma'aliyot, 5747/1987], pp. 120-121)

Appendix B

Rav Kook on Buddhism

Surveying the spiritual evolution of mankind, Rav Kook makes a brief foray into the variety of spirituality that developed in the Far East. To the best of this writer's knowledge, that an Orthodox rabbi should lavish such attention on Buddhism was unheard of until Rav Kook's time. Today, when so many Jews have explored Buddhism, Rav Kook's interest in that spiritual phenomenon will certainly strike the reader as far-sighted, though I do not imagine many will agree with his findings concerning Buddhism.

*

The divine pleasantness that is displayed in *K'nesset Israel* (Ecclesia Israel) in its simplicity and naturalness—in light of the divine idea implanted in her—makes for an agreeable, delicate, sweet life. Such life is not in question; not only will it continue to exist, but will even be renewed and replenished. This is the source of an inner *joie de vivre* that bonds with all the ideals of man's higher soul. The strong natural energies do not incite any moral protestation or opposition; these energies are viewed from the perspective of a higher science of eternal peace and divine joy.

This divine pleasantness that is imbibed with every draught of life enables one to view life and existence with a goodly eye and the joy of the righteous, to recognize that "all God made is very good."[305] At the other extreme, the pagan world that lacks this divine pleasantness—from the source of light of the divine idea innate in Israel—is unable to relate to the joy of life. Its dim view uncovers only misfortune; it becomes frustrated with itself, with its existence, with everything. It finds itself in opposition to its very self. As the pain increases, paganism finds a temporary relief (before it disappears from the earth) in a lifestyle that offers no resistance to all the barbaric elements. But it is impossible to stop up the spirit; the spiritual beauty of man and his inner morality demand their due. They are not to be pacified, especially after maturation of the worldview that inspects life inside and out. Therefore, paganism comes to the hiding place of Buddhism, which finds peace in nothingness and absolute negation. The cup of wrath—anger with life and its bitterness—is full to the brim; all the talents of intellect and emotion, faith and imagination, are summed up by a singular will: to self-annihilate.

(To the Process of Ideas in Israel)

*

There is a parallel piece in the collection *Hosafot le-Orot ha-Torah*, alternatively entitled *'Al Penimiyut ha-Torah* (edited by Rabbi Zevi

Yehudah Hakohen Kook and disseminated in stencil by Rabbi Shelomo Hakohen Aviner):

> Though the foundation of our being in the world is the fact we illuminated the divine light in its midst—the source of divine might we revealed in the world in a way tactical, practical, and national; in a way conducive to providing [spiritual] sustenance to many peoples—we did not adjust well, neither did the world adjust yet to receive the *pleasantness* of the divine splendor. Because of its magnitude, this requires great preparation of ethics, of strength, of knowledge, and of all life's assets that aid it. But the divine light is bound to the root of our souls! Thus, we are prepared to gaze on life and existence with a good eye; we are able to let know and to teach that *all God made is very good*,[306] because we recognize the sweetness of the light, of life that we create through the divine pleasantness. That makes life delicate and sweet, palatable and acceptable. The pagan world was unable to situate itself in life peaceably, but only through barbaric traits, without blocks or moral compunction. Once the outlook changed a bit, and morality was elevated, the pagan world came to the territory of Buddhism, which finds its peace in nothingness and annihilation, because life is tasted in all its bitterness, and the anger with life is full to the brim.

(*Al Penimiyut ha-Torah*, par. 17 [pp. 15-16]; reprinted in Rabbi Moshe Yehiel Zuriel, *Otserot ha-RAYaH*, vol. 2 [Rishon Lezion, 5762/2002], p. 328)

WHEN GOD BECOMES HISTORY

*

The previous piece is one of the passages in Rav Kook's literary *oeuvre* that treat Buddhism tangentially. In his *Letters* and in his magnum opus *Orot ha-Kodesh*, Rav Kook develops the theme at greater length:

> Regarding the existence of Nothing [Nirvana—BN] in the words of those leaning to Buddhism, it appears their intention is the existence of the power that aspires to absolute negation. So it follows that essentially, inwardly, it is being and existence, only that its being is a longing for negation, even self-negation. So it is possible for us to picture their *nothingness* such that it is nevertheless existence. By doing so, we in no way enter into incomprehensible mysticism. Now the Israelite consciousness of the goodness of the Lord brings to an awareness of absolute existence in its aspiration to full, complete being. Israelite consciousness delights in the Lord and His goodness. and trusts in Him with all its heart. This is the opposite of the arguments of those who despair, whose foundation is the vision of evil in existence. That leaves them with a bitter taste as long as they do not rise to the *pleasantness* of the Lord, whereby all bitterness turns to sweetness. We find that even this [supposed] opposition between Buddhism and Judaism is not an absolute opposition. Existence viewed *sans* God is totally evil and bitter; it harbors within an aspiration to absolute negation, that finally will be fulfilled. *The moon will be confounded and the sun ashamed* [Isaiah 24:23]. This refers to the sun and moon of *kelipah* (evil). *And the light of the moon will be as the light of the sun* [Isaiah 30:26]. This

refers to the sun and moon of *kedusha* (holiness). So it was explained in *Tikkunei Zohar*.

(*Igrot ha-RAYaH*, vol. 1 [Jerusalem: Mossad Harav Kook, 5722/1962], pp. 133-134)

This is a paraphrase of *Tikkunei Zohar*. The exact wording is: "It was said of the higher and lower *Shekhinah*, *The light of the moon will be as the light of the sun. The moon will be confounded and the sun ashamed*—These are the females of Samaël" (*tikkun* 8). This letter forms part of an ongoing correspondence with Samuel Aleksandrov of Bobroisk. See Aleksandrov's thoughts on the existence of nothing, the divine no-thing, and Buddhism in his collected letters, *Mikhtevei Mehkar u-Vikoret*, vol. 1 (Vilna: Romm, 5667/1907), pp. 18-19, 31-32 ; vol. 2 (Krakow: Ha-Mitspeh, 5670/ 1910), pp. 6-7. See also Tzvi Feldman, *Rav A.Y. Kook: Selected Letters* (Ma'aleh Adumim: Ma'aliot, 1986), pp. 108-111.

*

We recognize absolute good, whose existence is pure good and exalted pleasure; perfecting and broadening its existence are the paths of good and ecstasy. Pure, absolute evil is the absence of absolute good and the narrowing of its existence. Conversely, we recognize pure, absolute evil: Pure good is its absence and negation; narrowing its existence is the way to good.

Pessimism is looking into the depth of evil. The good in pessimism is the tendency to negation, which is redemption from the existence of evil. In the depth of its being, evil so longs for this negation. It should be understood that this longing [for self-negation] manifests in the higher aspect of evil, where it borders on good. It finds happiness in its self-destruction. *In the destruction of the wicked there is joy,*[307] even for the wicked themselves, who have ceased to be angry. The lower aspect of evil is incapable of being perfected. It is worse than the higher aspect. It does not yet recognize the fortune of its destruction; it yet longs for being and existence.

Buddhism has in it the good aspect of evil. It expressed well the longing for destruction. It was so imbued with this spirit that it guided an entire civilization to direct the lower aspect of evil to the higher aspect, which is the longing for destruction, ultimate self-destruction. It is understood that the innermost point of the good that is in evil combines with the good, and survives eternally. That longing for the destruction of evil that is within the domain of good continues to exist forever in infinite bliss.

The joy of the just is in the good aspect of good that surpasses all evil; they rejoice in good's existence and in the broadening of its being, empowered at the source of good, the source of life and existence, the light that vivifies worlds. *He spoke and it came into being.*[308]

(*Orot ha-Kodesh*, ed. Rabbi David Cohen, vol. 2 [Jerusalem: Mossad Harav Kook, 5724/1964], pp. 486-487)

Appendix C

Response to the Author of *Nitel u-Me'or'otav*[309]

Recently there appeared in print a scholarly work tracing the customs of "*Nitel nacht*" (Xmas night) when many Jews refrain from studying Torah. The author has collected much interesting and useful material, and has also reproduced some of the anti-Christian literature of a mythic nature that Jews penned over the ages (*Toledot Yeshu*, et al). The work joins the ranks of several recent scholarly studies that attempt to uncover the origins of this perplexing custom.

What comes as a shock to this reader, and probably many others as well, are the final pages of the book. There appear *face-à-face* photographs of a page from *Igrot ha-RAYaH* (*Letters of Rav Kook*) and the frontispiece of *Netivot 'Olam*, a notorious Christian missionary tract published in London in 1839. If we have any doubts why these two dissimilar documents have been juxtaposed, the author enlightens us in footnote 137 on pages 74-75:

> In the existence of *Kelal Israel* (the Jewish People) in exile for almost two thousand years, there appeared two books

in the holy tongue against the religion of Moses and Israel. One is *Netivot 'Olam* (London, 5599/1839), which heaped scorn on the religion of Moses and the prophets; the second, the books (!) of Abraham Isaac Hakohen Kook, who wrote many expressions in praise of the *Notsri* [i.e. Jesus] and Christianity. And these are his words in *Igrot RAYaH*, pp. 47-48: "Christianity truly desired to erase the trait of hate within the fabric of Israel's divine light,[310] but how well do we know that more than any system of hate, she shed blood and increased hatred for the sake of erasing hate."[311]

Let us examine rationally the author's allegations. The author has not told us where Rav Kook has written against the religion of Moses and Israel. In fact, in his writings, Rav Kook champions *dat moshe vi-yehudit*, Mosaic-Judaic religion. (See above, p. 110.)

As for the opposite contention that Rav Kook "wrote many expressions in praise of the *Notsri* and Christianity." Honestly, this writer, a lifelong student of Rav Kook's writings, knows but one passage where Rav Kook speaks in praise of the Nazarene, and even that is an example of what is known in the English language as an "underhanded compliment," designed to build up for the sake of demolishing. As Rav Kook explained in his letter to Rabbi Dov Milstein, the sages of old wrote that Bilʻam possessed some wonderful traits only to emphasize that with all of his gifts (which surpassed those of Moses) he ended a wicked man. So too Rav Kook wrote that Jesus possessed wonderful charisma which, unchecked and unbalanced by the discipline of formal learning, resulted in disaster for himself and his followers.

As for the passage from the *Letters* the author quotes, rather than constituting a tribute to Christianity, it actually points up the hypocrisy of this religion, which supposedly in the name of love, brutally tortured and sacrificed millions of innocent human beings. Its attempt to purge Judaism of the element of hate (Rav Kook refers earlier to the *mitsvah* to hate Amalek) resulted in one of the most hateful religions of all time.

No, Rav Kook did not write against the religion of Moses and Israel; neither did he write in praise of the *Notsri* and Christianity. The truth is that rarely in the millennia-old exile of *Kelal Israel* has so much Jewish genius been harnessed to exposing the spiritual nakedness, bankruptcy, hypocrisy, and turpitude of Christianity—as in the writings of Rav Kook, *zekher tsaddik ve-kadosh li-verakha*.

The reader is invited to examine these texts, from the earliest writings, the *'Eyn AYaH* commentary to the stories of Rabbah bar bar Hannah,[312] through the *Letters*, and *Orot*,[313] culminating in *Orot ha-Emunah*, where an entire section is devoted to demolishing *Minut* (Heresy, i.e. Christianity).[314]

Historians must not allow their anti-Zionism to color their perception of this man, Abraham Isaac Hakohen Kook. Let them content themselves with leveling at Rav Kook the charge of being a Zionist—an accusation he might or might not have accepted—and not paint this much maligned and misunderstood personality with the brush of Christianity, of which he is certainly not guilty.[315]

Notes

1. Rav Kook decries the fact that Jewish historians ape the European philosophy of history. In the case of European history, there is an upward progression "from the Teuton wandering the forests of Germany" to "the German sitting in a Berlin salon enjoying the splendor of the Enlightenment," but in the case of Jewish history, the progression is downward. Our remote ancestors were on a much higher level than we. See *Eder ha-Yekar* (Jerusalem: Mossad Harav Kook, 5745/1985), pp. 54-55. It is possible that when Rav Kook writes *philosophia historit* (philosophy of history), he has in mind the German philosopher Hegel. See below note 163.
2. Rabbi Shim'on Starelitz, *Me-ha-Makor*, pp. 119-126. Cited in Rabbi Moshe Zevi Neriyah, *Bi-Sdeh ha-RAYaH* (Kefar ha-Ro'eh, 5751/1991), p. 505.
3. *Erets Zevi: Zevi Glatt Memorial Volume* (Jerusalem, 5749/1989), p. 183.
4. *Shulhan 'Arukh, Yoreh De'ah* 345:5.

    In response to the request of editor Alexander Ziskind Rabinowitz (AZaR) that he contribute a eulogy for secular *halutsim* killed by Arab marauders, Rav Kook reveals his inner conflict in light of the Halakha. He cites the halakhic sources: *Semahot* 2:10; Maimonides, *Mishneh Torah, Hil. Evel* 1:10; *Shulhan 'Arukh, Yoreh De'ah* 345:5. Rav Kook suggests that these modern *porshim mi-darkhei ha-tsibbur* are not the religious renegades of yesteryear. First, they are *shogegim* (unintentional) not *mezidim* (deliberate) in their abandonment of Jewish observance. Second, Maimonides' classic *poresh mi-darkhei ha-tsibbur* "does not observe the commandments with the community, neither does he enter into their suffering, nor fast on their fast days, but goes on his way as one of the nations, as if he is not one of them" (*Mishneh Torah, Hil. Teshuvah* 3:11). Rav Kook notes that while these secularists do not observe commandments and fast days, they do nevertheless identify and empathize with the suffering of their people. But, Rav Kook writes, he is not thoroughly satisfied with these proposed differentials. In the case of martyrs however, there are clearcut halakhic grounds for eulogizing: "Some say that we mourn for an apostate (*mumar*) who was murdered by gentiles" (*Shulhan 'Arukh, Yoreh De'ah* 340:5). Certainly, the secularists are no worse, and actually a lot better than apostates! "'*Al bamoteinu halalim*," reprinted in *Ma'amrei ha-RAYaH*, vol. 1 (Jerusalem, 5740/1980), pp. 89-93.

Asher Erlich recorded an altercation that broke out in the synagogue of Rehovot between the visiting Rav Kook and the local residents whether the prayer *El Male Rahamim* should be recited for Herzl on the Sabbath preceding his *yahrzeit*. Despite Rav Kook's objections, the memorial prayer was recited. See *Asher Hayah: Sefer Zikaron le-Asher Erlich*, ed. Yitzhak Ogen (Tel-Aviv: Ahdut, 1959), p. 83. This reference was brought to my attention by Netanel Elyashiv.

5. Amos Perlmutter, *The Life and Times of Menachem Begin* (Garden City, NY: Doubleday, 1987), p. 35.

6. Rabbi Hayyim of Brisk and Rabbi Elijah of Pruzany were what is known as *mehutanim* (in-laws). Rabbi Elijah Feinstein's daughter Pesha was married to Rabbi Moshe Soloveichik, son of Rabbi Hayyim.

7. Heard from Rabbi Yosef Soloveichik of Jerusalem concerning his paternal grandmother Pesha Soloveichik (née Feinstein).

8. *Begroben* in Yiddish has a double connotation: To bury physically, but also to obliterate the memory. This anecdote was told to the author by Rabbi Matis Greenblatt.

9. "The historian Jawitz presented him with a scroll of the Torah; and the senior rabbi, the venerable Reb Schleimele [i.e., Rabbi Shelomo Hakohen], with trembling palms outstretched, pronounced the priestly blessing" (Israel Cohen, *History of Jews in Vilna* [Philadelphia: Jewish Publication

Society of America, 5704/1943], p. 350). So too Israel Klausner, *Vilna: "Jerusalem of Lithuania," 1881-1939*, vol. 2 (Hebrew) (Israel: Ghetto Fighters' House, 1983), p. 339.

Elsewhere, Klausner writes of Rabbi Shelomo Hakohen's pitiable involvement in the *'Or la-Yesharim* affair. (See following note.) The tract *'Or la-Yesharim* was published at the behest of the so-called "Black Office" (*Ha-Lishkah ha-Shehorah*), an anti-Zionist "watchdog committee" headed by Rabbi Yaakov Halevi Lipschutz of Kovno (Kaunas). Rabbi Shelomo Hakohen's sons and especially his son-in-law, Rabbi Nahum Greenhaus of Trok (Trakai), were ardent Zionists. It seems the latter prevailed upon his father-in-law to publish a scathing op-ed (*gilui da'at*) of *'Or la-Yesharim*. Subsequently, Hakohen's colleagues in the Vilna rabbinate, such as Rabbi Hayyim Ozer Grodzenski, brought pressure to bear on Hakohen to retract his blistering condemnation of *'Or la-Yesharim*. But in the end, Hakohen retracted even his retraction! Klausner, pp. 330-333.

10. Rabbi Shalom Dov Baer Schneersohn, *Kuntress u-Ma'ayan mi-Beit Hashem* (Brooklyn: Kehot, 5718/1958), p. 49. On 1 Shevat 5663/1903, a historic debate concerning Zionism took place between Rabbi Shalom Dov Baer (RaShaB) and a HaBaD follower with decidedly Zionist leanings, Rabbi Solomon Aronsohn (later to become Chief Rabbi of Tel-Aviv) in Nezhin, in the home of Rebbetzin Hannah Hishia, widow of RaShaB's uncle, Rabbi Israel Noah Schneersohn. The debate was recorded by RaShaB, *Kuntress u-Ma'ayan*, pp. 45-53. See also the letter of RaShaB anthologized in the anti-Zionist collection *'Or la-Yesharim* (Warsaw, 5660/1900), pp. 57-61, and the anti-Zionist pamphlet by RaShaB, *Ha-Ketav ve-ha-Mikhtav* (New York, 5677/1917). (A facsimile of the title page of *Ha-Ketav ve-ha-Mikhtav* appears in Rabbi Shaul Shimon Deutsch, *Larger than Life*, vol. 1 [New York: Chasidic Historical Productions, 1995], p. 47.)

11. See Marvin Lowenthal ed., *The Diaries of Theodor Herzl* (New York: Dial Press, 1956), pp. 33, 201, 232-233. Concerning Herzl and Czortkow, see Yitzchak Alfasi, "Hasidism and Political Zionism," in *Jubilee Volume in*

NOTES

Honor of Joseph B. Soloveitchik, ed. Israeli, Lamm and Raphael (Jerusalem: Mossad Harav Kook, 1984), vol. 2, pp. 695-698.

12. Rabbi Zevi Yehudah Hakohen Kook, *Li-Netivot Israel*, vol. 2 (Jerusalem, 5739/1979), p. 247. Rabbi Diskin related to Rabbi Zevi Yehudah that he once received a letter from Herzl. Evidently, this fact did not minimize his halakhic displeasure with paying tribute to a religious renegade.

On a more salutary note, Rabbi Isaac Jeruham Diskin once asked Samuel Kook, "Do you know that your brother was already in his youth a *gaon* and a *tsaddik*?" (Rabbi Diskin knew Rabbi Abraham Isaac Kook from Dvinsk. After his marriage, Rabbi Diskin resided there in the home of his father-in-law Rabbi Zechariah Batlan, and the young prodigy Abraham Isaac Kook of nearby Grieva would visit him to discuss Torah matters.) See Rabbi Moshe Zevi Neriyah, *Tal ha-RAYaH* (B'nei Berak, 5753/1993), pp. 18-19.

Rabbis Diskin and Sonnenfeld were opposed to Rav Kook as rabbi of Jerusalem. On the eleventh of Tevet, 5681/1921, Rabbi Jacob Moses Harlap dreamt that the deceased Rav of Brisk, Rabbi Joshua Leib Diskin, of blessed memory, appeared to him requesting that Rabbi Harlap implore his master Rav Kook not to dispute or disrespect his only son (Rabbi Isaac Jeruham Diskin). See *Hed Harim: Letters of Rabbi Jacob Moses Harlap to Rabbi Abraham Isaac Hakohen Kook*, ed. Zevi Yehudah Hakohen Kook (Jerusalem, 5731/1971), p. 86.

13. Rabbi Isaac Jeruham Diskin arrived in Jerusalem in the year 5669/1909. See Introduction to Rabbi Jacob Moses Harlap, *Beit Zevul*, vol. 1 (Jerusalem: Beit Zevul, 5747/1987), p. 7.

14. Rabbi Zevi Yehudah Hakohen Kook reminisced that "some Jerusalemites taunted him [i.e. the elder Rav Kook] for this and attempted to prevent him from doing this [i.e. eulogizing Herzl]." See Zevi Yehudah Hakohen Kook, *Li-Shelosha be-Ellul*, vol. 1 (Jerusalem, 5698/1938; reprinted Jerusalem, 5738/1978), pp. 14-15.

15. See *Letters of ADeReT* published as an appendix to Rabbi Abraham Isaac Hakohen Kook, *Eder ha-Yekar* (Jerusalem: Mossad Harav Kook, 5745/1985), pp. 90-95.

16. Leviticus 19:17.
17. *TB 'Arakhin* 16b.
18. Rabbi Nahman of Braslav, *Likkutei MOHaRaN* II 8:1.
19. *Igrot ha-RAYaH*, vol. 1 (Jerusalem: Mossad Harav Kook, 5722/1962), Letter 295, p. 336. See also the preceding Letter 294 on p. 335.
20. *Zikhron RAYaH*, ed. Yizhak Raphael (Jerusalem: Mossad Harav Kook, 5746/1986), pp. 5-14. Raphael erroneously assumed that the letter was written in 1912. Menahem Klein pointed out that actually it was penned a decade earlier in Boisk. See Rabbi Moshe Zuriel, *Otserot ha-RAYaH* (Rishon LeZion, 2002), vol. 1, p. 357.
21. *Zikhron RAYaH*, p. 10.
22. Ibid.
23. *TB Berakhot* 12a.
24. *TB Berakhot* 28b.
25. Lamentations 1:7.
26. "Lovers of Zion," a movement for rebuilding Zion, led by Rabbi Samuel Mohilever of Bialystok, Russia.
27. Genesis 28:17.
28. *TB Berakhot* 30b, 33a.
29. *TB Gittin* 56b.
30. Rabbi Abraham Isaac Hakohen Kook. "The Destiny of Israel and Its Nationalism" (*Te'udat Yisrael u-le'umiyuto*), *Ha-Peless* 5661/1901, Part One, pp. 45-52; reprinted in Rabbi Moshe Yehiel Zuriel, *Otserot ha-RAYaH*, vol. 2 (Tel-Aviv, 5748/1988), pp. 732-733.
31. Rav Kook's bitterest enemies were aware of the complex nature of his thought. One of the notorious *paskvillen* (posters) that appeared on the billboards of Jerusalem's religious districts, reads: "In general, he is a fickle person, today Zionist, tomorrow anti-Zionist" (Simha Raz, *Mal'akhim ki-b'nei adam* [Jerusalem: Kol Mevaser, 5762/2002], p. 203).

    The truth is that with time, Rav Kook's attitude to Zionism underwent a transformation. In his student days at the Volozhin Yeshiva, Rav Kook was not a member of Nes Ziyonah, the secret Zionist society, as was say, his fellow student, Moshe Mordechai Epstein, later to become dean of the famed Slabodka Yeshivah. According to Rabbi Yosef Soloveichik of Jerusalem, both Rabbi Moshe Mordechai Epstein and his future brother-in-law Rabbi Isser Zalman Meltzer (later *Rosh Yeshivah* of Slutsk and Yeshivah 'Ets Hayyim, Jerusalem) were members of Nes Ziyonah. Members of the society were sworn to secrecy. The *Rosh Yeshivah* of Volozhin, Rabbi Hayyim Soloveitchik found halakhic grounds for abrogating the oath, and thus, through his disciple Rabbi Isser Zalman Meltzer, was able to learn the identities of the group's members. (Rabbi Yosef Soloveichik is a great-grandson of Rabbi Hayyim. His father, the late Rabbi Ahron Soloveichik zt"l was the son of Rabbi Hayyim's son Rabbi Moshe Soloveichik.) The formula of the oath is transcribed in Israel Klausner, *Toledot ha-Agudah Nes Ziyonah be-Volozhin: Te'udot u-Mismakhim* (Jerusalem: Mossad Harav Kook, 5714/1954), p. 13. Concerning Rabbi Moshe Mordechai Epstein, see Klausner, pp. 25, 26, 65. On page 26, Rabbi Epstein appears in a group photo of members of Nes Ziyonah. On page 65, "Moshe Mordechai Epstein of Bakst" is signed on a letter together with other members of the central committee of Nes Ziyonah. Nes Ziyonah existed from 5645/1885 until its discovery by the Russian authorities in 5650/1890. Klausner, pp. 11, 17. Rav Kook studied in Volozhin during the year 5645/1885. Rabbi Moshe Zevi Neriyah writes that Rav Kook rebuffed the many overtures made to him to join the secret society on the grounds that the time spent in *yeshivah* should be devoted exclusively to study of Torah and not to political activity. Neriyah, *Tal ha-RAYaH* (B'nei Berak, 5753/1993), p. 68. Of course, Nes Ziyonah existed well before Herzlian Zionism came along in 1895. Nes Ziyonah interfaced with the Hovevei Zion Society in Odessa led by Rabbi Samuel Mohilever.

As late as 5663/1903, we find Samuel Aleksandrov of Bobroisk goading Rav Kook to come out in open support of the Zionists (or the religious wing of the movement, Mizrachi). Samuel Aleksandrov, *Mikhtevei Mehkar u-Vikkoret* I (Vilna: Romm, 5667/1907), pp. 16-17 (Aleksandrov was active in the Mizrachi movement founded by Rabbi Jacob Isaac Reines of Lida.

See Rabbi Zevi Yehudah Hakohen Kook, *Zemah Zevi*, vol. 1 [Jerusalem, 5751], p. 138.) It seems that what brought Rav Kook closer to the work of the Zionists was his encounter with the *halutsim* (pioneers) of Rehovot and the other settlements within his jurisdiction. However, it should be pointed out that for years to come, Rav Kook's attitude to Zionism would remain ambiguous, and to some, unintelligible. In 1914, Zevi Yehudah Kook (5651/1891-5742/1982), freshly arrived in Halberstadt, Germany, writes to his father that both the Zionists and anti-Zionists claim Rav Kook as one of their own. Zevi Yehudah responded to his German Jewish brethren: "When it comes to renewing the land and the language, we are with the Zionists; and when it comes to destruction of Judaism—atheism, throwing off the yoke of Torah and *mitsvot*, and assimilationist education—we fight with all our might." *Zemah Zevi*, p. 62. *Tout court*, Rav Kook was an independent spirit, a highly original individualist, whose thinking on Zionism and sundry other issues defied party lines. Samuel Aleksandrov rightly intuited that Rav Kook's vision was so unique that it warranted a platform of its own. He suggested that Rav Kook found a party, which he (Aleksandrov) would willingly join. Aleksandrov, *Mikhtevei Mehkar* I, p. 17.

32. If Rav Kook had to pick a flesh-and-blood candidate for the mythic "Messiah son of Joseph," it probably would have been the Vilna Gaon (5480/1720-5558/1797), not Theodor Herzl. Among the disciples of the Gaon, the belief was rampant that he was in some sense an embodiment of this Messianic ideal. See Rabbi Hillel of Shklov, *Kol ha-Tor*, ed. Yosef Rivlin (Jerusalem, 5754/1994), p. 20, n. 2-3 concerning the Gaon as *nehora de-Mashiah ben Yosef* (the light of Messiah son of Joseph). This tradition that the Gaon was Messiah son of Joseph is cited by the eminent disciple of Rav Kook, Rabbi Jacob Moses Harlap, "*Aliyat Eliyahu*," reprinted in *Amarot Tehorot*, ed. Hayyim Zaks (Jerusalem: Makhon Iyye ha-Yam, 5762/2002), pp. 168-169. Even closer to home, Rav Kook inherited the glosses to *Zohar* in the hand of his ancestor the kabbalist Rabbi Abraham of Preil and Sebezh. In the margin of the passage in *Zohar Hadash*, *Vayyeshev*

that speaks of the death of Messiah son of Joseph seventeen years after the dawn of redemption in the year 5540/1780, Rabbi Abraham penned this note: "This is a hint to the death of the Gaon." The Gaon died in 5758/1797. See Hayyim Avihu Schwarz ed., *Mi-Tokh ha-Torah ha-Goëlet: Lectures of Rabbi Zevi Yehudah Hakohen Kook* (Jerusalem, 5751/1991), p. 40. The glosses of Rabbi Abraham to *Zohar Hadash* were published under the title *Zehiruta de-Avraham* and appended to *Zohar Hadash*, ed. Reuven Margaliot (Jerusalem: Mossad Harav Kook, 5754/1994), 122b-123a. See the gloss to *Zohar Hadash* 29d. (In parentheses, Rabbi Zevi Yehudah Hakohen juxtaposed his ancestor's remark to that of Rabbi Menashe of Ilya in *Alfei Menashe*, chaps. 177 and 102. See below note 262.) According to Rabbi Moshe Zevi Neriyah, from earliest youth, Rav Kook delved into these writings of his ancestor. See M.Z. Neriyah, *Tal ha-RAYaH* (B'nei Berak, 5753/1993), p. 304. Concerning attempts to publish Rabbi Abraham's glosses to *Zohar* and *Tikkunei Zohar*, see *Igrot ha-RAYaH*, vol. 1 (Jerusalem: Mossad Harav Kook, 5722/1962), Letter 105, p. 129. Rabbi Abraham was the father of Rav Kook's maternal grandfather Rabbi Raphael. For a brief biographical sketch of Rabbi Abraham, see Rabbi Moshe Zevi Neriyah, *Sihot ha-RAYaH* (Tel-Aviv, 5739/1979), pp. 45-49, and Samuel Noah Gottlieb, *Oholei Shem* (Pinsk, 5672/1912), p. 492. For the mystical significance of the year 5540/1780, see Arie Morgenstern, *Mysticism and Messianism: From Luzzatto to the Vilna Gaon* [Hebrew] (Jerusalem: Maor, 5759/1999), pp. 205-206, 277-278. Concerning the last eighteen years of the Gaon's life, see Morgenstern, pp. 320-322.

What suggests the Vilna Gaon as a candidate for "Messiah son of Joseph" is the fact that (through his disciples) he spearheaded *'aliyah* (immigration) to Erets Israel at the beginning of the nineteenth century. See Schwarz, pp. 40-41. In a letter of congratulation to Rabbi Elijah Landau, a descendant of the Gaon, upon establishing in Tel-Aviv a synagogue named after the Gaon, Rav Kook likened the Vilna Gaon to Moses: Moses was barred from entering the Promised Land, but surely the longing in his soul provides the Jewish People throughout the ages with the strength to settle the land. Likewise, though the Vilna Gaon himself was unsuccessful in reaching Erets Israel, his holy aspiration to implant Torah in the Land, empowers us to achieve that goal. Published in *Erets Zevi: Zevi Glatt Memorial Volume* (Jerusalem, 5749/1989), pp. 184-185. Rabbi Zevi Yehudah Hakohen Kook went so far as to say Herzl's Zionist enterprise was a continuation of the arousal by the Vilna Gaon! Schwarz, pp. 41-42.

33.   TB *Sukkah* 52a.

34.   *Zohar* III, 276b. In the wake of Shabbetai Zevi's forced conversion to Islam, those Sabbatians who persisted in their belief in him as Messiah (perhaps Messiah son of Joseph) seized upon this passage in the *Zohar* as supposed proof that Messiah son of Joseph would one day be converted to another religion. Rabbi Moshe Hayyim Luzzatto (RaMHaL) dismantled this "proof" in his polemic work *Kin'at Adonai Zeva'ot*. The late Rabbi Hayyim Friedlander of B'nei Berak published Luzzatto's work from a manuscript in the Bodleian Library, Oxford. See Friedlandler ed., *Ginzei RaMHaL*, ed. Friedlander (B'nei Berak, 5740/1980), p. 101 ff.

35.   *Kin'at Adonai Zeva'ot*, pp. 104-105.

Rav Kook was familiar with *Kin'at Adonai Zeva'ot*. He cites from it almost as a postscript to a halakhic responsum (if only to qualify that one of Luzzatto's notions may work kabbalistically, but is not necessarily so, halakhically speaking). See Rabbi Abraham Isaac Hakohen Kook, *Mishpat Kohen* (Jerusalem: Mossad Harav Kook, 5745/1985), no. 148 (p. 359).

Rav Kook's disciple, Rabbi David Cohen (the "Nazirite") quotes this subtle distinction between *meshihut* (Messianism) and *anshei ha-meshihut* (Messianic figures). See Rabbi David Cohen, *Kol ha-Nevu'ah* (Jerusalem: Mossad Harav Kook, 5730/1970), p. 310. See also Rabbi Hillel of Shklov, *Kol ha-Tor*, ed. Yosef Rivlin (Jerusalem, 5754/1994), pp. 35-36: "Messiah son of Joseph resting in the entire House of Israel... a spark from the root of the soul of Messiah son of Joseph." Rabbi Hillel is fond of the phrase "the line(age) of Messiah son of Joseph" (*turya de-Mashiah ben Yosef*).

36.   See sources cited in Rabbi David Cohen, *Kol ha-Nevu'ah* (Jerusalem: Mossad Harav Kook, 5739/1979), pp. 309-310.

37. A random sampling produced the following references: See the Gaon's commentaries to Deuteronomy 33:17 (in *Aderet Eliyahu*, second method); Joshua 16:1; the Prayer of Hannah (1 Samuel 2:10); Habakkuk 2:3; 2 Chronicles 15:7; and the ditty recited at the conclusion of the Haggadah, *Had Gadya*. A more extensive bibliography is available in *Kol ha-Tor*, ed. Joseph Rivlin (Jerusalem, 5754/1994), p. 42, n. 3; p. 44, n. 13.

38. *Kol ha-Tor*, p. 79. See also Rabbi Isaac Haver (Wildmann), *Pithei She'arim, Netiv binyan ha-kelipot u-merkavah teme'ah* (ms.), published in Kalman Redisch, *Mi-Ginzei ha-GRA u-Veit Midrasho* (Lakewood, NJ, 5759/1999), pp. 240-241. The early kabbalist Abraham Abulafia wrote: "Messiah son of Joseph is born in nature, but Messiah son of David is born of that which is beyond nature" (Abraham Abulafia, *Otsar Eden Ganuz*, ed. Amnon Gross [Jerusalem, 5760/2000], p. 213).

39. *Midrash Tanhuma, Vayyigash*, par. 10, and commentary *'Ets Yosef* ad locum.

40. Cf. Rabbi Shneur Zalman of Liadi, *Tanya* (Brooklyn: Kehot, 5733/1973), chap. 2 (6b).

41. Had it gotten off the ground, Degel Yerushalayim would have offered an alternative to Agudah and Mizrachi, a third way. Rav Kook explains that though Mizrachi attempts to inject into Zionism some holy sentiments, since the foundation of Zionism remains essentially secular, Mizrachi is insufficient to press forcefully the demands of holiness. Agudah on the other hand, while determined to strengthen holiness throughout the world, is not sufficiently focused on Erets Israel. *Igrot ha-RAYaH*, vol. 4 (Jerusalem: Makhon RZYH Kook, 5744/1984), Letter 1000, p. 32.

42. Rabbi Abraham Isaac Hakohen Kook, *Orot* (Jerusalem: Mossad Harav Kook, 5745/1985), "*Le-Degel Yerushalayim*," pp. 185-186; *Igrot ha-RAYaH*, vol. 3 (Jerusalem: Mossad Harav Kook, 5725/ 1965), pp. 148-151, 315; vol. 4 (Jerusalem: Makhon RZYH Kook, 5744/1984), pp. 24-25; *Ma'amrei ha-RAYaH*, vol. 2 (Jerusalem, 5744/1984), pp. 333-335, 338-340; *Hed Harim: Letters of Rabbi Jacob Moses Harlap to Rabbi Abraham Isaac Hakohen Kook*, ed. Rabbi Zevi Yehudah Hakohen Kook (Jerusalem, 5731/1971), p. 76.

By the way, the version of the letter to Rabbi Hayyim Hirschensohn published in *Igrot ha-RAYaH*, vol. 4, p. 24 (Letter 994), omits a reference to Herzl. The version the recipient published contains the following passage: "This would complete the vision of Herzl in *Altneuland* concerning the temple to be erected not exactly on the site of the Holy Temple. It is as if he prophesied and knew not what he prophesied" (*niba ve-lo yada' mah niba*). There should be such a house close to the location of the Holy Temple until the Lord appears in His glory, and there will be fulfilled all the good promises concerning His people and His world that were conveyed through the prophets of truth and righteousness" (Rabbi Hayyim Hirschensohn, *Malki ba-Kodesh*, vol. 4 [St. Louis, MO: Moinester Printing, 5679-5682/1919-1922], p. 5).

43. Zechariah 12:11.
44. Traditionally, the area of Erets Israel is four hundred square parasangs.
45. TB *Megillah* 3a, *Mo'ed Katan* 28b.
46. TB *Megillah* 3a. Evidently, Rav Kook quoted from memory. The text of the Talmud reads *galuy ve-yadu'a le-fanekha*, "You know full well." No mention of "He who said and the world came into being." Also, Rav Kook omitted "*li-khevodekha 'asiti*" ("for Your honor I did [this]").
47. TB *Sukkah* 52a.
48. Ezekiel 37:25.
49. There occurs at this point in the text a digression: Material improvement is the right basis for all the great and holy plans that characterize Israel, whereby it is a nation holy to the Lord, "one nation in the land" [2 Samuel 7:23; Ezekiel 37:22]; "a light to the nations" [Isaiah 42:6; 49:6].
50. Deuteronomy 32:12.
51. Numbers 23:9.
52. *Midrash Tanhuma*, Lekh Lekha, 9; *Genesis Rabbah* 48:7; Nahmanides, Genesis 12:6.
53. Genesis 45:5,7; 50:20.
54. TB *Sotah* 36b.
55. Ibid.

56. *Genesis Rabbah* 73:7.

57. *TB Sanhedrin* 39b. The Talmud employs this adage to explain the fact that Ovadiah who prophesied the destruction of Edom was himself an Edomite proselyte. By the same token, David who vanquished Moab was himself descended from Ruth the Moabitess. Rav Kook's point is that Joseph's immersion in the society of the nations qualified him to be Esau's undoing. Perhaps it was Rav Kook's intention to reflect on the biography of Herzl; the latter was an assimilated Jew at home in European civilization.

58. Psalms 114:2. Rav Kook might have pointed out that in that generation of the descent to Egypt, Judah was emblematic of Torah. See RaShI, Genesis 46:28, citing Midrash.

59. Psalms 78:60. Cf. Rabbi Naphtali Zevi Yehudah Berlin, end *Haskamah* to *Ahavat Hesed* by Rabbi Yisrael Meir Kagan (Warsaw, 5648/1888); Rabbi Yehudah Aryeh Leib of Gur, *Sefat Emet, Vayyehi*, 5646, s.v. *ben porat yosef*.

60. Genesis 25:25; 1 Samuel 16:12; *Genesis Rabbah* 63:8. A ruddy complexion was thought to be the mark of a killer. The Sanhedrin is referred to as the "eyes of the congregation." See e.g. Leviticus 4:13; Numbers 15:24. Cf. Rabbi Zadok Hakohen of Lublin, *Zidkat ha-Zaddik* (Lublin, 5673/1913), chap. 258 (70d); idem, *Dover Zedek* (Piotrkow, 5671/1911), 40d-41a.

61. Ezekiel 37:19.

62. Psalms 47:4-5.

63. Isaiah 11:10.

64. 1 Kings 11:28.

65. Ibid. 14:9.

66. Hosea 7:8.

67. Ibid. 5:5.

68. Isaiah 3:8.

69. *TB Sanhedrin* 102a.

70. Deuteronomy 32:9.

71. Psalms 141:7.

72. At this point in the text there occurs a digression: The Kingdom of

David by dint of its distinctive nature subsumes as well the universal aspect. [This is the symbolism of] "ruddy with beautiful eyes" [1 Samuel 16:12].

73. Cf. the writings of Rabbi Moshe Hayyim Luzzatto, where Messiah son of Joseph is equated with *hitsoniyut* (outwardness) and Messiah son of David with *penimiyut* (inwardness). See *Kin'at Adonai Zeva'ot*, in *Ginzei RaMHaL*, ed. Rabbi Hayyim Friedlander (B'nei Berak, 5740/1980), pp. 101-102, and sources cited in Rabbi David Cohen, *Kol ha-Nevu'ah*, p. 309, n. 454-455.

74. Psalms 89:52.

75. *TB Sukkah* 52a.

76. Zechariah 12:10.

77. The manuscript has here the additional words "*be-tor kelalut ve-homriyut*" ("in terms of universality and the material"). See *Kevatsim me-Khetav Yad Kodsho*, vol. 1, ed. Boaz Ofen (Jerusalem, 2006), *Pinkas Rishon le-Yaffo*, par. 65 (p. 113).

78. *TB Sanhedrin* 102b.

79. 1 Kings 22:35; *TB Mo'ed Katan* 28b.

80. Psalms 108:9; *TB Sanhedrin* 104b.

81. *TB Sanhedrin* 102b.

82. 2 Kings 23:25.

83. 2 Kings 23:29–30; 2 Chronicles 35:20-25; *TB Ta'anit* 22.

84. Herzl died an untimely death at the age of forty-four.

85. Ezekiel 37:15-19.

86. The printed version of *Ma'amrei ha-RAYaH* has "*homriyim*" (material). The manuscript has "*enoshiyim*" (human). See *Kevatsim mi-Khetav Yad Kodsho*, vol. 1, p. 114.

87. Hosea 7:8.

88. Jeremiah 2:13.

89. Hosea 7:11.

90. Isaiah 46:13.

91. Isaiah 62:3.

NOTES

92. *TB Sanhedrin* 98b. Cf. Rabbi A.I. Hakohen Kook, *Orot* (Jerusalem: Mossad Harav Kook, 5745/1985), *Orot ha-Tehiyah*, end chap. 32; p. 80.

93. Daniel 9:24.

94. This sentence which occurs in the manuscript is missing in the printed version. See *Kevatsim mi-Khetav Yad Kodsho*, vol. 1, p. 115.

95. *TB Bava Batra* 4a.

96. Isaiah 16:3.

97. *Zohar* I, 4a.

98. The three weeks between the Seventeenth of Tammuz and the Ninth of Av, a time traditionally set aside for mourning, are referred to as *bein ha-metsarim* ("between the straits"), a reference to the verse in Lamentations 1:3.

99. *Mishnah, Avot* 1:12.

100. *Ha-Peless* was an anti-Zionist Journal published in Poltava, Ukraine by Rabbi Akiva Elijah Rabinowitz, a relation of Rav Kook's father-in-law Rabbi Elijah David Rabinowitz-Teʻomim (ADeReT). Rav Kook published three articles in *Ha-Peless* between the years 5661-5664 (1901-1904). They are reprinted in Rabbi Moshe Yehiel Zuriel, *Otserot ha-RAYaH*, vols. 1-2 (Tel-Aviv, 5748/1988), pp. 684-779.

101. Hosea 11:4.

102. *TB Nazir* 23b.

103. *Talmud Yerushalmi, Taʻanit* 2:6; *Yalkut Shimʻoni*, Joshua 7:9. (Rabbi Moshe Yehiel Halevi Zuriel)

104. *Zohar* I, 4a.

105. In other words, should we finalize his fall? (It would be the equivalent of the English expression "hammer a nail in his coffin.") The expression is based on *TB Kiddushin* 20b. The Talmud refers to a Jew who has become a priest in the service of idolatry. Even so, one must take pity and attempt to redeem him. "It was said in the studyhouse of Rabbi Ishmael: Since this individual went and became a priest of an idolatrous cult, perhaps a stone should be pushed down after the falling? Therefore it says, *After having*

been sold, redemption will come to him; one of his brothers will redeem him [Leviticus 25:48]."

106.   *TB Hullin* 124a.

107.   *TB 'Avodah Zarah* 3b; Maimonides, *Hil. Talmud Torah* 3:13.

108.   *TB Sanhedrin* 102a. Cf. *Likkutei ha-Shas me-ha-ARI z"l* (Zolkiew or Lemberg ca. 1815; photo offset B'nei Berak, 5732/1972), 15a, s.v. *amar lo HKB"H hazor bekha*; Rabbi Moshe Hayyim Luzzatto, *Ma'amar ha-Ge'ulah*, in *Yalkut Yedi'ot ha-Emet*, vol. 2, ed. Rabbi Yosef Begun (Tel-Aviv: Ahavah, 5726/1965), p. 239.

109.   *Talmud Yerushalmi, Berakhot* 1:1.

110.   Micah 7:15.

111.   *Orot ha-Kodesh*, vol. 2, ed. Rabbi David Cohen (Jerusalem: Mossad Harav Kook, 5745/1985), pp. 444-445. See now *Shemonah Kevatsim* 7:112.

112.   Zephaniah 3:9.

113.   Zechariah 12:10; *TB Sukkah* 52a. Cf. Rabbi Zadok Hakohen of Lublin, *Mahshevot Haruts* (Piotrkow, 5672/1912), 35c: "Messiah son of Joseph will be killed because in Joseph there was a bit of the root of what the brothers suspected... They detected the root of arrogance... But Messiah son of David... 'David is the smallest' [1 Sam 17:14]. In him, there is no arrogance whatsoever, not even in his kingship." See further idem, *Dover Zedek* (Piotrkow, 5671/1911), 41b.

There seems to be a glaring contradiction between the pensée published in *Orot* and the earlier address "The Lamentation in Jerusalem." In "The Lamentation in Jerusalem," Messiah son of Joseph symbolizes universalism, and Messiah son of David, Jewish particularism; in *Orot*, the roles are reversed, with Messiah son of Joseph embodying Jewish nationalism, and Messiah son of David, universalism. I have dealt with the complexity of this issue in my essay, "*Du-Partsufin shel ha-Meshihiyut*" ("The Two Faces of Messianism"), in Bezalel Naor, *Avirin* (Jerusalem: Zur-Ot, 5740/1980), pp. 16-24. Rav Kook's statement, "The Kingdom of David by dint of its distinctive nature subsumes as well the universal aspect" (note 72 above) is an invaluable key to the solution. See also the

NOTES

dream-communication from Rabbi Joshua Leib Diskin of Brisk for Rav Kook: "The difference between *Talmud Bavli* and *Talmud Yerushalmi* is that *Talmud Bavli* is a 'universal in need of a particular' (*kelal ha-tsarikh li-ferat*), and *Talmud Yerushalmi* is a 'particular in need of a universal' (*perat ha-tsarikh li-khelal*)" (*Hed Harim: Letters of Rabbi Jacob Moses Harlap to Rabbi Abraham Isaac Hakohen Kook*, ed. Rabbi Zevi Yehudah Hakohen Kook [Jerusalem, 5731/1971], p. 87).

114. See Rabbi Barukh Halevi Epstein, *Mekor Barukh* (Vilna: Romm, 1928), p. 1237 (619 in Hebrew pagination). Supposedly, this thought was confided by Rabbi Menahem Mendel Schneersohn to Epstein's father, Rabbi Yehiel Mikhel Halevi Epstein of Novahrodok, author of *'Arukh ha-Shulhan*.

115. *Talmud Yerushalmi, Ta'anit* 4:5.

116. See the diatribe reproduced in Simha Raz's biography of Rav Kook, *Mal'akhim ki-B'nei Adam* (Jerusalem: Kol Mevaser, 5762/2002), p. 203.

117. *Kitvei Polemos le-Profiat Duran* (Jerusalem, 5741/1981), cited in B.S. Hamburger, *Meshihei ha-Sheker u-Mitnagdeihem* (B'nei Berak: Makhon Moreshet Ashkenaz, 5749/1989), pp. 7-8. See further David Berger, "On the Uses of History in Medieval Jewish Polemic Against Christianity: The Quest for the Historical Jesus," in *Jewish History and Jewish Memory: Essays in Honor of Yosef Hayim Yerushalmi*, ed. Carlebach, Efron, and Myers (Hanover, NH: Brandeis Univ. Press, 1998), pp. 25-39.

118. *Sefer Yetsirah* 1:5.

119. Zechariah 8:22-23.

120. Psalms 89:15.

121. The paradigm shift in the Second Temple Period from prophecy to booklearning is one of the major themes of the enormously creative Hasidic thinker Rabbi Zadok Hakohen of Lublin (5583/1823-5660/1900). See below note 201.

122. *TB Sanhedrin* 21b-22a. See further the Introduction to *'Eyn AYaH*, vol. 1, ed. Filber (Jerusalem: Makhon RZYH Kook, 5747/1987), pp. 15-16; *Ma'amrei ha-RAYaH*, vol. 1 (Jerusalem, 5740/1980), pp. 209-210.

123. *TB Yoma* 69b. See at length Bezalel Naor, *Lights of Prophecy* (New York: Orthodox Union, 1990).

124. It is interesting to note in this connection the comment of the Vilna Gaon to the concluding song of the Passover Haggadah, *Had Gadya*:

> *Came the water and extinguished the fire. Water*, this is *K'nesset Israel* (Ecclesia Israel). *The fire*, this is the Evil Inclination that emerged from the Holy of Holies in the form of fire.

125. Rav Kook has much to say on the topic of sublimating the energy of paganism to authentic service of God. See his remarks concerning Abraham: *Igrot ha-RAYaH*, vol. 2 (Jerusalem: Mossad Harav Kook, 5722/1961), Letter 379, p. 43; *Orot ha-Emunah*, ed. Rabbi Moshe Gurevitz (Jerusalem, 5758/1998), pp. 109-110; *Siddur 'Olat RAYaH*, vol. 2 (Jerusalem: Mossad Harav Kook, 5749/1989), p. 261, s.v. *Maggid*; Bezalel Naor, *Ben Shanah Shaul* (Jerusalem: Zur-Ot, 5755/1995), pp. 43-46.

Based on Rav Kook's insight that the Binding of Isaac came to demonstrate that Abraham's monotheistic faith lacked none of the fervor, passion, and devotion of paganism, a contemporary scholar, Rabbi Joshua Hoffman explains the controversy in *Genesis Rabbah* 58:5 between Rabbi Levi and Rabbi Yosé whether Abraham was freshly arrived from the burial of Terah or from the binding of Isaac. The common denominator is that both ceremonies symbolize the new faith's ability to digest elements of pre-Abrahamitic paganism. Netvort: Parashat Hayyei Sarah, 5763. Netvort@aol.com. One might add that this resolution of the relationship with paganism would have been the necessary prelude to establishment of a Hebrew presence in Hebron, the first semblance of a permanent presence in the Holy Land.

126. According to the Talmud, the Second Temple was destroyed because of *sin'at hinam* (groundless hatred). See *TB Yoma* 9b.

127. Rabbi Zevi Yehudah Hakohen Kook commented on an anomaly in the *Mishnah*, *Avot* 1:6 and 1:16. The very same dictum, "Assign yourself a teacher," is attributed both to Rabbi Joshua ben Perahia and to Rabban

NOTES

Gamliel. Rabbi Zevi Yehudah explained that both these men contended with Christianity. According to the Talmud (*Sotah* 47a; *Sanhedrin* 107b in uncensored editions), Rabbi Joshua ben Perahia had been the teacher of Yeshu'a ha-Notsri (Jesus of Nazareth). Rabban Gamliel II, active in Yavneh in the second generation after the destruction of the Temple, was instrumental in combating the early Christians by instituting a special prayer against sectarians. See *TB Berakhot* 28b and the uncensored version of RaSHI ad locum; *Sefer Halakhot Gedolot*, ed. Azriel Hildesheimer (Jerusalem: Mekize Nirdamim, 1971), p. 54; (in Makhon Yerushalayim edition of *Sefer Halakhot Gedolot* [Jerusalem, 5752/1992], p. 50); Rabbi Abraham ben Isaac of Narbonne, *Sefer ha-Eshkol*, vol. 1, ed. Albeck (Jerusalem: Wagschal, 5744/1984), pp. 26-27; Maimonides, *MT, Hil. Tefillah* 2:1. [In the Cairo Genizah, there was unearthed a Palestinian version of the *Birkat ha-Minim* (curse of the sectarians) that singles out for mention *Notsrim* (Christians). Scholars are divided as to the dating of this version, and even as to the exact denotation of the term *Notsrim*. See Lawrence H. Schiffman and Reuven Kimelman in *Jewish and Christian Self-Definition*, vol. 2, ed. Sanders, Baumgarten, and Mendelson (Philadelphia: Fortress Press, 1981), pp. 150-152; 226-244.] Rabbi Joshua ben Perahia and Rabban Gamliel had the same sense about Christianity (both founder and adherents) that its flaw consisted in its failure to submit to rabbinic authority. In *TB Gittin* 57a, the essential flaw of Jesus is that he was wont to "ridicule the words of the sages" (*mal'ig 'al divrei hakhamim*). See further *TB Berakhot* 17b in uncensored editions; and B.M. Lewin, *Otsar ha-Ge'onim, Berakhot* 17b, citing Hai Gaon. See Hayyim Avihu Schwarz, *Mi-Tokh ha-Torah ha-Go'elet: Shi'urei Harav Zevi Yehudah Hakohen Kook*, vol. 4 (Jerusalem, 5751/1991), pp. 131-133.

The problem with this ingenious solution of Rabbi Zevi Yehudah Hakohen Kook is that there exists a consensus among commentators—Pseudo-RaShI, Me'iri, Rabbi Isaac ben Solomon of Toledo, Rabbi Solomon ben Zemah Duran of Algiers, Rabbi Joseph Hayyun, Abravanel, Rabbi Yom Tov Lipmann Heller, Rabbi Israel Lipschütz—that Rabban Gamliel in *Avot* 1:16 is not Rabban Gamliel II of Yavneh, who instituted *birkat ha-*

minim, but rather his grandfather, Rabban Gamliel I (grandson of Hillel), who lived before the destruction of the Temple. See *Seder ha-Kabbalah le-Rabbenu Menahem ha-Me'iri*, ed. S.Z. Havlin and A. Shoshana (Cleveland: Ofeq Institute, 5755/1995), pp. 88, 199; *Perushei Rishonim le-Massekhet Avot*, ed. M.S. Kasher and J.J. Blacherowitz (Jerusalem: Makhon Torah Shelemah, 5733/1973); *Perushei Rabbenu Yizhak bar Shelomo mi-Toledo*, ed. M.S. Kasher (Jerusalem: Makhon Torah Shelemah, 5743/1983); *Magen Avot le-RaShBaTs*, ed. Rabbi Elijah Rahamim Zini (Jerusalem: Erez, 5760/2000); *Abrabanel on Pirke Avot*, ed. Rabbi Abraham Chill (New York: Sepher-Hermon Press, 5751/1991), p. 71; Rabbi Menahem Azariah of Fano, *'Assarah Ma'amarot*, vol. 1 (Jerusalem: Yismah Lev, 5758/1998), *Ma'amar Hikkur Din*, Part 2, chap. 19 (pp. 140-143); Rabbi Yom Tov Lipmann Heller, *Tosafot Yom Tov*; and Rabbi Israel Lipschütz, *Tif'eret Yisrael*. However, see Hanokh Albeck, *Shishah Sidrei Mishnah* IV (Tel-Aviv: Devir, 5744/1984), p. 349. Rabbi David Zevi Hoffman argued convincingly that Rabban Gamliel of *Avot* 1:16 is indeed Rabban Gamliel II of Yavneh! See D. Hoffman, *The First Mishnah and the Controversies of the Tannaim*, trans. Paul Forchheimer (New York: Sepher-Hermon, 1977), pp. 45–46, 53.

This problem would exist even were we to assume that the Jesus described as a disciple of Rabbi Joshua ben Perahia in *Sotah* 47a and *Sanhedrin* 107b is one and the same as Jesus of Nazareth, founder of Christianity. The reader should be aware that the medieval Provencal authority Rabbi Menahem ha-Me'iri of Perpignan disputes this identification. His objection stems from the fact that Rabbi Joshua ben Perahia lived much earlier than the founder of Christianity. See Me'iri, Introduction to *Avot*; Rabbi Menahem ha-Me'iri, *Seder ha-Kabbalah*, ed. S.Z. Havlin and A. Shoshana (Jerusalem: Ofeq, 5755/1995), pp. 69–70. According to the contemporary historian Rabbi Shelomo Hakohen Rotenberg, though there were some medieval Jewish authorities who, like Meiri, posited two Jesuses because of the supposed discrepancy between the Talmudic dating and that in Christian sources, there really is no need. The Christians wilfully postdated Jesus, moving the year of his death closer to the destruction of the Temple, in order to supposedly create linkage between the two events and give credence to the notion that the destruction was punishment for having executed Jesus. Rabbi Rotenberg writes that today even Church authorities, though they may not publicize it, are fully aware that Jesus lived much earlier than they claimed. Rotenberg, *Toledot 'Am 'Olam*, vol. 2 (Brooklyn, NY: Keren Eliezer, 5733/1972), pp. 318, 420-421. The notion that Christians deliberately postdated Jesus to approach the date of the destruction of the Temple, first appears in Rabbi Abraham ibn Daud Halevi, *Sefer ha-Kabbalah* (Mantua, 1514), 3a. On the discrepancy between the Jewish and Christian dating of Jesus, see also Nahmanides, *Vikku'ah (Milhamot Hashem)* in *Kitvei RaMBaN*, vol. 1, ed. C.B. Chavel (Jerusalem: Mossad Harav Kook, 5728/1968), p. 306; and Rabbi Joseph Official, *Sefer Yosef Hamekane*, ed. Judah Rosenthal (Jerusalem: Mekize Nirdamim, 1970), p. 138.

128. Deuteronomy 10:20; *TB Pesahim* 22b; *Bava Kama* 41b.

Elsewhere, Rav Kook envisions Rabbi Akiva as the nemesis of emerging Christianity:

> The adversary of nascent Christianity, Rabbi Akiva, "interpreted on each crownlet piles of *halakhot*" [*TB Menahot* 29b]. It was he who appreciated the value of the nation as a whole, and her devotion to God in all her manifestations. He knew that even in her physical strength, "The portion of the Lord is His people" [Deuteronomy 32:9], and he bore the armor of Ben Koziba [Bar Kokhba], hoping that from him salvation would sprout forth for Israel [Maimonides, *MT, Hil. Melakhim* 11:2]. He endangered himself to ritually wash his hands [*TB 'Eruvin* 21b], and his soul departed with the word "One" [*TB Berakhot* 61b]. He was an Israelite man to the core, despite the fact that outwardly he was descended from converts to Judaism [*TB Berakhot* 27b, and Rav Nissim Gaon ad locum]. He is the power that protects against the utterance of the Name by the son of the Israelite woman.

"She was unique [in her adulterous relations with an Egyptian man] and Scripture publicized her: Shelomit daughter of Divri. Shelomit, because she was wanton, wishing 'Shalom' to all. Divri, because she would speak overly much" [*Leviticus Rabbah* 32:5]. "[And there went forth a son of an Israelite woman, but who was the son of an Egyptian man, among the children of Israel;] and there struggled in the camp, the son of the Israelite woman and an Israelite man" [Leviticus 24:10], until their judgment was explained. (*Orot ha-Emunah*, ed. Rabbi Moshe Gurevitz [Jerusalem, 5758/1998], pp. 35-36)

Rav Kook typecasts Jesus on the one hand, and Rabbi Akiva on the other, in the earlier roles of the son of the Israelite woman Shelomit bat Divri and an anonymous Israelite man struggling with one another. Rav Kook subscribed to the notion that the father of Jesus was a gentile. This was the opinion of Maimonides. (See Appendix A.) Also, Rav Kook took at face value the medieval anti-Christian work *Toledot Yeshu*, whereby Jesus made improper use of the divine name to achieve his wonders. (We should not be astonished that Rav Kook subscribed to the notion that Jesus performed signs by improper use of the divine name. As prestigious a philosopher as Rabbi Joseph Albo alludes to this notion as if it were historical fact. See Albo, *'Ikkarim* I, end chap. 18; Simha Bunim Orbach, *'Ammudei ha-Mahshavah ha-Yisraelit*, vol. 2 [Jerusalem: World Zionist Organization, 5732/1972], p. 560.) The irony of history is that Jesus, of a Jewish mother, was guilty of distorting Judaism, whereas Rabbi Akiva, of non-Jewish lineage, became Judaism's most faithful guardian. As opposed to Jesus who, according to the report in the Evangelium, made light of ritual washing of the hands before eating bread (Mark 7:2; Matthew 15:2), Rabbi Akiva endangered his life for this very rabbinic ordinance of *netillat yadayim*! (See Nahmanides, *Sefer ha-Mitsvot le-ha-RaMBaM 'im Hassagot ha-RaMBaN*, ed. C.B. Chavel [Jerusalem: Mossad Harav Kook, 5741/1981], *shoresh* 1, p. 18.)

NOTES

Rav Kook was not the first to envision the son of Shelomit bat Divri as the prototype of Jesus. See Rabbi Solomon Hakohen Rabinowitz of Radomsk, *Tif'eret Shelomo, Emor*, 87b. This classic Hasidic work by a nineteenth century Polish rebbe refers to a tradition that the initials of the words *ve-nokev shem YHWH* ("he that pronounces the name of the Lord") in Leviticus 24:16, spell Y-Sh-U, when reversed. Rav Kook attributes these initials to Rabbi Samson of Ostropolye. See *Pinkas Yod-Gimmel* (Jerusalem: Makhon RZYH Kook, 2004), par. 43 (p. 38); *Kevatsim mi-Khetav Yad Kodsho*, ed. Boaz Ofen, vol. 1 (Jerusalem, 2006), *Pinkas Rishon le-Yaffo*, par. 43 (p. 99). Concerning the son of Shelomit bat Divri as the "root" of the contemporary wicked, see Rabbi Isaac Haver (Wildmann), *Pithei She'arim, Netiv binyan ha-kelipot umerkavah teme'ah* (ms.), in Kalman Redisch, *Mi-Ginzei ha-GRA u-Veit Midrasho* (Lakewood, 5759/1999), p. 216ff.

129. Cf. Lamentations 2:9.

130. Cf. Rabbi Abraham Isaac Hakohen Kook, *Resh Millin* (Jerusalem: Mossad Harav Kook, 5745/1985), p. 8, "*Bet.*"

131. Cf. *Orot ha-Emunah*, ed. Rabbi Moshe Gurevitz (Jerusalem, 5758/1998), pp. 33-34.

132. Cf. the remark attributed to Rabbi Menahem Mendel Schneersohn of Lubavitch (5549/1789-5626/1866) by Rabbi Barukh Halevi Epstein:

> Our Hasidim do not know and cannot appreciate the favor the Vilna Gaon did for us by opposing us. Were it not for the controversy, there were truly grounds to worry that the new approach would gradually lead us over the border of Torah tradition. Not unfounded was the fear that as a result of the new way that swept up its founders, eventually the Talmud would be burnt by the fire of the Kabbalah, the hidden Torah would obscure the revealed Torah, and the practical commandments would be reduced in value in the face of emotions seething from the mysteries of *kavvanot* (kabbalistic meditations). (Barukh Halevi Epstein, *Mekor Barukh* III [Vilna: Romm, 1928], p. 1237)

133. *Mishnah, Avot* 5:17. That same year, Rav Kook published these lines:

> Hasidism, which came to raise up the holiness of character, of faith, the general awareness of the sanctity of Israel and their excellence, to enhance feelings of holiness that lay dormant in the heart through the value of prayer; and directly opposite, Mitnagdism, which worried that the practical foundation not totter as a result of overwhelming emotion, that the specifics not be blurred because of preoccupation with universals, and that the power of imagination aroused by the emotion brought on by good, holy, true feelings, not overstep its bounds and bring bitter results that would haunt the nation for generations to come—these two influences competed with one another. (*Eder ha-Yekar* [Jerusalem, 5666/1906; reprinted Jerusalem: Mossad Harav Kook, 5745/1985], p. 25)

134. Jeremiah 31:11.

135. Isaiah 62:2.

136. *Mishnah, Avot* 5:19.

137. Psalms 27:1.

138. In a letter to his soul-friend, the kabbalist Rabbi Pinhas Hakohen Lintop of Birzh, Lithuania, Rav Kook wrote:

> In the latter generations, all the conversation of the disciples of the Gaon Rabbi Elijah [the Vilna Gaon] taken together with the disciples of the Ba'al Shem Tov—who were so diametrically opposed to one another in their day—is very lovely to us. Not without toil and talent will there be created an entire literature that will have the capability of stitching together these tears in the spirit. But how precious will be the product that results from this work, which will be the actual stitching together of the nation, with a clear aspiration to her central goal: return to her strength

in her land. (*Igrot ha-RAYaH*, vol. 1 [Jerusalem: Mossad Harav Kook, 5722/1962], pp. 304-305)

The recipient of the letter, Rabbi Lintop, was himself struggling to unite—in terms of kabbalistic teachings—the two worlds of the disciples of the Gaon and the disciples of the Ba'al Shem Tov, specifically the masters of HaBaD. See Bezalel Naor, "*Gilgulei ketav-yad 'Adir ba-Marom' le-RaMHaL she-hayah be-ba'alut mishpahat ha-GRA*," *Sinai*, Tishrei-Heshvan 5759/1999, pp. 59- 62.

In his syllabus of Jewish Thought, Rav Kook included, "the books of the Gaon Rabbi Elijah and his disciples, the Gaon Rabbi Zalman of Liadi and all the *ba'alei hasbarah* (masters of explanation) in Hasidism" (Introduction to *Eder ha-Yekar* [Jerusalem, 5666/1906; reprinted Jerusalem: Mossad Harav Kook, 5745/1985], p. 16).

Recently, the thought occurred to this writer (BN) that the *yahrzeit* of the two adversaries is highly symbolic. Generally, we associate Hasidism with *simha* (joy) and *Mitnagdism* with Torah. We would have expected the *yahrzeit* of the Ba'al Shem Tov, founder of Hasidism, to take place on Sukkot, *zeman simhatenu* (the time of our rejoicing), and the *yahrzeit* of the Vilna Gaon, founder of Mitnagdism, to coincide with Shavu'ot, *zeman matan toratenu* (the time of the giving of our Torah). But divine providence willed the opposite: The Ba'al Shem Tov passed to his eternal reward on Shavu'ot, and the Vilna Gaon on the third day of *hol ha-mo'ed Sukkot*! The day the *tsaddik* departs from this world, there is revealed his inner essence. Inwardly, the Ba'al Shem Tov was the essence of Torah, and the Vilna Gaon, the essence of joy. Thus do the two halves of a "controversy for the sake of heaven" complement one another. (Continued below on page 232.)

139. Jeremiah 31:11.
140. Habakkuk 2:3.
141. Ibid. 2:4.
142. *'Ets Hayyim* (Tree of Life) by Rabbi Hayyim Vital is the *magnum opus* of Lurianic kabbalah. Rabbi Zevi Yehudah Hakohen Kook in his notes refers

to *'Ets Hayyim, hekhal* [6, *hekhal nukva de-z"a, sha'ar* 7], *sha'ar* 40 (*sha'ar penimiyut ve-hitsoniyut*). Subsequently, Rabbi Zevi Yehudah added the following sources: *'Ets Hayyim, hekhal* 1, *sha'ar* 3, chap. 3; *hekhal* 5, *sha'ar* 12, chaps. 1 and 2; *Sha'ar ha-Kavvanot, 'Inyan Rosh ha-Shanah, derush* 1 (*Igrot ha-RAYaH*, vol. 2 [Jerusalem: Mossad Harav Kook, 5722/1961], p. 343).

But truthfully, there is no reference there to the Nazarene. I believe the true source for Rav Kook's statement is the work by Rabbi Moses Hayyim Luzzatto, *Kin'at Adonai Zeva'ot*. Rav Kook's familiarity with the book is attested to by the responsum in *Mishpat Kohen* (Jerusalem: Mossad Harav Kook, 5745/1985), no. 148 (p. 359). The responsum was penned in 5676/1916. Rav Kook writes, "Many years ago I saw that the kabbalist RMH Luzzatto proved in his treatise *Kin'at Adonai Zeva'ot*..." Luzzatto speaks at great length concerning *hitsoniyut* (outwardness) and *penimiyut* (inwardness), and employing the code known as ATBaSh, mentions explicitly "*Notsri*." Rav Kook would have known these passages from the printed editions (Koenigsberg, 5628/1868; Rabbi Samuel Luria ed., Warsaw, 5648/1888). If by some stretch of the imagination he had access to the manuscript, he would have known yet another encrypted passage concerning the man of flesh and blood whom the Christians deified. See *Ginzei RaMHaL*, ed. Rabbi Hayyim Friedlander (B'nei Berak, 5740/1980), pp. 101-102, 104, 138-139.

143.   Hebrew, *mi-ko'ah ha-tohu*. RZYH Kook refers the reader to the article "*Ha-Neshamot shel 'Olam ha-Tohu*" ("The Souls of the World of Chaos"), which first appeared in *Ha-Tarbut ha-Yisraelit*, and was subsequently reprinted in *Orot* (1950 ed.), pp. 121-123. See the additional notes to *Igrot ha-RAYaH*, vol. 2, p. 343.

In *'Ets Hayyim* 49:3, Rabbi Hayyim Vital writes: "... and there begin in 'other gods,' and this is the mystery of 288 sparks that remain to be clarified in *Kelipat Nogah*, and from there is 'the *Mamzer*' ('the Bastard'), for he is numerically 288 (including the word)." The nickname "*Mamzer*" for Jesus of Nazareth was popular rather than rabbinic in origin. See the note of Rabbi Joseph Kafah to his edition of the *Epistle of Yemen* in Rabbenu

NOTES

Moshe ben Maimon, *Igrot* (Jerusalem: Mossad Harav Kook, 1994), p. 21, n. 26. The "288 sparks" are from the World of Chaos (*'Olam ha-Tohu*).

In the Kabbalistic writings of Rabbi Menahem Mendel of Shklov, a disciple of the Vilna Gaon, there is a passage that alludes to a "great secret" (*sod gadol*) of the one "who ridicules the words of the Sages" (*ha-mal'ig 'al divrei hakhamim*) [*TB Gittin* 57a]. This is followed by the epithet "*mamzer.*" The allusion to Jesus is rather transparent. See *Kitvei ha-GRMM z"l*, vol. 2 (Jerusalem, 5761), p. 163. Yehuda Liebes mistakenly interpreted the passage as referring to Shabbetai Zevi. See Y. Liebes, "*Talmidei ha-GRA, ha-Shabta'ut ve-ha-Nekudah ha-Yehudit,*" *Da'at* 50-52 (5763), pp. 255-290.

In *Kitvei ha-GRMM*, vol. 1, p. 66, RMM takes on both Christianity and Islam in the persons of *Yeshu* and *Mahmoud*. Their combined numerical value of 414 is equal to that of the enigmatic words "*et vahev*" in Numbers 21:14. Read through this eschatological lens, the Biblical verse reveals the following prophecy: "Therefore it is said in the Book of the Wars of the Lord: '*Mahmoud Yeshu* at the end.'"

144. *Sifré, Ve-Zot ha-Berakha*. One may wonder how Rav Kook segued from the topic of Jesus to that of Bil'am. There exists an entire literature juxtaposing these two figures from the rogues gallery of Jewish history, starting with the *Talmud Bavli* (*Gittin* 57a in the uncensored edition). See Peter Schäfer, *Jesus in the Talmud* (Princeton, 2007), pp. 30-33; *Toledot Yeshu: The Life Story of Jesus*, ed. Meerson and Schäfer, vol. 1 (Tübingen, 2014), p. 139, n. 12.

145. Psalms 119:126; *TB Gittin* 60b.

146. Zechariah 9:14.

147. Daniel 8:14.

148. Elhanan Kalmanson, *Sinai and Golgotha* [Hebrew] (Riga, 5685/1925), 40 pp. An historical survey of Judaism and Christianity.

149. Deuteronomy 7:26.

150. Nos. 9-12. Rabbi Meir Berlin (Bar Ilan), for many years the leader of the Mizrachi or Religious Zionist movement, was the *ben zekunim*, the son of old age of Rav Kook's mentor in the famed Volozhin Yeshiva, Rabbi Naphtali

Zevi Yehudah Berlin (NeZIV). Rav Kook's submission letter was published in *Igrot ha-RAYaH*, vol. 2, p. 67. In a letter to his friend Rabbi Jacob Moses Harlap, Rabbi Zevi Yehudah writes, "For two weeks I worked on it [i.e. "To the Process of Ideas in Israel"] assiduously and productively, thank God." *Zemah Zevi: Letters of Rabbi Zevi Yehudah Hakohen Kook*, vol. 1 (Jerusalem, 1991), p. 42. In other words, the editing was done by Rav Kook's only son.

151. It was removed from subsequent editions of the *Letters*.

152. The editor, Rabbi Zevi Yehudah Hakohen Kook, credited his brother-in-law (brother of Rabbi Zevi Yehudah's wife, Hava Leah née Hutner), Rabbi Abraham Joshua Hutner, with the suggestion of appending the essay to *Orot*. See the introduction to the 5710/1950 edition of *Orot*.

153. The views of the secular Zionists were summed up eloquently by Rabbi Shalom Dov Baer Schneersohn, writing in 1903. See the introduction to his *Kuntress U-Ma'ayan* (Brooklyn: Kehot, 5718/1958), pp. 45-53. Many years later, speaking before a group of disciples, Rabbi Zevi Yehudah Hakohen Kook would have occasion to bemoan the philosophy of secular education in Israel: "'*Torah* and *mitsvot* were necessary in Exile, but here in Erets Israel, in the generation of national revival, we do not need them.' This is a terrible, frightening counterfeit—counterfeit of the soul!" (Hayyim Avihu Schwarz, *Mi-Tokh ha-Torah ha-Go'elet*, vol. 4 [Jerusalem, 5751/1991], p. 68).

154. Sa'adyah Gaon, *Beliefs and Opinions* (Judeo-Arabic and Hebrew trans.), ed. Kafah (Jerusalem, 5753/1993), III, 7 (p. 132).

155. This point was made by Rabbi El'azar Menahem Man Shach of B'nei Berak in a public address in the 1980s.

156. Parenthetically, it has been observed that an Orthodox rabbi typified as a proto-Zionist, the Sephardic Rabbi Judah Hai Alkalay of Semlin, Croatia, may have been influenced by the example of Serbian nationalism. The same goes for Alkalay's mentor, Rabbi Judah Bibas of Corfu, who held up Greek nationalism as an example. "Just as the Greeks took their land by force from the Turks, so must the Jews seize Palestine." Quoted in David Benvenisti and Hayyim Mizrahi, "Rabbi Yehudah Bibas and the community of Corfu during his lifetime," *Sefunot* II (5718/1958), p. 310.

157. However, at the conclusion of chapter V, Rav Kook does quote a few

lines from Halevi's poem, *Zion Halo Tish'ali*. As I have written elsewhere, further proof that the essay was informed by the ideology of the *Kuzari* is its concluding theme that especially the so-called *mitsvot shim'iyot* (non-rational commandments) serve to connect Israel to the divine. See *Kuzari* II, 48.

158. Diana Lobel recently translated *al-'amr al-ilahi* as "the divine thing." See Lobel, *Between Mysticism and Philosophy: Sufi Language of Religious Experience in Judah Ha-Levi's Kuzari* (Albany: State University of New York Press, 2000), p. 7.

159. This seems consonant with the *Zohar*'s vision of the Third Temple as a synthesis of the First and Second Temples. See *Zohar* II, 9b; III, 221a; Rabbi Hayyim Vital, *'Ets Hayyim*, Gate 36, *Sha'ar Mi'ut ha-Yare'ah*, chap. 2. However, in his famous responsum concerning the sanctity of the Temple Mount nowadays, Rav Kook cites a different kabbalistic interpretation based on Rabbi Moses Cordovero's work *Elimah* (*'Eyn kol tamar*, V, chaps. 22, 25). See *Mishpat Kohen* (Jerusalem: Mossad Harav Kook, 5745/1985), no. 96 (pp. 209-210).

160. See Commentary of Rabbenu Ezra of Gerona to Song of Songs, in *Kitvei RaMBaN*, ed. Chavel, vol. 2 (Jerusalem: Mossad Harav Kook, 5728/1968), p. 517; Rabbenu Nissim ben Reuben Gerondi, *Derashot ha-RaN*, ed. Leon A. Feldman (Jerusalem: Shalem, 5734/1974), *derush* 7 (p. 123); Hasdai Crescas, *'Or Adonai* 3:8:2.

161. See *TB Yoma* 21b.

162. Elsewhere, Rav Kook ventures the opinion that the Sadducees of the Second Temple Period carried individualism to an extreme. They conceived of the Jewish People as some sort of partnership, denying the collective sanctity of *K'nesset Israel*, a whole greater than the sum of its parts. See Rav Kook's letter to Rabbi Meir Dan Plotski, published in *Mishpat Kohen* (Jerusalem: Mossad Harav Kook, 5745/1985), no. 124 (273b-274b). Cf. *Ma'amrei ha-RAYaH*, vol. 1 (Jerusalem, 5740/1980), pp. 177-181. However, the Sadducees were infamous for denying the existence of the World to Come. See *Avot de-Rabbi Nathan*, chap. 5, and Maimonides' commentary to

Mishnah, *Avot* 1:3.

163. Eliezer Goldman speculated that in "To the Process of Ideas in Israel," Rav Kook was responding to Moses Hess's *Rome and Jerusalem* (Leipzig, 1862), which he could have read in Hebrew translation, and to various writings of Ahad ha-'Am (Asher Ginsberg). See Eliezer Goldman, "*Tsiyonut hilonit, te'udat Yisrael ve-takhlit ha-Torah*," *Da'at*, Summer 5743/1983, pp. 115-117.

Actually, the assertion that individuality and the belief in an afterlife are absent from Judaism turns up in Hegel (1822):

> The individual never comes to the consciousness of independence; on that account we do not find among the Jews any belief in the immortality of the soul; for individuality does not exist in and for itself. But though in Judaism the *Individual* is not respected, the *Family* has inherent value; for the worship of Jehovah is attached to the *Family*, and it is consequently viewed as a substantial existence" (Georg W.F. Hegel, *The Philosophy of History*, trans. J. Sibree [Buffalo, NY: Prometheus Books, 1991], p. 197).

See also Benjamin Ish-Shalom, *Rabbi Abraham Isaac Kook: Between Rationalism and Mysticism* (Hebrew) (Tel-Aviv: 'Am 'Oved, 5750/1990), p. 284, n. 137; 326, n. 51.

In the generation following Rav Kook, Simon Rawidowicz devoted much thought to the subject of First and Second Temples. See his essay, "Israel's Two Beginnings: The First and Second 'Houses,'" in Simon Rawidowicz, *Studies in Jewish Thought*, ed. N. Glatzer (Philadelphia: Jewish Publication Society of America, 1974), pp. 81-209.

164. 1 Samuel 25:29.
165. 2 Samuel 14:14.
166. Genesis 15:15; Judges 2:10; 2 Kings 22:20; 2 Chronicles 34:28.
167. Maimonides, *MT, Hil. Teshuvah* 8:3; Crescas, *'Or Adonai* 3:2:2. See also Menasseh ben Israel, *Nishmat Hayyim* I, 7.

NOTES

168. Rabbi Abraham Isaac Hakohen Kook, *Igrot ha-RAYaH*, vol. 1 (Jerusalem: Mossad Harav Kook, 5722/1962), p. 134.
169. *Mishnah, Sanhedrin* 10:1.
170. See *TB* Menahot 110a:

> From Tyre to Carthage they recognize Israel and their Father in Heaven; and from Tyre westward, and from Carthage eastward, they recognize neither Israel nor their Father in Heaven. Rav Shimi questioned Rav, "Does it not say, *For from the rising of the sun unto its going down My name is great among the nations* [Malachi 1:11]?" Rav responded, "Can you be Shimi [the wise man]? They call Him, God of gods!"

Cf. also these lines from Rabbi Solomon ibn Gabirol's poem, *Keter Malkhut* (The Royal Crown):

> You are God,
> And all the creatures are Your servants and worshipers.
> Your glory is not lessened on account of those who worship other gods,
> Because the intention of all is to reach You.
> But they are as blind men.
> Their goal is the way of the King,
> And they have strayed from the way.
> One has drowned in a bottomless well.
> Another has fallen in a ditch.
> All thought they arrived at their destination,
> And they strove for nought.
> But Your servants are seeing;
> They go in a straight way.
> They deviate from the path neither right nor left,
> Until they reach the courtyard of the King.
> —Solomon ibn Gabirol (ca. 1021-ca. 1058)

171. Cf. *Zohar* III, 135b; *Likkutei ha-Shas me-ha-ARI z"l* (Zolkiew or Lemberg ca. 1815; photo offset B'nei Berak, 5732/1972), 20b, s.v. *tanna devei Eliyahu shit alfei shenin* (*'Avodah Zarah* 9a); Rabbi Menahem Azariah of Fano, *Ma'amar Ma'ayan Ganim* in *Ma'amrei ha-RaMA mi-Fano*, vol. 2 (Jerusalem: Yishmah Lev, 5757/1997), 170a, 172b.
172. Many years later, the Existential writer Sartre would speak of "nausea" in this vein. See Jean-Paul Sartre, *Nausea* (1938).
173. Hosea 4:1.
174. Isaiah 24:20, 21.
175. With one fell swoop, Rav Kook dismisses both Marxism (dialectical materialism) and Freudian psychology.
176. Habakkuk 2:19.
177. Genesis 18:19.
178. Deuteronomy 4:6.
179. Rav Kook quotes the verse, "the kindness of your youth, the love of your betrothal" (Jeremiah 2:2). The reference is to the generation of the Exodus from Egypt.
180. *TB Hullin* 60b.
181. Proverbs 27:8; *Tikkunei Zohar*, Introduction.
182. *Zohar* II, 85a.
183. *Mishnah, Yadayim* 3:5.
184. *Zohar* II, 20a; III, 37b; *Tikkunei Zohar, tikkun* 25, 26.
185. The author conflates three verses: 2 Samuel 23:1; 1 Chronicles 29:23; and Psalms 122:5.
186. Hosea 10:1.
187. *TB Pesahim* 87a.
188. Hosea 2:4.
189. Hosea 2:18-22.
190. See *TB Gittin* 58a, and Rabbi Judah Löw, *Netsah Israel*, end chap. 7.
190*. Cf. Lamentations 2:1.
191. Jeremiah 2:21.
192. Jeremiah 31:20; *Sifré, 'Ekev*, par. 7.
193. Psalms 14:7.

194. Jeremiah 17:12.

195. *TB Yoma* 54a; *'Ets Hayyim, sha'ar he'arat ha-mohin*, chap. 5. Regarding the kabbalistic symbolism of Zion, see Rav Kook's response to Rabb Menashe Adler in *Igrot ha-RAYH*, vol. 4 (Jerusalem, 1984), Letter 1277 (p. 217).

196. The author conflates three texts: Isaiah 49:13=52:9; 44:23; and Jeremiah 50:19.

197. Cf. Rav Kook's article *"Te'udat Israel u-le'umiyuto"* ("The Destiny of Israel and Its Nationalism") published in *Ha-Peless* (Poltava), 5662/1902.

198. Ezra 6:21; Nehemiah 10:29.

199. *TB Hullin* 60b.

200. Rabbi Zevi Yehudah Kook was wont to point out that the word for religion, *dat*, is a Persian loanword that first occurs in the Bible in the Scroll of Esther. Thus, the entire expression given to Godliness that goes by the name of religion is of exilic origin. The landed form of the divine idea is much too holistic to be subsumed under religion. See Hayyim A. Schwarz, *Mi-Tokh ha-Torah ha-Go'elet*, vol. 3 (Jerusalem, 5747/1987), p. 225.

See Rav Kook's own objection to the use of the word *"dat"* when referring to Judaism, in *Igrot ha-RAYaH*, vol. 1 (Jerusalem, 1962), Letter 164 (p. 215); and *Kevatsim mi-Khetav Yad Kodsho*, ed. Boaz Ofen, vol. 2 (Jerusalem, 2008), *Pinkas ha-Dapim* 1, par. 20 (pp. 59-60).

201. Song of Songs 7:14; *TB 'Eruvin* 21b. Cf. Introduction to *'Eyn AYaH*, ed. Filber, vol. 1 (Jerusalem: Makhon RZYH Kook, 5747/1987), p. 16; *Ma'amrei ha-RAYaH*, vol. 1 (Jerusalem, 5740/1980), p. 210.

In the generation preceding Rav Kook, the highly original Hasidic thinker Rabbi Zadok Hakohen of Lublin developed the theme that though the Oral Law goes back to Sinai, it certainly gained prominence in the Second Temple Period. Rabbi Zadok's source for this assertion is *Pirkei Hekhalot*, chap. 27. See Rabbi Zadok Hakohen, *Takkanat ha-Shavin* (Beit El, 5748/1988) 6:24 (p. 48); *Mahshevot Haruts* (Piotrkow, 5672/1912), 71d; *Resisei Laylah* (Lublin, 5663/1903), 81b; *Peri Zaddik*, vol. 1 (Lublin, 5661/1901), *Hannukah*, 69a; *Vayyigash*, 106b-d; vol. 5 (Lublin, 5694/1934),

Devarim, 8c; *Poked 'Akarim* (Piotrkow, 1922), 26a-b; *Likkutei Ma'amarim* (appended to *Divrei Soferim*, Lublin 1913), 118d-119a. These texts were collected in Bezalel Naor, *Lights of Prophecy* (New York: Orthodox Union, 5750/1990).

202. Leviticus 26:12.
203. Sa'adyah Gaon, *Beliefs and Opinions*, Introduction.
204. Rav Kook attempts to answer the oft-asked question why there is no mention of the afterlife in the Bible. Numerous solutions have been offered over the centuries. See Sa'adyah, *Beliefs and Opinions* 9:2; Judah Halevi, *Kuzari* I, 104-117; Ibn Ezra, *Deuteronomy* 32:39 (citing Hai Gaon); Maimonides, *Mishneh Torah, Hil. Teshuvah* 9:1; Nahmanides, Exodus 6:2; Leviticus 18:29; 26:11; Deuteronomy 11:13; Rabbi Nissim ben Reuben of Gerona, *Derashot ha-RaN*, end *Derush* 1 ("*Bereshit*"); anonymous, *Hinukh*, Introduction; Rabbi Joseph Albo, *'Ikkarim* IV, 39-41; Rabbi Isaac Arama, *'Akedat Yizhak* III, *Sha'ar* 70 (144a-b); Rabbi Isaac Abravanel, Leviticus 26; Rabbi Shem Tov ben Joseph, ms. commentary to *Avot*, 109r.-110v. (published by Michael Shmidman in *Rabbi Dr. Leo Jung Memorial Volume*); Rabbi Joseph Ya'avets, *Yesod ha-Emunah* (Piotrkow, 5671/1911), 12b; Rabbi Meir ibn Gabbai, *'Avodat ha-Kodesh* II, 17; Rabbi Judah Löw of Prague, *Gevurot Hashem*, First Introduction; Rabbi Isaiah Halevi Horowitz, *Shnei Luhot ha-Berit, Ma'amar Bayit Aharon*; Rabbi Menasseh ben Israel, *Nishmat Hayyim* 1:2; Rabbi Zadok Hakohen of Lublin, *Resisei Laylah* (Lublin, 5663/1903), 80b-c; idem, *'Or Zaru'a la-Zaddik* (Lublin, 5689/1929), 17c; Rabbi Abraham Isaac Hakohen Kook, *Orot ha-Torah* 8:5.
205. Elsewhere, Rav Kook writes that *Minut* (Heresy, the rabbinic term for Christianity) inverted the values of Judaism, giving priority to the Prophets over the Torah (Pentateuch), which is tantamount to a prioritization of *Aggadah* (ethics) over *Halakha* (law). In the process, the morality of the Prophets as well becomes perverted. See *Orot ha-Emunah*, ed. Rabbi Moshe Gurevitz (Jerusalem 5758/ 1998), p. 33.

Rav Kook, employing the technique known as *remez*, expressed this thought by way of pun. "If a thief be found while breaking in" (Exodus 22:1).

NOTES

The Hebrew word for break-in or underground is *mahteret*. Traditionally, there were forty-eight prophets over the ages. (See *TB Megillah* 14a. RaShI there cites *Seder 'Olam*. However, according to Chaim Milikowsky the number 48 does not occur in the original text of *Seder 'Olam* but is rather a later interpolation. See *Seder 'Olam*, ed. Chaim Milikowsky, vol. 2 [Jerusalem: Yad Ben-Zvi, 2013], pp. 333, 350.) The natural order would be *trt* (Torah) first, followed by *mh* (48), the Prophets. The thief is found out by his tendency to reverse the order. What characterizes the spiritual thief is the fact that he gives precedence to *mh* (the Prophets) over *trt* (Torah). This pun was transmitted by Rabbi Zevi Yehudah Hakohen Kook to his students. See Hayyim A. Schwarz, *Mi-Tokh ha-Torah ha-Go'elet*, vol. 3 (Jerusalem. 5747/1987), p. 225; Rabbi Zevi Yehudah Hakohen Kook, *Judaism and Christianity* (Hebrew), ed. Shelomo Hayyim Hakohen Aviner (Jerusalem, 5761/2001), pp. 26-28. It has since been published in *Pinkas Yod-Gimmel* (Jerusalem: Makhon RZYH Kook, 2004), par. 43 (pp. 37-39) and in *Kevatsim mi-Khetav Yad Kodsho*, ed. Boaz Ofen, vol. 1 (Jerusalem, 2006), *Pinkas Rishon le-Yaffo*, par. 43 (pp. 98-99).

Rav Kook portrays the founder of Christianity as a *gonev shem shamayim*, literally one who "steals the name of heaven." This is an allusion to the fable told in *Toledot Yeshu* that Jesus made off with the *shem ha-meforash* (ineffable name of God) preserved in the Temple, by incising it in his skin. Supposedly, the "miracles" he later wrought were accomplished by improper use of the divine name. (According to Talmudic tradition, Ben Stada surreptitiously brought magic inscriptions out of Egypt by incising them in his skin. See *Tosefta, Shabbat* 12:9; *Talmud Yerushalmi, Shabbat* 12:4; *TB Shabbat* 104b. *Toledot Yeshu* metamorphosed the magical inscriptions of the Egyptian sorcerers into the divine name safekept in the Temple in Jerusalem.)

Rav Kook believed, as did earlier Maimonides, that the distortion of Judaism originated already with Jesus. See Appendix A. (A contemporary writer tries to make the case that the undermining of *halakha* came about later through the machinations of Paul. See Hyam Maccoby, *The Mythmaker: Paul and the Invention of Christianity* [New York: Harper and

Row, 1986].)

The Lithuanian kabbalist Rabbi Isaac Haver (Wildmann) also observed that Christianity capitalized on the Prophets:

> Their primary hold is on the Prophets, the "hips." "He struck the socket of his hip" (Genesis 32:26), specifically the Later Prophets.... There is the hold of the primordial kings of Edom (Rabbi Isaac Haver, *Pithei She'arim* I [Tel-Aviv: Sinai, 5724/1964], *Netiv 'Olam ha-Tikkun*, chap. 22 [76a]).

Edom is a trope for Christianity. In Kabbalah, the two hips, the *sefirot* of *Netsah* and *Hod*, are the level of prophecy. (See *Tikkunei Zohar*, Introduction, *Patah Eliyahu*.) The seizing of Jacob's thigh by the *saro shel Esav* (guardian angel of Esau) adumbrates that in the future Christianity will appropriate the Prophets. Although it is not clear whether Rabbi Isaac Haver refers, as does later Rav Kook, to the fact that Christianity makes claims on the moral exhortation of the Prophets, or to the fact that the Churchmen read Christological meaning into specific passages of the Prophets, such as Isaiah 53 concerning the "Suffering Servant." (By the way, in an early work of Rav Kook that contains bibliographic references, Rav Kook cites another kabbalistic work of Rabbi Isaac Haver [Wildmann], *Beit 'Olamim* on the *Idra*. See Rav Kook's commentary to the stories of Rabbah bar bar Hannah, in *Ma'amrei ha-RAYaH* II [Jerusalem, 5744/1984], p. 445.)

Concerning the struggle between Jacob and the guardian angel of Esau as a trope for Jewish-Christian relations, see further *Orot ha-Emunah*, ed. Rabbi Moshe Gurevitz (Jerusalem, 5758/ 1998), p. 110.

206.   No doubt Rav Kook has in mind Paul (Saul) of Tarsus. Cf. *Eder ha-Yekar* (Jerusalem: Mossad Harav Kook, 5745/1985), p. 31, where Rav Kook takes a jab at "those who sprang to force the End; to make *K'nesset Israel* against her will into a 'student who is unfit to teach but teaches anyway,' concerning whom it is said, 'many corpses she fell' [Proverbs 7:26; *'Avodah Zarah* 19b], the result being that in many peoples the general religion

assumed the trembling, weak form—incapable of mixing with life, and confined to dark monasticism—that is less capable of confronting life than any idolatry."

207. Exodus 19:4.
208. *TB Pesahim* 49.
209. Genesis 1:31. See *Zohar* III, 107a.
210. See Appendix B.
211. Psalms 27:1.
212. *Tikkunei Zohar, tikkun* 22. Cf. *TB Shabbat* 104a.
213. See above note 200. Cf. *Eder ha-Yekar* (Jerusalem: Mossad Harav Kook, 5745/ 1985), p. 34.
214. *TB Sotah* 22b.
215. Isaiah 43:21.
216. Isaiah 2:17-18.
217. Judah Halevi, *Zion ha-lo tish'ali*.

Rav Kook vocalizes the word *nezirayikh* (your nazirites). Today, in the wake of ShaDaL (Samuel David Luzzatto), it has become customary to vocalize *nezarayikh* (your crowns), and to interpret *kalil* (or rather *kelil*) as "crown" rather than "utterly." See Simon Bernstein, *Jehuda Halevi: Selected Liturgical and Secular Poems* (New York: Ogen Publishing, 5705/1944), p. 234; and Hayyim Schirmann, *Yehudah Halevi: Shirim Nivharim* (Jerusalem: Schocken, 5723/1963), pp. 74, 147. However, there is merit to Rav Kook's reading as well. "Your nazirites" connects to "your prophets" (*nevi'ayikh*) in the line above. Cf. Amos 2:11.

218. Malachi 1:5
219. Isaiah 40:2.
220. Jeremiah 31:8.
221. Isaiah 35:10.
222. *Mishnah, Ketubot* 7:6. Cf. *'Ikvei ha-Tson* (Jerusalem: Mossad Harav Kook, 5745/1985), p. 148; *Igrot ha-RAYaH*, vol. 1 (Jerusalem: Mossad Harav Kook, 5722/ 1962), p. 128. The term *dat moshe ve-yehudit* was also used in this sense by Nahmanides. See *Viku'ah ha-RaMBaN* (*Milhamot Hashem*)

in *Kitvei RaMBaN*, ed. C.B. Chavel, vol. 1 (Jerusalem: Mossad Harav Kook, 5728/1968), p. 303, n. 19.

223. Cf. Judah Halevi, *Kuzari* II, 48; III, 7; Rabbi Nissim ben Reuben of Gerona, *Derashot ha-RaN*, ed. Leon A. Feldman (Jerusalem: Shalem, 5734/1973), end *Derush* 1 (pp. 19-20). The source for the RaN is the earlier *Kuzari*.

224. *Zohar* II, 216a; Rabbi Hayyim Vital, *Sha'ar ha-Mitsvot*, Introduction.

225. Psalms 90:17.

226. Psalms 102:19.

227. *TB 'Arakhin* 29a.

228. *TB Yoma* 69b, *Sanhedrin* 64a. See Bezalel Naor, *Lights of Prophecy* (New York: Orthodox Union, 1990).

229. Deuteronomy 6:5.

230. *TB Berakhot* 54a.

231. Haggai 1:8; *TB Yoma* 21b. This statement requires qualification. To say that there was no divine presence in the Second Temple would be to adopt an indefensible position. We must clarify that the type or kind of *Shekhinah* that manifested in the First Temple was absent in the Second Temple. See Rabbi Shneur Zalman of Liadi, *Tanya*, chap. 53 (74b); Rabbi Jacob Ettlinger, Responsa *Binyan Zion* I, no. 3.

232. *TB Yoma* 21b.

233. Lamentations 3:6.

234. Isaiah 54:1.

235. *TB Berakhot* 10a. In an earlier work, *'Eyn AYaH*, Rav Kook accepted at face value the printed version of the Talmud, "Said that Sadducee to Beruriah." See *Eyn AYaH*, ed. Filber, vol. 1 (Jerusalem: Makhon RZYH Kook, 5747/1987), pp. 48-49, par. 124. This reading is highly unlikely because it is generally accepted that the Sadducees disappeared from the political arena at the time of the destruction of the Second Temple. Clearly, "Sadducee" is a censored version. Rav Nissim Gaon preserves the original text: *"mina"* (heretic). In our passage in *Eder ha-Yekar*, Rav Kook draws the reasonable inference that Beruriah was drawn into a disputation with a

Christian.

By the way, in *'Eyn AYaH* to *Shabbat* 89a, Rav Kook restored the original reading *ha-hu mina* where the censored, printed edition of the Talmud reads, *ha-hu zadoki*. See *'Eyn AYaH*, ed. Filber, vol. 4 (Jerusalem: Makhon RZYH Kook, 5760/2000), p. 197, par. 78. Concerning the common substitution of *zadokim* for *minim*, see Rabbi David Cohen, *He-'Akov le-Mishor* (Brooklyn, NY: Morashah Le-hanhil, 5753/ 1993), p. 28. Rabbi Cohen's assertion that Rabbi Zvi Hirsch Chajes fell into the trap of believing that *"zadokim"* in *Berakhot* 54a is the genuine reading, is gratuitous. MaHaRaTs Chajes asks the same question in his glosses to Maimonides' commentary to *Avot*, and there he quotes the correct reading of *Berakhot* 54a, *"minim"*! Chajes' question is conceptual by nature, and was not motivated by a censor's doctored version, as Rabbi Cohen *shelit"a* contends.

236. Proverbs 7:26; TB *'Avodah Zarah* 19b.

237. In *'Ikvei ha-Tson*, p. 134, Rav Kook wrote that Spinoza's philosophy engendered antisemitism. Rivkah Schatz-Uffenheimer published a manuscript version of the piece where Rav Kook goes to far as to say: "It [i.e. Spinozism] wrought the age of modernity with all its evils, including antisemitism, so that Spinoza and Bismarck are like Bil'am and Haman of old." Rivkah Schatz-Uffenheimer, "The Contribution of Rav Kook's Philosophy to Modern Jewish Thought" (Hebrew) in *Yovel Orot*, ed. Benjamin Ish-Shalom (Jerusalem, 5745/1985), p. 353. Spinoza's book *Tractatus Theologico-Politicus* contains some vicious attacks on Judaism and the Jewish People. See Rabbi David Cohen, *Kol ha-Nevu'ah* (Jerusalem: Mossad Harav Kook, 5739/1979), p. 116.

Rav Kook's point in *'Ikvei ha-Tson*, pp. 133-135, was that Spinoza deviated from Jewish theology inasmuch as he focused on the *'Atsmut* (Essence) of divinity rather than on God's activity in the world and manifestation in life (which Rav Kook sums up by "divine ideals"). Cf. *Orot* (Jerusalem: Mossad Harav Kook, 5710/1950), p. 119. Regarding Rav Kook's critique of Spinoza, see also *Eder ha-Yekar* (Jerusalem, 5666/1906; reprinted Jerusalem: Mossad Harav Kook, 5745/ 1985), p. 40, and Bezalel

Naor, "Plumbing Rav Kook's Panentheism," in *Engaging Modernity: Rabbinic Leaders and the Challenge of the Twentieth Century*, ed. Moshe Z. Sokol (Northvale, NJ: Jason Aronson, 1997), pp. 87-88.

By the way, there exists an interesting parallel between Spinoza's concept of the Substance and his Hebrew grammar, in which—in defiance of accepted theory—the noun rather than the verb is the root of the Hebrew word. Spinoza's philology matches his philosophy. See Cohen, p. 118, n. 134, citing Jacob Bernays.

238. Exodus 32:16; *Mishnah, Avot* 6:2. Rav Kook is alluding to the fact that in Spinoza's *Ethics* the divine will is not free but determined. Neither is there any provision in Spinoza's philosophical system for human free will. See the work of Rav Kook's disciple, Rabbi David Cohen (the "Nazirite"), *Kol ha-Nevu'ah* (Jerusalem: Mossad Harav Kook, 5739/1979), pp. 117-118.

239. Deuteronomy 32:6; *TB Berakhot* 12b and RaShI *ad locum*.

240. *Zemah Zevi*, p. 181. That Rabbi Zevi Yehudah Kook was conversant with Nietzsche's philosophy is borne out in other passages in his printed oeuvre. See Rabbi Zevi Yehudah Hakohen Kook, *Li-Netivot Israel*, vol. 2 (Jerusalem, 5739/1979), p. 120; and Hayyim Avihu Schwarz, *Mi-Tokh ha-Torah ha-Go'elet*, vol. 3 (Jerusalem, 5747/1987), pp. 226-227. The quotations there are from Nietzsche, *Beyond Good and Evil*, aphorism 52; idem, *Dawn of Day*, aphorism 205.

In the recently discovered manuscript *Li-Nevukhei ha-Dor*, Rav Kook himself mentions the term "*mussar ha-'avadim*," the Hebrew translation of the German "*Sklavenmoral*" (slave morality), but it is inconclusive that Rav Kook read Nietzsche in the original. His knowledge of the new philosophy might have been acquired from the Hebrew literature of the day. See RAYH Kook, *Li-Nevukhei ha-Dor*, ed. Rabbi Shahar Rahmani (Tel-Aviv: Yedi'ot Aharonot, 2014), chap. 29 (p. 152).

In what might be construed as a proto-Nietzschean jab at Christianity, the thirteenth-century founder of the school of "Prophetic Kabbalah," Abraham Abulafia satirized that by substituting baptism for circumcision, Jesus (!) had turned Christians from males into females. The piece is

NOTES

outrageously ahistorical. See Abraham Abulafia, *Sitrei Torah*, ed. Amnon Gross (Jerusalem, 2002), p. 97; Moshe Idel, *Studies in Ecstatic Kabbalah* (Albany: State University of New York Press, 1988), p. 54.

241.   Maimonides, *Mishneh Torah, Hil. Melakhim* 11:4 in uncensored versions. As astounding as it may seem, this idea of Maimonides is not a minority opinion. This very passage from *Mishneh Torah* was cited verbatim and approvingly by Nahmanides. See Nahmanides, *Torat Hashem Temimah*, in *Kitvei Rabbenu Moshe ben Nahman*, ed. C.B. Chavel, vol. 1 (Jerusalem: Mossad Harav Kook, 5728/1968), p. 144. (Cf. Rabbi Judah Halevi, *Kuzari* IV, 23.) The elder Rav Kook would seem to concur with Maimonides that the spread of Christianity was a part of the divine plan for humanity:

> However, it was brought about by the Lord; the Holy One, blessed be He, assisted those who sprang to force the End; to make *K'nesset Israel* against her will into a "student who is unfit to teach but teaches anyway," concerning whom it is said, "Many corpses she fell" [Proverbs 7:26; *'Avodah Zarah* 19b], the result being that in many peoples the general religion assumed the trembling, weak form—incapable of mixing with life, and confined to dark monasticism—that is less capable of confronting life than any idolatry. (*Eder ha-Yekar* [Jerusalem, 5666/1906; reprinted Jerusalem: Mossad Harav Kook, 5745/1985], p. 31)

The following passage would seem to be an exact paraphrase of Maimonides' statement concerning Christianity and Islam:

> As much as these two dark clouds [i.e. Christianity and Islam] obscure the pure light that shines and flows in *K'nesset Israel* (Ecclesia Israel), at the same time, they disconnect a vast multitude from the abyss of paganism and its thick roots. (*Orot ha-Emunah*, ed. Rabbi Moshe Gurevitz [Jerusalem, 5758/1998], p. 111)

242. The editors of the collection have omitted the name of the recipient of the letter. Most probably the letter was addressed to Rabbi David Cohen (the Nazirite). Cf. the letter published in *Dodi li-Zevi: Letters of Rabbi David Cohen to Rabbi Zevi Yehudah Hakohen Kook* (Jerusalem: Nezer David, 5735/1975), pp. 44-45. There, as in our letter, Rabbi Zevi Yehudah refers the recipient to his father's article, "Seminal Ideas" ("*Zer'onim*") and to his own article "The Israelite Civilization" ("*Ha-Tarbut ha-Yisraelit*"). See *Zemah Zevi*, p. 182.

243. Exodus 19:6.

244. This is reminiscent of Rabbi Nahman of Braslav's statement regarding *Erets Israel*, "*mit die shtiblakh un die heizlakh*" (with these houses). Quoted in *Hayyei MOHaRaN*, talks pertaining to the teachings, par. 15; cited by Rabbi Zevi Yehudah Kook, *Zemah Zevi* (Jerusalem 5751 /1991), Letter 41 (p. 109). In other words, Rabbi Nahman's conception of Erets Israel was not an abstraction but a very concrete reality.

245. *Mishnah, Avot* 4:22; Additional prayer for Rosh ha-Shanah, *Atah zokher ma'aseh 'olam*: "There is no forgetfulness before the throne of Your glory."

246. Psalms 33:11.

247. See H.J. Zimmels, *Ashkenazim and Sephardim* (London: Oxford University Press, 1958), pp. 151-155. See also Meyer Waxman, *A History of Jewish Literature*, vol. I (New York, Bloch Publishing Company, 1938), p. 264.

Isaac Hirsch Weiss wrote:

Nahmanides, Sepharadi by birth, was by temperament and character the image of the French sages. By nature, he was sharp of intellect, pilpulistic as all the great sages of France; he was a master at reconciling contradictions and harmonizing oppositions by the acuity of his mind (*Dor Dor ve-Doreshav* [Vienna, 1891], Pt. 5, p. 8).

NOTES

248.   Heschel wrote:

> Sephardic books are distinguished by their strict logical arrangement. Composed according to a clear plan, every one of their details has its assigned place, and the transitions from one subject to another are clear and simple. Ashkenazic writers forego clarity for the sake of depth. The contours of their thoughts are irregular, vague, and often perplexingly entangled; their content is restless, animated by inner wrestling and a kind of baroque emotion.
>
> Sephardic books are like Raphaelesque paintings; Ashkenazic books like the works of Rembrandt—profound, allusive, and full of hidden meanings. The former favor the harmony of a system, the latter the tension of dialectic; the former are sustained by a balanced solemnity, the latter by impulsive inspiration. The strength of the Sephardic scholars lies in their mastery of expression, that of the Ashkenazim in the unexpressed overtones of their words. A spasm of feeling, a passionate movement of thought, an explosive enthusiasm, will break through the form.
>
> Sephardic books are like neatly trimmed and cultivated parks, Ashkenazic writings like enchanted ancient forests; the former are like a story with a beginning and an end, the latter have a beginning but frequently turn into a story without an end (Abraham Joshua Heschel, *The Earth Is the Lord's* [1950], pp. 30-31).

249.   *Kana'uteh de-Pinhas*, ed. Bezalel Naor (Spring Valley, NY: Orot, 2013), p. 126, n. 104:

> Our French and German rabbis…detest [rational] inquiry and criticism in regard to divine beliefs and opinions…They are sharp

of intellect, lovers of depth and *pilpul*, and far from the confines of the logical and orderly...After the Holy Torah permitted anthropomorphic language, her descendants were also permitted to speak in anthropomorphic language. The understanding shall understand. These things are visible to us in Rashi and his disciples the Tosafists.

The Sephardic sages are their exact opposite...They made obligatory rational inquiry into the ancestral faith. They are lovers of logic and order, and detest deep *pilpul*...Their desire and goal...is to explain the secrets of the anthropomorphic language of the Torah, to teach the Children of Israel the secret of His unity by stripping away the corporeality.

When we contemplate the spirit of this Godly man, Rabbi Isaac [Luria], of blessed memory, as he is described by his faithful disciple Rabbi Hayyim Vital, his spirit was really that of one of the sages of France and Germany...He distanced intellectual and logical inquiry into the Wisdom of Truth [i.e., Kabbalah], which had greatly exercised Rabbi Moses Cordovero. He said that all the novellae of Rabbi Moses Cordovero are suspended in the realm of *Belimah* [i.e., they are without substance]. He did not study with his students in an orderly, disciplined fashion. He revealed to them the last *derush* of *ABY"A* before the first. He loved sharpness of intellect and *pilpul* so much that he taught six different "faces" of the Talmud, causing him to break out in a sweat...He spoke much in anthropomorphic parables, not fretting to explicate them and remove from them the accidents of matter.

Both Rav Kook and the older Rabbi Lintop were students of the Volozhin Yeshiva (at different times). Both may have been influenced by the historiosophy of the Rosh Yeshivah of Volozhin, Rabbi Naphtali Zevi Yehudah Berlin (NeZIV). See "*Kidmat ha-'Emek*," the sprawling introduction to *Ha'amek She'elah*, the commentary of NeZIV to *She'iltot de-Rav Ahai*

Gaon, (Vilna, 1861). See Rabbi Aaron Eisenthal, "*Mishnat ha-NeZIV*" in *Eretz Tvi* (*Tzvi Menahem Glatt Memorial Volume*) (Jerusalem, 1989), pp. 82-84 (esp. n. 66); Bezalel Naor, "Rav Kook's Role in the Rebirth of Aggadah" in *Orot: A Multidisciplinary Journal of Judaism* 1 (1991), pp. 101-104.

However, where both Rabbis Kook and Lintop differ from their master NeZIV, is in attributing the different methods of study in Sepharad and Ashkenaz to their inherent character traits. For NeZIV, the determining factor was whether a community of scholars possessed or lacked a "*kabbalah*" (oral tradition) concerning the proper interpretation of the Talmud. The Geʹonim possessed such a *kabbalah*; therefore they were able to resolve halakhic issues without recourse to dialectic or *pilpul*. Maimonides followed the tradition of the early Geʹonim. French Jewry had no such *kabbalah* reaching back to the Geʹonim. Therefore the *Hakhmei Tsarfat* were forced, for lack of better alternative, to resort to their own ingenuity and develop dialectic. See *Kidmat ha-ʹEmek*, pp. 9-11, par. 12-16.

250. *En passant*, many years ago, an erudite Sephardic rabbi confided to me that among Sephardic scholars it is widely held that one may find in the seven volumes of *Hikrei Lev* (arranged according to the order of the *Shulhan ʹArukh*) of Rabbi Joseph Raphael Hazan of Izmir and Jerusalem (1741-1819), conceptual novellae on a par with those of Rabbi Hayyim Soloveitchik of Brisk!

251. For a "vertical perspective" of the "dialectical movement" of the two enterprises—the codificatory and the commentarial—that "characterizes much of the history of post-Talmudic rabbinic literature," see Isadore Twersky, "The *Shulhan ʹAruk*: Enduring Code of Jewish Law," in The *Jewish Expression*, ed. Judah Goldin [New Haven: Yale University Press, 1976], p. 329.

252. These marginalia first appeared in the Giustiniani (Justinian) edition of the Talmud, printed in Venice between the years 1546-1551. Penned by the distinguished Italian sage Rabbi Joshua Boaz Baruch, they comprised references to Maimonides, *Semag* and *Tur*. Later editions of the Talmud

supplemented references to Rabbi Joseph Karo's *Shulhan 'Arukh* (*editio princeps* Venice 1565). Since Rabbi Joseph Karo adopted the *"simanim"* (chapters) of the earlier *Arba'ah Turim*, conveniently enough, the same references are valid for both *Tur* and *Shulhan 'Arukh*. See Marvin J. Heller, *Further Studies in the Making of the Early Hebrew Book* (Leiden: Brill, 2013), pp. 447-448.

Isaiah Sonne wrote that each of these three codes appealed to a different community within Italian Jewry: Maimonides to the Spanish exiles; *Semag* to the French or Provencal Jews; and *Tur* to the German Jews. See Isaiah Sonne, *"Tiyyulim be-historiyah u-bibliografia,"* in *Sefer ha-Yovel li-Khevod Alexander Marx* (Philadelphia: Jewish Publication Society, 1950), pp. 209-221. Concerning Rabbi Joshua Boaz Baruch, see there p. 218.

253. In a private communication, Prof. Ephraim Kanarfogel shared with me (=BN) a valuable insight concerning a fundamental difference between the Sephardic and Ashkenazic codes. Even when engaging in codification, the Ashkenazim tend to present a panoply of different opinions. Rabbi Moses of Coucy's *Sefer Mitsvot Gadol* and Rabbi Jacob ben Asher's *Arba'ah Turim* abound in different opinions. And not only do they cite various opinions, but they engage with them as well.

On the other side of the aisle, Maimonides' code *Mishneh Torah* is virtually monolithic. Only on very rare occasions does Maimonides cite the opinion of the Ge'onim. Although not as ironclad as *Mishneh Torah*, Rabbi Joseph Karo's *Shulhan 'Arukh* might also be termed "monolithic" when compared to the Ashkenazic codes.

In the latter regard, see Benayahu's reaction to Eliav Shohetman, who argued, based on the multiplicity of opinions in *Shulhan 'Arukh*, that the author did not intend the book to be authoritative; Meir Benayahu, *Yosef Behiri* (Jerusalem, 1991), pp. 382-383.

254. This was the informed opinion of Freimann. See A.H. Freimann, *Ha-Rosh, Rabbenu Asher ben Rabbi Yehiel ve-Tse'etsa'av* (Jerusalem: Mossad Harav Kook, 1986), p. 133.

Rabbi Jacob ben Asher, as earlier his father Rabbenu Asher (Rosh),

NOTES

was claimed by both Ashkenazim and Sepharadim. Though clearly father and son retained their German identity (as reflected in the contents of their codes which reflect Ashkenazic tradition), the fact that Rabbenu Asher served as Rabbi of Toledo, Spain, won the *Tur* to the hearts of Sephardic Jewry. See Sonne, op. cit., p. 211; Meir Benayahu, *Yosef Behiri* (Jerusalem, 1991), p. 338. Concerning Rabbenu Asher, Rabbi Joseph Karo quoted approvingly on numerous occasions a responsum of Rabbi Levi ibn Habib, who wrote: "...the custom of Sepharad, who held the Rosh to be their Rabbi" (*Beit Yosef, Orah Hayyim*, chaps. 51 and 215; *Avkat Rokhel*, no. 18). (The wording of Twersky's quote, "Spanish rabbi," is a bit misleading. See Isadore Twersky, "The *Shulhan 'Aruk*," p. 340, n. 15.) Freimann went so far as to write a panegyric to Rabbi Jacob's *Tur*, extolling its universality: "The *Turim* became the possession of the nation and the book of Halakha of *Kelal Yisrael*" (*Ha-Rosh*, p. 160). See ibid. pp. 13, 157-162.

255. A decade earlier, Rabbi Joseph Karo had composed his *Beit Yosef* as a commentary to the *Turim*. (*Shulhan 'Arukh* is an extract of *Beit Yosef*.) Why he chose the *Turim* as his platform and not Maimonides' *Mishneh Torah* is open to speculation. See Isadore Twersky, "The *Shulhan 'Aruk*," p. 339, n. 9.

256. Rabbenu Asher (*She'elot u-Teshuvot Rosh* 43:8) witnessed that in Spain, Talmudic study was for the most part limited to *RIF* (Alfasi). The exclusive preoccupation with Alfasi was also noted by Rabbi Menahem ben Zerah in his Introduction to *Tsedah la-Derekh*. Cited in A.H. Freimann, *Ha-Rosh*, p. 39, n. 84. See also *She'elot u-Teshuvot Rosh* 32:11: "Most of the lands decide and adjudicate based upon *RIF* and Maimonides' code."

Ta-Shema observed that whereas the study of Alfasi did not catch on in Germany and Northern France; it did gain wide acceptance in Provence. Israel M. Ta-Shema, *Rabbi Zerahiah Halevi Ba'al ha-Ma'or u-B'nei Hugo: Le-Toledot ha-Sifrut ha-Rabbanit be-Provence* (Jerusalem: Mossad Harav Kook, 1992), p. 68. (Continued below on page 232.)

Rabbi Harlap thought that Maimonides had conceived of his Code originally as a companion to Alfasi's *Halakhot*. Rabbi Harlap based this contention on Maimonides' advice to his student Rabbi Joseph ben Judah ibn Shim'on:

> Concerning what you mentioned about your going to Bavel (Baghdad). I already allowed you to open a *Midrash* (academy) and to teach Torah by assiduous application to the study of the Code. Delve only into the *Halakhot* of the Rabbi [Isaac Alfasi] and spread it out alongside the Code. (*Kovets Teshuvot ha-Rambam* [Leipzig, 1859], Part Two [*Igrot ha-Rambam*], 31c)

By the same token, Rabbi Harlap believed that the *Tur* was written by Rabbi Jacob expressly to serve as a companion to his father Rabbi Asher's code of the Talmud. This latter insight was derived in a roundabout way from Rabbi Ya'ir Hayyim Bacharach, *She'elot u-Teshuvot Havvot Ya'ir*, no. 124. See Rabbi Ya'akov Moshe Harlap, "*Halakha Berurah*" (1941), in *Amarot Tehorot*, ed. Hayyim Zaks (Jerusalem, 2002), p. 157.

257.   Nahmanides expressed his high regard for the French sages in poetic form in his introduction to *Dina de-Garmei*: "They are the teachers, they are the instructors, they are the ones who reveal to us the hidden" (*Kitvei Rabbenu Moshe ben Nahman*, ed. C.B. Chavel, vol. I [Jerusalem: Mossad Harav Kook, 1968], p. 417).

Concerning Nahmanides' being the first Spanish sage to place himself in the French orbit in terms of conceptual study, see Isadore Twersky, *Rabad of Posquières* (Cambridge, Mass: Harvard University Press, 1962), p. 57. For Nahmanides' unabated continuation of the Spanish tradition of codification, see ibid. pp. 84-85.

Rabbi Joseph B. Soloveitchik was effusive in his praise of Nahmanides as "the pioneer in the analytic approach to halakhah which stressed conceptualization." In his mind's eye, he could very well see his grandfather Rabbi Hayyim Soloveitchik (founder of the famous "Brisker Derekh," a revolutionary method of Talmudic analysis) saying the passage from *Hiddushei Ramban*. See Rabbi Aaron Rakeffet-Rothkoff, *The Rav*, vol. 2 (Ktav, 1999), pp. 195-196.

NOTES

Tsvi Groner observed that unlike the Tosafists, who translated their theoretical novellae into practical halakha, the Sephardic luminaries—Nahmanides, Rashba, Ritba, Ran, et al—evidently lacked confidence in the novellae they arrived at using the dialectic method of the Tosafists, and for practical halakha, would inevitably fall back on the time-honored decisions of the Geonim. See Tsvi Groner, "Legal Decisions of *Rishonim*, and Their Attitudes Towards Their Predecessors" (Hebrew), in *Me'ah She'arim: Studies in Medieval Jewish Spiritual Life in Memory of Isadore Twersky*, ed. Fleischer, Blidstein, Horowitz, and Septimus (Jerusalem: Hebrew University Press, 2001), pp. 267-278.

258. Concerning the *Hiddushei ha-Ritba*, see Ephraim Kanarfogel, "Between Ashkenaz and Sefarad: Tosafist Teachings in the Talmudic Commentaries of Ritva," *Between Rashi and Maimonides*, ed. E. Kanarfogel and M. Sokolow (New York, 2010), pp. 237-273. (The article addresses Ritba's predecessors as well.)

259. In a recent newspaper interview, Prof. Haym Soloveitchik observed that generally, halakhic texts moved from North to South; from Ashkenaz to Sepharad, and not vice versa. The one notable exception was Maimonides' code which merited *Hagahot Maimoniyot*, the glosses penned by a disciple of Rabbi Meir (Maharam) of Rothenburg.

> In the volume that already appeared [Collected Essays, vol. 1] I address the "one way street" that you mention. For example, the Rosh moved from Germany to Spain in the beginning of the fourteenth century. His *Pesakim* and the *Tur*, the work of his son, made their way swiftly to Ashkenaz, but the *Hiddushei HaRamban* or those of the Rashba never did. The same caravans or boats which brought the *Piskei HaRosh* to Cologne could have brought the *Hiddushei HaRashba*, had people in Germany been interested in them. Apparently, they weren't. With one exception, they also ignored the Rambam…By "one exception," I meant Maharam mi-Rothenburg…I assume that the *Hagahot Maimoniyot*, written

by his pupil, was inspired by him...As I pointed out in my book, the *Hagahot Maimoniyot* never "Ashkenized" *Mishneh Torah*, as the *Hagahot* of the Rama succeeded in "Ashkenizing" the *Shulhan 'Arukh* of R. Yosef Karo and enabled its reception in Ashkenaz.

("Interview with Professor Haym Soloveitchik by Rabbi Yair Hoffman," *Five Towns Jewish Times*, Wednesday, January 8, 2014) Available at: http://www.theyeshivaworld.com/news/headlines-breaking-stories/209453/interview-with-professor-haym-soloveitchik-by-rabbi-yair-hoffman.html

Concerning Rabbi Meir of Rothenburg and Maimonides, see Abraham Grossman, "From Andalusia to Europe: The Attitude of Rabbis in Germany and France in the Twelfth-Thirteenth Centuries towards the Halakhic Writings of Alfasi and Maimonides" (Hebrew), *Pe'amim* 80 (Summer 1999), pp. 14-32; and Ephraim Kanarfogel, "Preservation, Creativity and Courage: The Life and Works of R. Meir of Rothenburg," *Jewish Book Annual* 50 (1992-1993), pp. 249-259.

Tosafot quote Maimonides in but two instances. See *Tosafot, Berakhot* 44a, s.v. *'al ha-'ets*; and *Menahot* 42b, s.v. *tefillin yesh lahen bedikah*. Regarding the latter instance and the attribution of the *Tosafot* to Tractate *Menahot* to Rabbi Samson of Sens, see E.E. Urbach, *The Tosaphists: Their History, Writings and Methods (Ba'alei ha-Tosafot)*, 5th Enlarged Edition (Jerusalem: Bialik Institute, 1986), pp. 663-664. For an incorrect identification of Maimonides in *Tosafot, Megillah*, see Urbach, p. 618, n. 99. (See further at page 233.)

Inter alia, Shamma Friedman has recently militated for the view that Maimonides may have made use of Rashi's commentary in his revisions to *Mishneh Torah*. See Shamma Yehudah Friedman, "*Kelum lo nitsnets perush Rashi be-beit midrasho shel ha-Rambam?*" in *Rashi: Demuto vi-Yetsirato*, ed. Abraham Grossman and Sarah Yefet (Jerusalem, 5769/2009), pp. 403-464.

260.   In his travelogue *Ma'agal Tov*, Rabbi Hayyim Yosef David Azulai (*HIDA*) explained how this innovation came about in Tunis.

NOTES

Rabbi Abraham Taïeb was the great man of the generation and a student of Rabbis Abraham Cohen (called "Baba Rabbi") and Tsemah Tsarfati. Before them, they did not study *Tosafot* in Tunis, just Gemara and Rashi. And the aforementioned Rabbis did wonders in the study of *Tosafot, Maharasha* [i.e., Rabbi Samuel Edels] and *Maharashal* [i.e., Rabbi Solomon Luria]. They would delve very deeply into the words of *Maharashal* and held his words in great affection…The outcome was that the aforementioned Rabbis spread Torah and "kids became goats." Based on what I heard, today there are close to three hundred Torah scholars in Tunis. I also saw lads of fourteen years of age who were sharp-witted and able to hit the mark with their analysis. Their entire focus is upon Talmud and *Maharasha* and novellae of the Rabbis of Ashkenaz, and a bit upon Maimonides' phraseology, but they are not so familiar with the *Posekim* and responsa literature. (*Ma'agal Tov ha-Shalem*, ed. Aharon Freimann [Jerusalem, 1983], Tishri, 5534/1773 [p. 57])

See further Shalom Bar-Asher, "*Ha-Sifrut ha-rabbanit bi-tsefon Afrika 1700-1948*," *Pe'amim* 86-87 (5761), pp. 237-238.

Today, the major advocate for this method of Talmudic study is Rabbi Meir Mazuz of B'nei Berak, a native of Tunis. Quite coincidentally, the renowned Ashkenazic sage of B'nei Berak, Rabbi Abraham Isaiah Karelitz ("Hazon Ish") advocated the study of *Maharasha*, the most important supercommentary on *Tosafot*. I once heard the late Rabbi Ahron Soloveichik say that people have a wrong picture of his grandfather Rabbi Hayyim Soloveitchik of Brisk. Rabbi Ahron wanted to set the historical record straight. "They imagine that Reb Hayyim paid no attention to *Aharonim*. Reb Hayyim was well aware of *Maharasha*'s analysis of *Tosafot*."

261. Rav Kook's two exceptions to the rule are Nahmanides and the Vilna Gaon. By pure happenstance, the eminent disciple of the Gaon,

Rabbi Hayyim of Volozhin, once compared his master's greatness to that of Nahmanides! See Dov Eliach, *Avi ha-Yeshivot: Rabbenu Hayyim mi-Volozhin* (Jerusalem, 5772/2011), pp. 63-64, n. 38.

Recently, Rabbi Nehemiah Feffer supposed some similarities between the *"derekh ha-limmud"* (methodology) of the Vilna Gaon and that of the Sephardic sages. See his biography of Rabbi Menahem Mendel of Shklov in *Bi'urei ha-RaMaM mi-Shklov 'al Temunat ha-Otiyot* (New York: Makhon ha-GRA, 5772/2012), *"Toledot ha-Mehaber,"* pp. 24-36. However, in one crucial respect the Vilna Gaon and his disciples differed sharply with the representatives of Sephardic tradition. In the matter of *pesikah* (halakhic ruling), the Sephardic authorities tended to rely on the earlier rulings of their predecessors. The Vilna Gaon believed that he and at least some of his disciples (the most noteworthy being Rabbi Hayyim of Volozhin) were competent to decide the halakha based on their own independent examination of the Talmud. This difference in ideology came to a head in a famous controversy in Jerusalem between the Rishon le-Zion, Rabbi Joseph Raphael Hazan (author *Hikrei Lev*) and the Gaon's disciples Rabbi Menahem Mendel (Ashkenazi) of Shklov and Rabbi Israel (Ashkenazi) of Shklov. Rabbi Hazan cited in this regard the responsum of the medieval authority Rabbi Joseph Migash (no. 114) who favored decisions based on Geonica over those rendered directly from the source of the Talmud. See Feffer, pp. 21-24; Eliach, pp. 539-544; Kahana, pp. 153-161.

In regard to Rabbi Hayyim of Volozhin's method of deciding halakha, Rabbi Zevi Yehudah Hakohen Kook transmitted in his father's name that before issuing a novel leniency allowing an *'agunah* to remarry, Rabbi Hayyim would review the entire Talmud for three days! Quoted in Eliach, p. 543, note 10.

262. In direct opposition to the method of the Vilna Gaon was that of his contemporary Rabbi Aryeh Leib Günzberg, author *Sha'agat Aryeh*. (In addition to providing the author's formal name, the title page of the *editio princeps* of *Sha'agat Aryeh* [Frankfurt on Oder, 1756] states that he is referred to popularly as "Rabbi Leib Rosh Yeshivah." Rabbi Aryeh Leib

served for a time as Rosh Yeshivah in Minsk.) His namesake and paternal grandfather was given the sobriquet "Rabbi Leib Baʻal ha-Tosafot." The latter died and was buried in Minsk. (See the Introduction by the author's sons to *Keren Orah* of Rabbi Isaac Schick of Karlin, another descendant of Rabbi Leib Baʻal ha-Tosafot.) In the *Shaʼagat Aryeh* too we witness the spirit of *pilpul* commonly associated with the medieval French Tosafists. Rabbi J.B. Soloveitchik of Boston reported hearing in his youth from his fellow schoolchildren that the *Shaʼagat Aryeh* was a *gilgul* (reincarnation) of Rabbenu Tam! (Repeated to the writer by Prof. Haym Soloveitchik)

Rabbi Hayyim of Volozhin studied under both men, the *Shaʼagat Aryeh* and the Vilna Gaon. He recorded that the Vilna Gaon criticized the *Shaʼagat Aryeh* for engaging overly much in *pilpul* or dialectic, while the *Shaʼagat Aryeh* criticized the Vilna Gaon for focusing too much on the *peshat* or simple sense. See Rabbi Asher Hakohen of Tiktin, *Orhot Hayyim/ Keter Rosh*, ed. Elijah Landau (Jerusalem, n.d.); Eliach, op. cit., p. 70.

Writing in a mystical vein, Rabbi Menashe of Ilya, a student of sorts of the Vilna Gaon, saw Messianic significance in the Gaon's insistence on *peshat* or the plain meaning:

> The famous Gaon, our teacher Rabbi Elijah of Vilna, of blessed memory—if not for him, Torah would have been forgotten from Israel, for he returned the crown to its former position. With all of his sharpness and encyclopedic knowledge, he paid attention to the plain meaning and directed his gaze to interpreting everything in a plain and simple manner. Most of his studies proceed in this way. (*Alfei Menashe* [Vilna, 1822], chap. 102)

> It appears based on the length of our Exile, that the footsteps of the Messiah approach, and that it is necessary to clear for him the way of truth, as I have written, for our main striving consists in our serving as a vessel prepared to receive light and good… And

it appears that the Lord sent us an angel from heaven, the famous Gaon, our teacher Rabbi Elijah of Vilna, of blessed memory, who began a bit to return the crown of the Torah to its former position, according to his way, the way of plain truth. (Ibid., chap. 177)

Rabbi Ya'akov Moshe Harlap, eminent disciple of Rav Kook, wrote (based upon what he received "from mouth to ear") that the soul of the Vilna Gaon appeared in the world for three things: 1) to preserve the supremacy of Torah (as opposed to prophecy); 2) to teach the proper method of studying Torah, at a time when many had fallen into the pitfall of *pilpul*; and 3) to stir hearts to settle in Zion. See Rabbi Y.M. Harlap, "'*Aliyat Eliyahu*," in *Amarot Tehorot*, pp. 168-169.

263. Rabbi Issachar Baer ben Tanhum, *Ma'aseh Rav* (Zolkiew, 1808), chap. 60; Rabbi Pinhas ben Judah of Polotsk, *Rosh ha-Giv'ah* (Vilna, 1820), f.11r., quoting his master the Vilna Gaon; RAYH Kook, *Orot ha-Torah* 9:3.

Earlier, Maimonides recommended the study of Alfasi's *Halakhot* in an epistle to his student Rabbi Joseph ben Judah ibn Shim'on who was about to establish a *[beit] midrash* in Bavel (Baghdad); see *Kovets Teshuvot ha-Rambam* [Leipzig, 1859], Part Two [*Igrot ha-Rambam*], 31c. (Cited in *Orot ha-Torah* 9:13.) See also Maimonides' letter to Rabbi Pinhas ha-Dayyan of Alexandria concerning the practice of studying Alfasi's *Halakhot* in Maimonides' own academy; *Igrot ha-Rambam*, ed. Shilat (Jerusalem, 1988), vol. II, p. 439.

According to anecdote, one Friday night in the Volozhin Yeshiva, the lights went out, yet NeZIV was able to continue studying, having committed Alfasi to memory. (Heard from my teacher Rabbi Aharon Rakeffet-Rothkoff.)

Rabbi Shim'on Glitzenstein, who acted as Rav Kook's secretary during the latter's stay in London, attested that an Alfasi in small format never left the Rav's hands during his medically prescribed walks. See Rabbi Moshe Zevi Neriyah, *Sihot ha-RAYaH* (Jerusalem, 5755/2015), pp. 184-185. (In the earlier edition of *Sihot ha-RAYaH*, Tel-Aviv 1979, p. 200.)

In the introduction to *Shevil ha-Yashar* (Vilna, 1839), a commentary to the RIF, the author, Rabbi Shaul Shiskes, relates how Rabbi Shelomo Zalman of Volozhin (disciple of the Vilna Gaon and younger brother of Rabbi Hayyim of Volozhin) proofread this work on three orders of RIF. Quoted in Rabbi Joshua Heschel Levin, *'Aliyot Eliyahu* (Jerusalem, 1989), p. 92, note 64.

Lest we imagine that the Vilna Gaon was the first Ashkenazic authority to recommend the study of Alfasi's *Halakhot*, we have this testimony of Rabbi Ya'ir Hayyim Bacharach:

> About the time of his arrival in Worms, which was at the end of 5410/1650, he [i.e., my father, Moses Samson Bacharach] would study RIF (Alfasi) with me and with companions, excellent young men...and this is the good and straight way, more effective than any other study. And so was the custom of the early greats. And so I was told by my father-in-law Rabbi Zussman, of blessed memory, who passed in Fulda, where he presided, that so had he received from his rabbis. And so he wrote and trained his son the Gaon Rabbi Itsak, of blessed memory, and he succeeded at it, for one can easily complete it [i.e., study of Alfasi's *Halakhot*] in three years. (*She'elot u-Teshuvot Havvot Ya'ir*, no. 124)

After completing the study of RIF, the author counsels the study of *Rosh* (Rabbenu Asher):

> There is no study more delectable and proper than the study of *Rosh*, after one has in hand the RIF...And I received that the elderly Gaon Rabbi Pinhas Horowitz, who was Av Beit Din of Fulda, and at the end of his days an Appelant in Prague—outstanding in rulings and decisions—his entire study was in *Rosh*, and he followed his decision as if it were given at Sinai, not caring whether it opposed

the determination of Rabbi Moses Isserles, for he said that he too was worthy of making a determination. (Ibid.)

(Many years ago, the elder Rabbi of Springfield, Mass., Rabbi Moshe Don Sheinkopf imparted to the writer [BN] the importance of studying *Rosh* as the key to Talmudic success.)

Isadore Twersky noted Rabbi Bacharach's concern about correct methods of study and his criticism of undisciplined methods. See I. Twersky, "Law and Spirituality in the Seventeenth Century: A Case Study in Rabbi Yair Hayyim Bacharach," in *Jewish Thought in the Seventeenth Century*, ed. Isadore Twersky and Bernard Septimus (Cambridge, Mass.: Harvard University Press, 1987), p. 452.

Inter alia, in his autobiography, Chaim Tchernowitz recorded that Rav Kook (unlike some more conservative-minded rabbis) lauded his projected *Kitsur ha-Talmud*, in which Rav Kook saw a valuable tool for acquiring knowledge of Talmud. See Ch. Tchernowitz ("Rav Tsa'ir"), *Pirkei Hayyim* (New York: Bitsaron, 1954), p. 133; *Haskamot ha-RAYaH*, ed. Chwat and Hallamish (Jerusalem, 2017), no. 83 (p. 178). And see Rav Kook's letter to Tchernowitz (in another regard) in *Igrot ha-RAYaH*, vol. 1, pp. 363-364 (Letter 325).

264.   Rabbi Harlap wrote that the Vilna Gaon paved the way to "breadth" ("*hekef*"), this being the unique contribution of the Gaon's *Bi'ur* to *Shulhan 'Arukh*. See "*Halakha Berurah*" (1941), in *Amarot Tehorot*, p. 160.

Rabbi Yosef Soloveichik of Jerusalem once shared with this writer (BN) a family tradition from Rabbi Hayyim Soloveitchik of Brisk that true novellae are possible only against the background of the entire Talmud.

265.   From the Introduction of Rabbi Abraham and Rabbi Judah Leib, sons of the Gaon of Vilna, to *Be'ur ha-Gra* on *Orah Hayyim* (Shklov, 1803).

Yehuda Liebes explored the Gaon of Vilna's self-perception in light of the Moses figure of *Tikkunei Zohar* and *Ra'aya Mehemna*. In that literature, Moses' messianic role is portrayed as that of the halakhist *par excellence* who distances *pilpul*. See Yehuda Liebes, "The Self-Perception of the Gaon of Vilna and his Attitude towards Sabbateanism" (Hebrew), *The Flint into a Fountain of Waters [Hallamish le-Maʿayeno Mayim]: Studies in Kabbalah, Jewish Law, Custom and Philosophy Submitted to Prof. Moshe Hallamish* (Jerusalem, 2016), p. 608.

266. This reservation was expressed earlier by the *Dayyanim* of Vilna in their *Haskamah* to Rabbi Z.H. Lampert's *Piskei ha*-GRA (Vilna, 1904); quoted in Rabbi M.Z. Neriyah, *Sihot ha-RAYaH* (Tel-Aviv, 1979), p. 206 (footnote).

267. *Beʾer Eliyahu* first appeared in *Sefer ha-GRA* (Jerusalem, 1954). Initially the book covered the first twenty-seven chapters of *Hoshen Mishpat*. Subsequently, in the year 2000, Makhon RZYH issued Part Two of the work on *Hilkhot ʿEdut* and the beginning of *Hilkhot Halvaʾah*.

In an article published in *Sefer ha-Yovel li-Mekhon Harry Fischel* (Jerusalem, 1935) and reprinted in Rabbi Moshe Zuriel's collection *Otserot ha-RAYaH*, vol. 4 (5753/1992), p. 116, Rav Kook lauded the GRA's contribution to halakhic methodology:

> The greatest factor in strengthening Torah and returning the way of learning to the straightforward and truthful, was the appearance of our great teacher, the GRA, of blessed memory. In his instruction to his disciples, the geniuses, and in the way paved in his books that have come down to us, *and especially in his* Beʾur *to the four sections of* Shulhan ʿArukh, *he spread out before the community of Torah scholars the straightforward and simple way, which is at the same time incisive, penetrating to the depth of halakhic analysis—without complications and pitfalls along the way* (italics—BN).

According to Rabbi Moshe Zevi Neriyah, this was the last article that Rav Kook published in his lifetime; see *Sihot ha-RAYaH* (Tel-Aviv, 1979), p. 205. For an overall appreciation of the *Beʾur ha-GRA* and of Rav Kook's commentary to *Hoshen Mishpat*, *Beʾer Eliyahu*, see *Sihot ha-RAYaH*, pp. 206-

209; and Avinoam Rosenak, *The Prophetic Halakhah: Rabbi A.I.H. Kook's Philosophy of Halakhah* (Hebrew) (Jerusalem: Magnes, 2007), pp. 406-409.

Rabbi Hayyim of Volozhin recommended to his disciples in-depth study of *Be'ur ha-GRA*; Rabbi Yosef Zundel of Salant acted upon this recommendation. In the introduction to *Mishnah Berurah*, a commentary to *Shulhan 'Arukh, Orah Hayyim*, Rabbi Israel Meir Kagan singled out *Be'ur ha-GRA*, "for he is the light of Israel and the stake upon which all depends and worthy to decide [between two differing opinions of *Aharonim*]." See Eliach, op. cit., p. 91.

Perhaps inspired by Rav Kook's example, Rabbi Baruch Rakover has published a multivolume super-commentary to the *Be'ur ha-Gra* to *Shulhan 'Arukh*, entitled *Birkat Eliyahu*. Recently, Rabbi Hillel Goldberg of Denver published a supercommentary to *Be'ur ha-Gra, Yoreh De'ah*, chap. 201 (*Hilkhot Mikv'aot*), entitled *Hallel Hakohen* (Lakewood, 2008).

268. Rabbi Moshe Zevi Neriyah, *Sihot ha-RAYaH* (Tel-Aviv, 1979), p. 208.
269. See Simon L. Eckstein, *Toldot ha-Chabif: The Work, Life and Influence of Rabbi Hayim Palaggi (1787-1868), Chief Rabbi of Izmir, Turkey* (Hebrew) (Jerusalem, 1999), p. 412, no. 41.

In *Hartsa'at Harav* (Jerusalem, 1921), Rav Kook called for the composition of an encyclopedia of Talmudic concepts expressed in clear, concise language, devoid of *pilpul*, and arranged in alphabetical order. (*Hartsa'at Harav* was later appended to *Orot ha-Torah*.) This was the vision that inspired the *Encyclopedia Talmudica*. See Rosenak, pp. 409-410.

The two halakhic encyclopedias (of note) that preceded *ET* were Rabbi Isaac Lampronti's *Pahad Yitshak* and Rabbi Hayyim Hezekiah Medini's *Sedei Hemed*. Lampronti was an Italian sage; Medini, a Sephardic sage of Hebron. While yet in Europe, Rav Kook contributed to *Sedei Hemed* the article "*Rihata de-Hakla'i*" (later reprinted as an appendix to Rav Kook's '*Ittur Soferim* [Jerusalem, 1974]).

270. Letter to Israel Shim'on Rabinowitz, datelined "Jaffa, 27 Tevet, 5669/1909," in Moshe Zuriel, *Otserot ha-RAYaH*, vol. 1 (2002), p. 379. The passage in its entirety reads:

NOTES

> I very much desire that you accustom yourself to study specific *sugyot*, not to seek lengthy *pilpulim* but rather the pure essence that arises from the words of the *Gemara*, *Tosafot* and *Rishonim*, and also the *Aharonim* that speak thereof. And how good would it be if you would commit the abstract to writing, even without originality, but rather according to *the way of the Sephardic summarists* [italics mine—BN]. Except that they tend to gather from the *Aharonim* more than from the *Rishonim*, while the methodology that brings true blessing makes the words of the *Rishonim* the main dish, with the words of the *Aharonim* thrown in for spice.

In effect, Rav Kook has described the method of the *Birur Halakha*, a project to which Rav Kook devoted the final years of his life, and which continues to this day, as witnessed by the many volumes of *Halakha Berurah* produced by the scholars of Merkaz Harav. At my very first meeting with Rabbi Zevi Yehudah Hakohen Kook in the winter of 5738/1978, he extended an invitation to work on this ongoing project. At that time, he revealed to me that his father, of blessed memory, said that the same *"tsav"* ("command") that prompted him to write his mystical work *Resh Millin*, prompted him to write the *Halakha Berurah*. See also Rosenak, op. cit., p. 404. Rosenak provides an overview of *Halakha Berurah* (penned by Rav Kook himself) and *Birur Halakha* (inspired by Rav Kook and penned by his disciples) on pp. 399-406. See further Rabbi Yitshak Arieli, *'Eynayim le-Mishpat, Kiddushin* (Jerusalem, 1936), Introduction.

271. Philosophy (to be certain Jewish Philosophy) would eventually gain some acceptance in Ashkenaz of the sixteenth century, which by then had gravitated eastward to Poland. Witness the infusion of Maimonidean philosophy in Rabbi Moses Isserles' *Torat ha-'Olah*, and Isserles' disciple Rabbi Mordekhai Jaffe's commentary to Maimonides' *Guide*. As for the intervening fourteenth and fifteenth centuries in Germany proper, this is the subject of much debate among historians. Ephraim Kupfer's

pronouncement that interest in philosophy abounded in Ashkenaz during that period has been contested. See Ephraim Kupfer, "Concerning the Cultural Image of German Jewry and Its Rabbis in the Fourteenth and Fifteenth Centuries" (Hebrew), *Tarbiz* 42 (1972-1973), pp. 113-147; Joseph Dan, "Fourteenth-Century Ashkenazi *Yihud* Tractate," *Tarbiz* 44 (1974-1975), pp. 204-206; Israel Jacob Yuval, *Scholars in Their Time: The Religious Leadership of German Jewry in the Late Middle Ages* (Jerusalem, 1988), pp. 289-290, 300-311; Haym Soloveitchik, "Religious Law and Change: The Medieval Ashkenazic Example," *AJS Review* 12:2 (Fall 1987), pp. 213-214, n. 12; Lawrence Kaplan, "Rabbi Mordekhai Jaffe and the Evolution of Jewish Culture in Poland in the Sixteenth Century," in *Jewish Thought in the Sixteenth Century*, ed. Bernard Dov Cooperman (Cambridge, Mass.: Harvard University Press, 1983), pp. 267-268; 281, n. 5; Daniel J. Lasker, "Jewish Philosophical Polemics in Ashkenaz," in *Contra Iudaeos: Ancient and Medieval Polemics Between Christians and Jews*, ed. Ora Limor and Guy G. Stroumsa (Tübingen: J.C.B. Mohr, 1996), pp. 198-199, n. 17.

272. In recent years, scholars have done much "spade work" to unearth the Islamic institution of the *Majlis*, a kind of Parliament of Religions (or more likely, a forum for religious disputation) that was in vogue in Baghdad. See *The Majlis: Interreligious Encounters in Medieval Islam*, ed. Hava Lazarus-Yafeh, et al (Wiesbaden: Harrassowitz, 1999).

Though it might be convenient to view the relative openness of the Cordoban court as somehow beholding to the institution of the *Majlis*, the distance from Abbasid Baghdad to Omayyad Cordoba is daunting in more ways than one.

273. Of late, Warren Zev Harvey has recast Rashi as a philosopher conversant with Plato's *Timaeus* in Latin translation. This is a Derridan "trace" or "specter." Professor Harvey would have done well to leave Rashi standing on the *terra firma* of *Sefer Yetsirah*, by which his cosmology is indisputably informed. See Warren Zev Harvey, "Rashi on Creation: Beyond Plato and Derrida" (Hebrew), *The Flint into a Fountain of Waters [Hallamish le-Ma'ayeno Mayim]: Studies in Kabbalah, Jewish Law, Custom and Philosophy Submitted to Prof. Moshe Hallamish* (Jerusalem, 2016), pp. 167-181.

274. See José Faur, "The Legal Thinking of the Tosafot: An Historical Approach," *Dinei Yisrael* 6 (1975), p. 54; E.E. Urbach, *Ba'alei ha-Tosafot*, p. 87, n. 9; I.M. Ta-Shema, "Halakha and Reality: The Tosafist Experience," in *Rashi et la culture juive en France du Nord au moyen age,* ed. Dahan, Nahon and Nicolas (Paris: E. Peeters, 1997), pp. 313-329; Ephraim Kanarfogel, *Jewish Education and Society in the High Middle Ages* (Detroit: Wayne State University Press, 1992), especially chapter 5. (Continued on page 233.)

275. See the Introduction to Maimonides' *Sefer ha-Mitsvot*. There he writes that he will choose Mishnaic Hebrew rather than Biblical Hebrew or the Aramaic of the Talmud as the language of the future code; likewise it will be divided into chapters and *halakhot* after the arrangement of the *Mishnah* (with *Halakhot* substituting for the *Masekhtot* of the *Mishnah*).

276. See Saul Lieberman, "The Publication of the *Mishnah*," in idem, *Hellenism in Jewish Palestine* (New York and Jerusalem, 1994), pp. 83-99; Shaye J.D. Cohen, *From the Maccabees to the Mishnah* (Philadelphia: Westminster Press, 1987), pp. 216-217; Daniel Sperber, *Greek in Talmudic Palestine* (Ramat Gan: Bar Ilan University, 2012); Chaim Milikowsky, *Seder 'Olam: Critical Edition, Commentary, and Introduction* (Jerusalem: Yad Ben-Zvi, 2013), vol. 1, pp. 144-147; Amram Tropper, *Wisdom, Politics, and Historiography: Tractate Avot in the Context of the Graeco-Roman Near East* (Oxford and New York: Oxford University Press, 2004); Yakir Paz, *Mi-Soferim li-Melumadim: Parshanut Hazal la-Mikra le-'Or ha-Parshanut ha-Homerit* (Ph.D. Thesis, Hebrew University, December 2014).

277. Gideon Libson, *Jewish and Islamic Law: A Comparative Study of Custom During the Geonic Period* (Cambridge, MA, 2003); idem, "Parallels Between Maimonides and Islamic Law" in *The Thought of Moses Maimonides: Philosophical and Legal Studies*, ed. I. Robinson, L. Kaplan and J. Bauer (Lewiston, NY, 1990); idem, "Two Sureties: A Comparative Study of R. Shmuel ben Hofni Gaon, Maimonides and Analogous Muslim Legal Literature" (Hebrew), *Shnaton ha-Mishpat ha-Ivri* 11-12 (1984-1986): 337-392.

278. David E. Sklare, *Samuel ben Hofni Gaon and His Cultural World: Texts and Studies* (Leiden: Brill, 1996).

279. 2 Samuel 7:23; 1 Chronicles 17:21.

280. See Arthur A. Goren, "Sanctifying Scopus: Locating the Hebrew University on Mount Scopus" in *Jewish History and Jewish Memory: Essays in Honor of Yosef Hayim Yerushalmi*, ed. Carlebach, Efron and Myers (Hanover, NH: Brandeis Univ. Press, 1998), pp. 330–347.

281. Originally, Rabbi Kook was to be joined at the occasion by his entire court (*beit din*) including Rabbi Zevi Pesah Frank, but the vehicle carrying the members of Rabbi Kook's entourage broke down en route. This anecdote was told to the writer [BN] by Rabbi Zevulun Charlop, whose grandfather Rabbi Jacob Moses Harlap was Rav Kook's closest disciple.

282. Isaiah 2:3.

283. It should be noted that if Rav Kook's remarks aroused the ire of his opponents to the right, they did not pass without comment from the left. The American rabbi, Mordecai M. Kaplan, who later founded the Reconstructionist movement, attended the ceremony in Jerusalem. Kaplan recorded in his memoirs his displeasure with the Chief Rabbi:

> But the splendid impression was lost because of Rabbi Kook who promised to speak about eight minutes but went on for half an hour and more. When Magnes asked him to begin the [opening] prayer, Kook agreed only on the condition that he be allowed to continue speaking; but he tired out the audience. I don't know why but I felt that this man is a fakir, and this feeling grew today when I saw him and listened to him for the first time (*Communings of the Spirit: The Journals of Mordecai M. Kaplan, Volume I 1913-1934*, ed. Mel Scult [Detroit: Wayne State University Press, 2001], pp. 204-205).

284. In a letter to Rabbi Dr. Bernard Revel, President of Yeshiva University in New York, dated 11 Kislev 5680/1920, Rav Kook wrote: "It is inconceivable

that the Holy City of Jerusalem should serve through the university as a center for the secular youth, while the holy youth consecrated to Torah learning and awe of heaven, should remain scattered without a center" (*Igrot ha-RAYaH*, vol. 4 [Jerusalem: Makhon RZYH Kook, 5744/1984], p. 21, Letter 992). In an appeal for the Universal Central Yeshivah, dated Ellul 5682/1922, Rav Kook expressed his pain: "Secular life floods us all about. Gymnasia, universities... are going to be established sooner or later. Students from all over the Diaspora, not distinguished by their positive attitude to the life of holiness, will come to us from all sides. And we are totally unprepared to set up a mighty holy force to serve as a defense against swelling secularism" (ibid. p. 136, Letter 1143). In a later appeal for the Universal Central Yeshivah, dated Shevat 5685/1925, just two months before the opening of Hebrew University, he wrote: "It is impossible that the movement of national renascence should develop only in secular forms, such as gymnasia and universities; the main thing we need is that the light of Torah in its holy source should illumine from Jerusalem the entire Diaspora" (ibid. p. 231, Letter 1294, par. 4).

By the way, *gymnasia* in this context does not refer to a sports complex but rather to a secular school. For Rav Kook's attitude to the *gymnasia* in Jaffa, see Rabbi M.Z. Neriyah, *Likkutei ha-RAYaH* (Kefar ha-Ro'eh: Hai Ro'i, 5750/1990), pp. 105-108. Rabbi Jacob Moses Harlap related that on one of his visits to Jaffa, he and Rav Kook happened to pass by the building of the Herzliyah Gymnasia. Rav Kook told him, "We should recite in this place two blessings. On the beautiful building we should say, 'Blessed He who erects the border of a widow,' but regarding what goes on inside this building, we should say, 'Blessed He who will uproot idolatry from our land!'" Neriyah, ibid. p. 108.

285. Leaving biology aside, from an angle of intellectual history, Rav Kook's point is well taken. Philo Judaeus, the flower of Alexandrian genius, remained virtually unknown to Jews until he was rediscovered by Azariah dei Rossi in the sixteenth century and renamed "Yedidyah ha-Alexandroni." Philo's works were preserved in the patristic literature.

286. Isaiah 60:4, 5. This passage in Isaiah is from the *haftarah* (reading from the Prophets) for *Ki Tavo*, one of the seven *haftarot* of consolation read between the Ninth of Av and New Year (*shev di-nehamata*).

287. Psalms 119:165.

288. *Mishnah, Berakhot* 4:2.

289. The reference is to the Septuagint, a Greek translation of the Hebrew Bible commissioned by Ptolemy II Philadelphus of Egypt (285-246 B.C.E.).

290. End *Megillat Ta'anit*. Cf. Tractate *Soferim* 1:7; *Ma'amrei ha-RAYaH*, vol. 2 (Jerusalem, 5744/1984), pp. 499-501, Tevet.

291. Isaiah 32:18.

292. Isaiah 2:3.

293. "Sinai" signifies thorough familiarity with the laws of the Torah as they were given on Mount Sinai. "Uprooter of mountains" refers to the ability to overturn accepted notions and arrive at new understandings in Torah. See *TB Berakhot* 64a; *Horayot* 14a.

294. Rabbi Isaac Kosovsky went on to become Chief Rabbi of South Africa.

295. Jeremiah 30:18; Isaiah 33:17.

296. *TB Sanhedrin* 99b.

297. Isaiah 2:6.

298. Jeremiah 2:13.

299. Eventually, Torczyner would Hebraize his name to Tur-Sinai.

300. While on the topic of non-verbal communication, in what is undoubtedly one of the most profound of his *ma'amarim* (discourses), Rabbi Isaac Hutner employs the following example culled from life's experiences to explain the words of the *Talmud Yerushalmi, Berakhot* 7:3: "This One is deserving of the appellation *gibbor* (mighty) for He sees the destruction [of the Temple] and remains silent."

> A group of disciples sit before their master and thirstily drink in his words. One of the members of this group has a special gift for being able to grasp the thought of the master when the master is silent. The content of the master's thoughts when he is silent is

much deeper than the content of the thoughts that he verbalizes to the disciples. The reason being, that the thoughts in which the master is sunk during his silence are "for himself," whereas the thoughts that make up his spoken remarks always take into account the level of the disciples, which is below the level of "his self." We find therefore that though the transition from speech to silence spells an absolute break in communication between master and disciples—for that special disciple who has the gift of grasping the master's thoughts at the time he is silent, the moment of transition from speech to silence is an opportunity for ascent. At that moment, he rises from the level of the master as he exists for the other, to the level of the master as he exists for himself. And the insights of the master "for himself" are deeper than the insights of the master "for the other." (Rabbi Isaac Hutner, *Pahad Yizhak: Hanukkah* [n.p.: Gur Aryeh, 5749/1989], pp. 64-65)

301. This is based on the tradition that the father of Jesus was his mother's seducer, (a Roman soldier) named Pandera. See *TB Shabbat* 104b and *Sanhedrin* 67a in uncensored editions. Normally, the child of an adulterous union is considered halakhically a *mamzer* (bastard). In this case, since the seducer was a non-Jew, the child is halakhically "kosher." RaShI (*Shabbat* 104b in uncensored editions), who refers to Ben Stada as a *mamzer*, does so colloquially, unless RaShI understood the seducer Pandera to be a Jew, in which case the term *mamzer* is used halakhically. Rabbenu Tam (*Tosafot, Shabbat* 104b, s.v. *Ben Stada* in uncensored version) makes the point that Ben Stada or Ben Pandera, contemporaneous with Pappus ben Judah and therefore with Rabbi Akiva, is not to be confused with the much earlier Yeshu'a ha-Notsri. It seems the way this identification came about was that both Jesus and Ben Stada were hung on the eve of Passover. See *Sanhedrin* 43b and 67a in uncensored editions of Talmud. A certain Jacob of Kefar Sekhanya (evidently an early Christian) would supposedly heal in the name of his master Yeshu'a ben Pandera. See *Tosefta, Hullin* 2:6; *Talmud*

Yerushalmi, Shabbat 14:4 (Kefar Samma instead of Kefar Sekhanya); *TB 'Avodah Zarah* 27b; *Ecclesiastes Rabbah* 1:8. By the way, in Yiddish slang, Jesus was referred to as "Yoshke Pondrik" (Jesus son of Pandera).

302. *TB Yevamot* 45b.

303. Daniel 11:14. Cf. Maimonides, *MT, Hil. Melakhim* 11:4 in uncensored editions.

304. Cf. Rabbi Abraham Maimonides, *Commentary to the Pentateuch*, trans. E.J. Wiesenberg (Jerusalem: 5744/1984), *Toledot*, p. 27.

305. Genesis 1:31.

306. Ibid.

307. Proverbs 11:10.

308. Hebrew. *Hu sah vayyehi*. From the Ashkenazic hymn for the High Holy Days, *Atah hu Eloheinu ba-shamayim u-va'arets*.

309. Israel Barukh Messinger, *Nitel u-Me'or'otav: hasifat mekorot, te'amim ve-nimmukim, 'im he'arot ve-tsiyyunim* (Union City, NJ: Tevet, 5760/'00).

310. In the author's faulty transcription of the passage from *Igrot ha-RAYaH*, *'or* (light) has become *avir* (air).

311. Letter 11 in the first edition of *Igrot ha-RAYaH* (5683/1923), it does not appear in subsequent editions of the Letters. However, it was reprinted in *Ma'amrei ha-RAYaH*, vol. 2 (Jerusalem, 5744/1984), pp. 507-510. It is also available in English translation in Tzvi Feldman, *Rav A.Y. Kook: Selected Letters* (Ma'aleh Adumim: Ma'aliot, 1986), pp. 162-172. Feldman translates the passage in question as follows: "Indeed, Christianity wished to eliminate the attribute of hate, woven into the tapestry of the divine light of Israel, but have we not come to realize that it shed blood and magnified malevolence in the name of the elimination of hatred, more than any battle of hatred [ever did]?" (p. 167).

312. Published in *Ma'amrei ha-RAYaH*, vol. 2, pp. 419-448. In Rav Kook's interpretation of the first story, Christianity, with its abolition of the *mitsvot ma'asiyot* (practical commandments), threatens to sink the historic ship of Israel. Ibid. pp. 421-422.

313. See Bezalel Naor ed., *Orot: The Annotated Translation of Rabbi Abraham Isaac Kook's Seminal Work* (Northvale, NJ: Jason Aronson, 1993), pp. 50-51.

314. *Orot ha-Emunah*, ed. Rabbi Moshe Gurevitz (Jerusalem, 5758/1998), pp. 28-38.

315. Messinger's juxtaposition of Rav Kook's literary oeuvre to *Netivot 'Olam* is indeed ironic inasmuch as Rav Kook on several occasions (citing his father-in-law ADeReT) decried this very missionary tract! See S.B. Shulman, *Ha-RAYaH Kook* (Jerusalem, 1976), pp. 5-9; Rabbi Judah Leib Maimon (Fishman), *Sarei ha-Me'ah*, vol. 1 (Jerusalem, 1955), pp. 180-191; Shnayer Z. Leiman, "The *Ba'al Teshuvah* and the Emden-Eibeschuetz Controversy," *Judaic Studies* 1 (1985), pp. 1-9.

Addenda

Continued from page 130: Recently, Haym Soloveitchik has argued that Ashkenazic Jewry's eschewal of the surrounding "higher culture" was a deliberate, conscious decision rather than force of circumstance. He envisions Ashkenaz as a puritanical society. Though Soloveitchik's theory will no doubt raise considerable controversy, it is interesting that earlier Rav Kook arrived at the same conclusion, albeit by a quite different process. See Haym Soloveitchik, "The 'Third Yeshivah of Bavel'" in idem, *Collected Essays*, Vol. II (Portland, Oregon, 2014), pp. 177-178, 192-193.

Continued from page 189, note 138: I see now that the same observation concerning the "role reversal" of the Ba'al Shem Tov and the Vilna Gaon was made by none other than Rabbi Isaac Hutner, a noted thinker much influenced in his youth by Rav Kook. See *Sefer ha-Zikaron le-Maran Ba'al "Pahad Yitzhak,"* second edition (Brooklyn, NY, 2014), p. 86.

Continued from page 211, note 256: *Par contre*, Elalouf distinguished between France and Germany. *Hakhmei Tsarfat*, whose *oeuvre* was for the most part commentarial, had little use for Alfasi's *Halakhot*. On the other hand, later *Hakhmei Ashkenaz*, whose *oeuvre* was codificatory in nature, often referenced the *Halakhot* in their own *pesakim*. See Emmanuel Elalouf, *Ha-RIF, Bein Sefarad*

ADDENDA

le-Ashkenaz: Hishtalshelut ha-halakhah ve-darkhei ha-limmud bi-Sefarad u-be-Ashkenaz u-mekomo shel ha-RIF ki-megasher beinehem (Jerusalem, 5776/2016), pp. 501-507.

Continued from page 214, note 259: Recently, Rabbi Avraham Wasserman of Ashdod has demonstrated that the great Tosafist, Rabbi Samson ben Abraham of Sens made ample use of Maimonides' *Mishneh Torah* in his own commentaries to the Mishnaic orders of *Zera'im* and *Toharot*. See A. Wasserman, "*Muva'ot mi-'Mishneh Torah' la-Rambam be-Pherushei Rash mi-Sens*" in: *Hitsei Gibborim* 10 (Nissan 5777), pp. 799-819. (However, Rabbi Samson does not mention Maimonides' name.) This is consistent with Urbach's finding that the author of the *Tosafot* to *Tractate Menahot* (wherein Maimonides is cited explicitly, *Menahot* 42b, s.v. *tefillin*) is none other than—Rabbi Samson of Sens! See E.E. Urbach, *The Tosaphists: Their History, Writings and Methods* (Hebrew) (Jerusalem: Bialik Institute, 1986), vol. 2, pp. 663-664.

Continued from page 225, note 274: See now Haym Soloveitchik, *Collected Essays*, Vol. II (Portland, Oregon, 2014), chap. 2 ("Dialectics, Scholasticism, and the Origin of the *Tosafot*"), pp. 23-28.

Passages Omitted from Rav Kook's Letter to Aderet

(Pagination refers to 2016 edition of *When God Becomes History*)

EXPLANATION:

In *When God Becomes History*, I translated the text of the letter as it appeared in *Ginzei RAYaH*, vol. 3 (n.p.: Makhon RZYH Kook, n.d.), pp. 16-18. (The ellipses that occur in *Ginzei RAYaH* are an indication of omissions from the original text of the letter.)

Since then, there has come to my attention that an unexpurgated version of the letter was published by Rabbi Ya'akov Filber in his collection *Kokhvei 'Or* (Jerusalem, 1993), pp. 170-174.

The words in **bold** appear in the body of the book. The words in plain typeface are supplied from Rabbi Filber's *Kokhvei 'Or*.

Page 52:

Now there came to me two gentlemen, one a Sephardi by the name of Amzalag, who was the English consul here [in Jaffa],[1] **and requested me** with entreaty and due humility **since they were planning**

---

1. Haim Amzalag (or Amzalak) (1828-1916) was appointed British Vice-Consul at Jaffa in 1872. (This appointment was considered by contemporary Jewry a great honor and distinction.) It was Amzalag who purchased the land for the early settlements of Petah Tikvah and Rishon le-Zion.

such as the Anglo-Palestine Bank here. And if I would not go there, then in their opinion, I would be humiliating the entire public gathering, for they have invited all the notables of the city. By the same token, such a grave insult could not pass without [engendering] a deep-seated hatred whose fruits would be felt by me in particular and by all Torah scholars and the God-fearing in general.

Now with my great pain that I had arrived at this situation whereby many of the remaining God-fearing, who are dear to me as my own body and soul, would wonder about me, I could not refuse these notables. It would have been tantamount to driving them out, especially as they went out of their way [to meet me] before sending a written invitation and a carriage, for they feared being rebuffed.

I knew to what extent such a symbolic "slap in the face" would stir up animosity and prevent the good influence likely to be exerted—with the help of the Lord—upon the state of Judaism in the city [of Jaffa] and the [surrounding] settlements, by adhering to the way of peace and righteousness which I have always upheld. I decided that there is no justification for causing hatred and competition, and [financial setback] to the charitable institutions of the city [of Jaffa], especially to the Talmud Torah "Sha'arei Torah," for all sectors participate in its continued existence, thank God. **Therefore I promised them I would attend.**

Bottom page 55:

This too would have produced great controversy and eternal enmity, and also a reduction of income to the Talmud Torah, to which many of the Zionists contribute. But there did not occur to me the thought of being present there, and I was not.

Page 56:

After [the address], others came to me and reported that some read into my words ideas I never intended and attributed to me nonsense and deemed the remarks heresy, and I explained that the report is inaccurate and the reporters erred. But it is worthy that every sage of Israel differentiate between opinions that in his estimation are incorrect and in error (though they are not injurious to the foundations of Torah)—and words of heresy. One must not lump together all incorrect opinions and treat their exponents as renegades, for this rash judgment is a grave misreading [of Talmudic law] and brings about many stumbling blocks. And though it be obligatory upon us to straighten out opinions so that they be free of mistakes, nevertheless we must act with moderation. If someone expresses an opinion that is not true to Torah, one must bring that individual close with gentle words and inform him of the truth. **By using good reason**

Bibliography

Abrabanel, Isaac. *Abrabanel on Pirke Avot*, ed. Abraham Chill. New York, 1991.

Abraham ben Isaac of Narbonne. *Sefer ha-Eshkol*, ed. Albeck, Vol. 1. Jerusalem, 1984.

Abraham ibn Daud Halevi. *Sefer ha-Kabbalah*. Mantua, 1514.

Abulafia, Abraham. *Otsar Eden Ganuz*, ed. Amnon Gross. Jerusalem, 2000.

Albeck, Hanokh. *Shishah Sidrei Mishnah*. Vol. 4. Tel-Aviv, 1984.

Albo, Joseph. *Sefer ha-'Ikkarim*. Warsaw, 1877; photo offset Jerusalem, 1960.

Aleksandrov, Samuel. *Mikhtevei Mehkar u-Vikkoret*. 2 vols. Vol. 1. Vilna, 1907. Vol. 2. Cracow, 1910.

Alfasi, Yitzhak. "Hasidism and Political Zionism," in *Jubilee Volume in Honor of Joseph B. Soloveitchik*, ed. Israel, Lamm, and Raphael. Jerusalem, 1984.

Alter, Yehudah Aryeh Leib (of Gur). *Sefat Emet*. Piotrkow and Cracow, 1905-1908.

Anonymous. *Netivot 'Olam*. Christian missionary tract. London, 1839.

Arama, Isaac. *'Akedat Yitzhak*. Warsaw, 1883.

Arieli, Yitzhak. *'Eynayim le-Mishpat: Kiddushin*. Jerusalem, 1936.

Ashkenazi, Asher Hakohen (of Tiktin), *Orhot Hayyim/ Keter Rosh*, ed. Elijah Landau. Jerusalem, n.d.

Ashkenazi, Hillel (of Shklov). *Kol ha-Tor*, ed. Yosef Rivlin. Jerusalem, 1994.

Ashkenazi, Menahem Mendel (of Shklov). *Bi'urei ha-RMM mi-Shklov 'al Temunat ha-Otiyot*, ed. Nehemiah Feffer. New York, 2012.

———. *Kitvei ha-GRMM z"l*. 2 vols. Jerusalem, 2001.

Azulai, Hayyim Yosef David. *Ma'agal Tov ha-Shalem*, ed. Aharon Freimann. Jerusalem, 1983.

Bacharach, Ya'ir Hayyim. *Havot Ya'ir*. Frankfurt am-Main, 1699. Reprinted Jerusalem, 1987 (photo offset of Lemberg, 1896).

Bar-Asher, Shalom. "*Ha-Sifrut ha-rabbanit bi-tsefon Afrika* 1700-1948," *Pe'amim* 86-87 (5761).

Benayahu, Meir. *Yosef Behiri*. Jerusalem, 1991.

Ben Johanan, Karma. "Wreaking Judgment on Mount Esau: Christianity in R. Kook's Thought." *Jewish Quarterly Review*, Vol. 106, No. 1 (Winter 2016).

Ben Porat, Menashe (of Ilya). *Alfei Menashe*. Vilna, 1822.

Benvenisti, David and Mizrahi, Hayyim. "Rabbi Yehudah Bibas and the community of Corfu during his lifetime," *Sefunot*, vol. 2 (5718/1958).

Berger, David. "On the Uses of History in Medieval Jewish Polemic against Christianity: The Quest for the Historical Jesus," in *Jewish History and Jewish Memory: Essays in Honor of Yosef Hayim Yerushalmi*, ed. Carlebach, Efron and Myers. Hanover, NH, 1998.

Berlin, Naphtali Zevi. *Haskamah* to *Ahavat Hesed* of Israel Meir Kagan. Warsaw, 1888.

———. "*Kidmat ha-'Emek*." Introduction to *Ha'amek She'elah*, commentary to *She'iltot de-Rav Ahai Gaon*. Vilna, 1861.

Bernstein, Simon. *Jehuda Halevi: Selected Liturgical and Secular Poems*. New York, 1944.

Borukhovich, Shneur Zalman (of Liozhna and Liadi). *Shulhan 'Arukh*. Shklov and Kopyst, 1814-1816.

———. *Tanya*. Slavuta, 1796. Expanded edition Vilna, 1900.

Cohen, David. *Dodi li-Zevi: Letters of Rabbi David Cohen to Rabbi Zevi Yehudah Hakohen Kook*. Jerusalem, 1975; expanded edition Jerusalem, 2005.

———. *Kol ha-Nevu'ah*. Jerusalem, 1970.

Cohen, David. *He-'Akov le-Mishor*. Brooklyn, NY, 1993.

Cohen, Israel. *History of Jews in Vilna*. Philadelphia, 1943.

BIBLIOGRAPHY

Cohen, Shaye J.D. *From the Maccabees to the Mishnah.* Philadelphia, 1987.

Crescas, Hasdai. *'Or Adonai*, ed. Shelomo Fisher. Jerusalem, 1990.

Dan, Joseph. "Fourteenth-Century Ashkenazi *Yihud* Tractate," *Tarbiz* 44 (1974-1975).

Deutsch, Shaul Shimon. *Larger than Life.* Vol. 1. New York, 1995.

Duran, Isaac. *Kelimat ha-Goyim.* In *Kitvei Polemos le-Profiat Duran,* ed. Efraim Talmage. Jerusalem, 1981.

Duran, Shim'on ben Tzemah. *Magen Avot*, ed. Elijah Rahamim Zini. Jerusalem, 2000.

Eckstein, Simon L. *Toldot ha-Chabif: The Work, Life and Influence of Rabbi Hayim Palaggi* (1787-1868) (Hebrew). Jerusalem, 1999.

Eisenthal, Aaron. "*Mishnat ha-Netsiv*" in *Eretz Tvi: Tzvi Menahem Glatt Memorial Volume.* Jerusalem, 1989.

Elalouf, Emmanuel. *Ha-RIF, Bein Sefarad le-Ashkenaz: Hishtalshelut ha-halakhah bi-Sefarad u-be-Ashkenaz u-mekomo shel ha-RIF ki-megasher beinehem.* Jerusalem, 2016.

Elharar, Moshe. *Li-Khevodah shel Torah.* Jerusalem, 1988.

Eliach, Dov. *Avi ha-Yeshivot: Rabbenu Hayyim mi-Volozhin.* Jerusalem, 2011.

Epstein, Barukh Halevi. *Mekor Barukh.* 3 vols. Vilna, 1928.

Erlich, Asher. *Asher Hayah: Sefer Zikaron le-Asher Erlich,* ed. Yitzhak Ogen. Tel-Aviv, 1959.

Ettlinger, Jacob. *Binyan Zion.* Altona, 1868.

Ezra of Gerona. Commentary to Song of Songs. In *Kitvei Ramban*, ed. Chavel, vol. 2. Jerusalem, 1968.

Fano, Menahem Azariah. *Ma'amar Hikkur Din* in *'Assarah Ma'amarot,* ed. Pinhas 'Ovadyah. Jerusalem, 1998.

———. *Ma'amar Ma'ayan Ganim* in *Ma'amrei ha-Rama' mi-Fano,* ed. Pinhas 'Ovadyah. Vol. 2. Jerusalem, 1997.

Faur, José. "The Legal Thinking of the *Tosafot*: An Historical Approach," *Dinei Yisrael* 6 (1975).

Felman, Abraham (of Preil and Sebezh). *Zehiruta de-Avraham*. Appended to *Zohar Hadash*, ed. Reuven Margaliot. Jerusalem, 1994.

Feldman, Tzvi. *Rav A.Y. Kook: Selected Letters*. Ma'aleh Adumim, 1986.

Freimann, A.H. *Ha-Rosh: Rabbenu Asher ben Rabbi Yehiel ve-Tse'etsa'av*. Jerusalem, 1986.

Friedman, Shamma Yehudah. "*Kelum lo nitsnets perush Rashi be-beit midrasho shel ha-Rambam?*" In *Rashi: Demuto vi- Yetsirato*, ed. Abraham Grossman and Sarah Yefet. Jerusalem, 2009.

Gabbai, Meir ibn. *'Avodat ha-Kodesh*. Warsaw, 1883; photo offset Jerusalem, 1973.

Glatt, Zevi. *Erets Zevi: Zevi Glatt Memorial Volume*. Jerusalem, 1989.

Goldberg, Hillel. *Hallel Hakohen*. Lakewood, 2008.

Goldman, Eliezer. "*Tsiyonut hilonit, te'udat Yisrael ve-takhlit ha-Torah*," *Da'at*, Summer 5743/1983.

Goren, Arthur A. "Sanctifying Scopus: Locating the Hebrew University on Mount Scopus" in *Jewish History and Jewish Memory: Essays in Honor of Yosef Hayim Yerushalmi*, ed. Carlebach, Efron and Myers. Hanover, NH, 1998.

Gottlieb, Samuel Noah. *Oholei Shem*. Pinsk, 1912.

Groner, Tsvi. "Legal Decisions of Rishonim, and Their Attitudes Towards Their Predecessors" (Hebrew). In *Me'ah She'arim: Studies in Medieval Jewish Spiritual Life in Memory of Isadore Twersky*, ed. Fleischer, Blidstein, Horowitz, and Septimus. Jerusalem, 2001.

Grossman, Abraham. "From Andalusia to Europe: The Attitude of Rabbis in Germany and France in the Twelfth-Thirteenth Centuries towards the Halakhic Writings of Alfasi and Maimonides" (Hebrew), *Pe'amim* 80 (Summer 1999).

Günzberg, Aryeh Leib. *Sha'agat Aryeh*. Frankfurt on Oder, 1756.

Hamburger, B.S. *Meshihei ha-Sheker u-Mitnagdeihem*. B'nei Berak, 1989.

Harlap, Jacob Moses. "*'Aliyat Eliyahu*," reprinted in *Amarot Tehorot*, ed. Hayyim Zaks. Jerusalem, 2002.

———. *Beit Zevul*. Vol. 1. Jerusalem, 1942-1948; photo offset Jerusalem, 1987.

———. "*Halakha Berurah*" (1941). Reprinted in *Amarot Tehorot*, ed. Hayyim Zaks. Jerusalem, 2002.

———. *Hed Harim: Letters of Rabbi Jacob Moses Harlap to Rabbi Abraham Isaac Hakohen Kook*, ed. Zevi Yehudah Hakohen Kook. Jerusalem, 1971.

Harvey, Warren Zev. "Rashi on Creation: Beyond Plato and Derrida" (Hebrew). In *The Flint into a Fountain of Waters* [*Hallamish le- Ma'ayeno Mayim*]: *Studies in Kabbalah, Jewish Law, Custom and Philosophy Submitted to Prof. Moshe Hallamish*. Jerusalem, 2016.

Haver (Wildmann), Isaac. *Beit 'Olamim*. Warsaw, 1889.

———. *Pithei She'arim*. Warsaw, 1888; photo offset Tel-Aviv, 1964.

———. *Pithei She'arim: Netiv binyan ha-kelipot u-merkavah teme'ah*, in Kalman Redisch, *Mi-Ginzei ha-Gra u-Veit Midrasho*. Lakewood, NJ, 1999.

Hegel, Georg W.F. *The Philosophy of History*, trans. J. Sibree. Buffalo, NY, 1991.

Heller, Marvin J. *Further Studies in the Making of the Early Hebrew Book*. Leiden, 2013.

Heschel, Abraham Joshua. *The Earth Is the Lord's*. New York, 1950.

Hess, Moses. *Rome and Jerusalem*. Leipzig, 1862.

Hirschensohn, Hayyim. *Malki ba-Kodesh*. Vol. 4. St. Louis, MO, 1919-1922.

Hoffman, David. *The First Mishnah and the Controversies of the Tannaim*, trans. Paul Forchheimer. New York, 1977.

Hoffman, Joshua. Netvort: *Parashat Hayyei Sarah*, 5763. Netvort @ aol.com

Horowitz, Isaiah Halevi. *Shnei Luhot ha-Berit*. Amsterdam, 1648.

Hutner, Isaac. *Pahad Yizhak: Hanukkah*. New York, 1989.

———. *Sefer ha-Zikaron le-Maran Ba'al "Pahad Yitzhak."* Second Edition. Brooklyn, NY, 2014.

Isaac ben Solomon of Toledo. *Perushei Rabbenu Yitzhak bar Shelomo mi-Toledo*, ed. M.S. Kasher and J.J. Blacherowitz. Jerusalem, 1983.

Ish-Shalom, Benjamin. *Rabbi Abraham Isaac Kook: Between Rationalism and Mysticism* (Hebrew). Tel-Aviv, 1990.

Issachar Baer ben Tanhum. *Ma'aseh Rav*. Zolkiew, 1808.

Isserles, Moses. *Torat ha-'Olah*. Prague, 1570.

Jaffe, Mordechai. *Levush Pinat Yikrat*. Commentary to Maimonides' *Guide*. Lublin, 1595. Reprinted Jerusalem 2000.

Judah Halevi. *Kuzari*. Judeo-Arabic and Hebrew translation by Yosef Kafah. Kiryat Ono, 2013.

Kagan, Israel Meir. *Mishnah Berurah*. Warsaw, 1891.

Kahana, Maoz. *From the Noda BeYehudah to the Chatam Sofer: Halakha and Thought in Their Historical Moment* (Hebrew). Jerusalem, 2015.

Kalmanson, Elhanan. *Sinai ve-Golgotha*. Riga, 1925.

Kanarfogel, Ephraim. "Between Ashkenaz and Sefarad: Tosafist Teachings in the Talmudic Commentaries of Ritva," *Between Rashi and Maimonides*, ed. E. Kanarfogel and M. Sokolow. New York, 2010.

———. *Jewish Education and Society in the High Middle Ages*. Detroit, 1992.

———. "Preservation, Creativity and Courage: The Life and Works of R. Meir of Rothenburg," *Jewish Book Annual* 50 (1992-1993).

Kaplan, Lawrence. "Rabbi Mordekhai Jaffe and the Evolution of Jewish Culture in Poland in the Sixteenth Century," in *Jewish Thought in the Sixteenth Century*, ed. Bernard Dov Cooperman. Cambridge, Mass, 1983.

Kaplan, Mordecai M. *Communings of the Spirit: The Journals of Mordecai M. Kaplan, Volume I: 1913-1934*, ed. Mel Scult. Detroit, 2001.

Kasher, Moshe Shelomo and J.J. Blacherowitz (ed.), *Perushei Rishonim le-Masekhet Avot*. Jerusalem, 1973.

[Kayyara, Shim'on]. *Sefer Halakhot Gedolot*, ed. Azriel Hildesheimer. Jerusalem, 1971; Makhon Yerushalayim edition. Jerusalem, 1992.

Kimelman, Reuven. "*Birkat Ha-Minim* and the Lack of Evidence for an Anti-Christian Jewish Prayer in Late Antiquity." In *Jewish and Christian Self-Definition*, ed. Sanders, Baumgarten, and Mendelson. Vol. 2. Philadelphia, 1981.

Klausner, Israel. *Toledot ha-Agudah Nes Ziyonah be-Volozhin: Te'udot u-Mismakhim*. Jerusalem, 1954.

———. *Vilna: "Jerusalem of Lithuania," 1881-1939*. Hebrew. 2 vols. Lohamei ha-Geta'ot, 1983.

Kook, Abraham Isaac Hakohen. *Be'er Eliyahu*. In *Sefer ha-Gra*, ed. Judah Leib Maimon. Jerusalem, 1954. Part Two: *Hilkhot 'Edut* and *Hilkhot Halva'ah*. Jerusalem 2000.

BIBLIOGRAPHY

——. *Eder ha-Yekar*. 1906. Reprinted Jerusalem, 1985.

——. *'Eyn Ayah*, ed. Ya'akov Filber. 4 vols. Jerusalem, 1987-2000.

——. *Ginzei Rayah*. Vol. 3. n.p., n.d.

——. *Hartsa'at Harav*. Jerusalem, 1921.

——. *Hosafot le-Orot ha-Torah*, alternatively entitled *'Al Penimiyut ha-Torah* Edited by Zevi Yehudah Hakohen Kook and disseminated in stencil by Shelomo Hakohen Aviner. Reprinted in Rabbi Moshe Yehiel Zuriel, *Otsrot ha-RAYaH*, vol. 2. Rishon Lezion, 2002.

——. *Igrot ha-RAYaH*, ed. Zevi Yehudah Hakohen Kook, Vol. 1. Jerusalem, 1923.

——. *Igrot ha-RAYaH*. New Series. 4 vols. Vols. 1-3 edited by Zevi Yehudah Hakohen Kook. Vols. 1-2. Jerusalem, 1961. Vol. 3. Jerusalem, 1965. Vol. 4. Edited by Ya'akov Filber. Jerusalem, 1984.

——. *'Ikvei ha-Tson*. 1906. Reprinted Jerusalem, 1985.

——. *Kevatsim me-Khetav Yad Kodsho*, ed. Boaz Ofen. Vol. 1. Jerusalem, 2006. Vol. 2. Jerusalem, 2008.

——. "Le-Mahalakh ha-Ide'ot be-Yisrael," *Ha-'Ivri*, 5672/1912, nos. 9-12. Reprinted in the first edition of *Igrot ha-Rayah* (1923); and in the expanded edition of *Orot* (1950).

——. *Li-Nevukhei ha-Dor*, ed. Shahar Rahmani. Tel-Aviv, 2014.

——. *Ma'amrei ha-RAYaH*. Vol. 1, ed. Elisha Langenauer and David Landau. Jerusalem, 1980. Vol. 2, ed. Elisha Aviner (Langenauer). Jerusalem, 1984.

——. *Mishpat Kohen*. Jerusalem, 1937; reprinted Jerusalem, 1985.

——. "Ha-Neshamot shel 'Olam ha-Tohu" ("The Souls of the World of Chaos"), *Ha-Tarbut ha-Yisraelit*. 1913. Reprinted in 1950 edition of *Orot*.

——. *Orot*, ed. Zevi Yehudah Hakohen Kook. Jerusalem, 1920. Expanded edition Jerusalem, 1950; reprinted Jerusalem, 1985.

——. *Orot: The Annotated Translation of Rabbi Abraham Isaac Kook's Seminal Work*. Introduction, translation and notes by Bezalel Naor. Northvale, NJ, 1993. [Based on text of 1st edition, Jerusalem, 1920.]

——. *Orot ha-Emunah*, ed. Moshe Gurevitz. Brooklyn, NY, 1985. Second corrected edition. Jerusalem, 1998.

——. *Orot ha-Kodesh*. ed. David Cohen. 4 vols. Vol. 2. Jerusalem, 1964.

———. *Orot ha-Teshuvah*, ed. Zevi Yehudah Hakohen Kook. Jerusalem, 1924.

———. *Orot ha-Torah*, ed. Zevi Yehudah Hakohen Kook. Jerusalem, 1940.

———. *Pinkas Yod-Gimmel*. Jerusalem, 2004.

———. *Resh Millin*. London, 1917. Reprinted Jerusalem, 1985.

———. *Rihata de-Hakla'i*. In Hayyim Hezekiah Medini, *Sedei Hemed*. Reprinted as appendix to Abraham Isaac Hakohen Kook, *'Ittur Soferim*. Jerusalem, 1974.

———. *Shabbat ha-Arets*. 1910. Reprinted Jerusalem, 1985.

———. *Shemonah Kevatsim*. 2 vols. 2nd edition. Jerusalem, 2004.

———. *Siddur 'Olat RAYaH*, ed. Zevi Yehudah Hakohen Kook. 2 vols. Jerusalem, 1939. Reprinted Jerusalem, 1989.

———. "*Te'udat Yisrael u-Le'umiyuto*" ("The Destiny of Israel and Its Nationalism"), *Ha-Peless* 5661/1901; reprinted in Moshe Yehiel Zuriel, *Otserot ha-Rayah*, Vols. 1-2. Tel-Aviv, 1988.

———. "*Zer'onim*" ("Seminal Ideas"). In *Ha-Tarbut ha-Yisraelit*. 1913.

Kook, Zevi Yehudah Hakohen. *Judaism and Christianity* (Hebrew), ed. Shelomo Hayyim Hakohen Aviner. Jerusalem, 2001.

———. *Li-Netivot Israel*. 2 vols. Jerusalem, 1967-1979. 2nd edition. Beit El, 2002.

———. *Li-Shelosha be-Ellul*. Vol. 1. Jerusalem, 1938. Vol. 2. Jerusalem, 1947. Both vols. reprinted Jerusalem, 1978.

———. "*Ha-Tarbut ha-Yisraelit*" ("The Israelite Civilization"). In *Ha-Tarbut ha-Yisraelit* (journal by same name). 1913. Reprinted in *Li-Netivot Yisrael*, Vol. 1.

———. *Zemah Zevi: Letters of Rabbi Zevi Yehudah Hakohen Kook*. Jerusalem, 1991.

Kramer, Elijah ben Solomon (Gaon of Vilna). *Be'ur ha-Gra* on *Orah Hayyim*. Shklov, 1803.

Kupfer, Ephraim. "Concerning the Cultural Image of German Jewry and Its Rabbis in the Fourteenth and Fifteenth Centuries" (Hebrew), *Tarbiz* 42 (1972-1973).

Lampert, Zevi Hirsch. *Piskei ha-Gra*. Vilna, 1904.

Lampronti, Isaac. *Pahad Yitzhak*. Venice, 1750.

Lasker, Daniel J. "Jewish Philosophical Polemics in Ashkenaz," in *Contra Iudaeos: Ancient and Medieval Polemics Between Christians and Jews*, ed. Ora Limor and Guy G. Stroumsa. Tübingen, 1996.

Lazarus-Yafeh, Hava, ed. *The Majlis: Interreligious Encounters in Medieval Islam.* Wiesbaden, 1999.

Leiman, Shnayer Z. "The *Ba'al Teshuvah* and the Emden-Eibeschuetz Controversy," *Judaic Studies* 1 (1985).

Levin, Joshua Heschel. *'Aliyot Eliyahu.* Vilna, 1856. Jerusalem, 1989.

Lewin, Benjamin Menashe. *Otsar ha-Ge'onim: Berakhot.* Haifa, 1928.

Libson, Gideon. *Jewish and Islamic Law: A Comparative Study of Custom During the Geonic Period.* Cambridge, MA, 2003.

———. "Parallels Between Maimonides and Islamic Law," *The Thought of Moses Maimonides: Philosophical and Legal Studies*, ed. I. Robinson, L. Kaplan and J. Bauer. Lewiston, NY, 1990.

———. "Two Sureties: A Comparative Study of R. Shmuel ben Hofni Gaon, Maimonides and Analogous Muslim Legal Literature" (Hebrew), *Shnaton ha-Mishpat ha-Ivri* 11-12 (1984-1986).

Lieberman, Saul. "The Publication of the *Mishnah*," in idem, *Hellenism in Jewish Palestine.* New York and Jerusalem, 1994.

Liebes, Yehuda. "Mysticism and Reality: Towards a Portrait of the Martyr and Kabbalist, R. Samson Ostropoler." In *Jewish Thought in the Seventeenth Century*, ed. I. Twersky and B. Septimus. Cambridge, Mass., 1987.

———. "The Self-Perception of the Gaon of Vilna and his Attitude towards Sabbateanism" (Hebrew). In *The Flint into a Fountain of Waters [Hallamish le-Ma'ayeno Mayim]: Studies in Kabbalah, Jewish Law, Custom and Philosophy Submitted to Prof. Moshe Hallamish*, ed. A. Elqayam and H. Pedaya. Jerusalem, 2016.

———. "*Talmidei ha-Gra, ha-Shabta'ut ve-ha-Nekudah ha-Yehudit*," *Da'at* 50-52 (5763/2003).

Lintop, Pinhas Hakohen. *Kana'uteh de-Pinhas*, ed. Bezalel Naor. Spring Valley, NY, 2013.

Lobel, Diana. *Between Mysticism and Philosophy: Sufi Language of Religious Experience in Judah Ha-Levi's Kuzari.* Albany, 2000.

Löw, Judah (of Prague). *Gevurot Hashem*. Cracow, 1582. Reprinted London, 1954.

Lowenthal, Marvin, ed. *The Diaries of Theodor Herzl*. New York, 1956.

Luria, Isaac. *Likkutei ha-Shas me-ha-ARI z"l*. Zolkiew or Lemberg, ca. 1815; photo offset B'nei Berak, 1972.

Luzzatto, Moses Hayyim. *Kin'at Adonai Tzeva'ot*. 1st edition. Koenigsberg, 1868. 2nd edition. Edited by Samuel Luria. Warsaw, 1888. 3rd edition in *Ginzei Ramhal*, ed. Friedlander. B'nei Berak, 1980.

——. *Ma'amar ha-Ge'ulah*, in *Yalkut Yedi'ot ha-Emet*, ed. Yosef Begun, vol. 2. Tel-Aviv, 1965.

Maccoby, Hyam. *The Mythmaker: Paul and the Invention of Christianity*. New York, 1986.

Maimon (Fishman), Judah Leib. *Sarei ha-Me'ah*. Vol. 1. Jerusalem, 1955.

Maimonides, Abraham. *Commentary to the Pentateuch*, trans. E.J. Wiesenberg. Jerusalem, 1984.

Maimonides, Moses. *Epistle to Yemen*. In *Igrot ha-Rambam*, ed. Yitzhak Shilat. Vol. 1. Jerusalem, 1987. In *Igrot ha-Rambam*, ed. Yosef Kafah. Jerusalem, 1994.

——. *Guide of the Perplexed*, trans. Shlomo Pines. Chicago, 1964.

——. *Igrot ha-Rambam*, ed. Yitzhak Shilat. 2 Vols. Jerusalem, 1987-1988.

——. *Kovets Teshuvot ha-Rambam*. Leipzig, 1859. Part Two: *Igrot ha-Rambam*.

Medini, Hayyim Hezekiah. *Sedei Hemed*. Warsaw, 1896-1911.

Me'iri, Menahem. *Seder ha-Kabbalah*, ed. S.Z. Havlin and A. Shoshana. Cleveland and Jerusalem, 1995.

Menasseh ben Israel. *Nishmat Hayyim*. Amsterdam, 1652.

Messinger, Israel Baruch. *Nitel u-Me'or'otav: Hasifat mekorot, te'amim ve-nimmukim, 'im he'arot ve-tsiyyunim*. Union City, NJ, 2000.

Milikowsky, Chaim. *Seder 'Olam: Critical Edition, Commentary, and Introduction*. 2 vols. Jerusalem, 2013.

Morgenstern, Arie. *Mysticism and Messianism: From Luzzatto to the Vilna Gaon* (Hebrew). Jerusalem, 1999.

Nahmanides, Moses. *Dina de-Garmei* in *Kitvei Rabbenu Moshe ben Nahman*, ed. C.B. Chavel. Jerusalem: 1968.

BIBLIOGRAPHY

———. *Kitvei Rabbenu Moshe ben Nahman*, ed. C.B. Chavel. 2 vols. Jerusalem, 1968.

———. *Sefer ha-Mitsvot le-ha-Rambam 'im Hassagot ha-Ramban*, ed. C.B. Chavel. Jerusalem, 1981.

———. *Torat Hashem Temimah*, in *Kitvei Rabbenu Moshe ben Nahman*, ed. C.B. Chavel. Jerusalem, 1968.

———. *Viku'ah ha-Ramban (Milhamot Hashem)* in *Kitvei Rabbenu Moshe ben Nahman*, ed. C.B. Chavel. Jerusalem, 1968.

Naor, Bezalel. *Ben Shanah Shaul*. Jerusalem, 1995.

———. "*Du-Partsufin shel ha-Meshihiyut*" ("The Two Faces of Messianism"), in Bezalel Naor. *Avirin*. Jerusalem, 1980.

———."*Gilgulei ketav-yad 'Adir ba-Marom' le-Ramhal she-hayah be-ba'alut mishpahat ha-GRA*," *Sinai*, Tishrei-Heshvan 5759/1999.

———. *Lights of Prophecy* (*Orot ha-Nevu'ah*). New York, 1990.

———. "Plumbing Rav Kook's Panentheism," in *Engaging Modernity: Rabbinic Leaders and the Challenge of the Twentieth Century*, ed. Moshe Z. Sokol. Northvale, NJ, 1997.

———. "Rav Kook's Role in the Rebirth of Aggadah," in *Orot: A Multidisciplinary Journal of Judaism* 1 (1991).

Neriyah, Moshe Zevi. *Bi-Sdeh ha-RAYaH*. Kefar ha-Ro'eh, 1991.

———. *Likkutei ha-RAYaH*. Kefar ha-Ro'eh, 1990.

———. *Sihot ha-Rayah*. Tel-Aviv, 1979. Second expanded edition. Jerusalem, 2015.

———. *Tal ha-RAYaH*. B'nei Berak, 1993.

Nietzsche, Friedrich. *Beyond Good and Evil*. Leipzig, 1886.

Nissim ben Reuben Gerondi. *Derashot ha-Ran*, ed. Leon A. Feldman. Jerusalem, 1974.

Official, Joseph. *Sefer Yosef Hamekane*, ed. Judah Rosenthal. Jerusalem, 1970.

Orbach, Simha Bunim. *'Ammudei ha-Mahshavah ha-Yisraelit*, 2 vols. Jerusalem, 1971-1972.

'Or la-Yesharim, ed. Shelomo Zalman Landau and Joseph Rabinowitz (of Kovno). Anti-Zionist collection. Warsaw, 1900.

Paz, Yakir. *Mi-Soferim li-Melumadim: Parshanut Hazal la-Mikra le-'Or ha-Parshanut ha-Homerit*. Ph.D. Thesis, Hebrew University, December 2014.

Perlmutter, Amos. *The Life and Times of Menachem Begin*. Garden City, NY, 1987.

Pinhas ben Judah (of Polotsk). *Rosh ha-Giv'ah*. Vilna, 1820.

Rabinowitz, Solomon Hakohen (of Radomsk). *Tif'eret Shelomo*. 2 volumes. Warsaw, 1867, 1869. Reprinted Jerusalem, 1992.

Rabinowitz, Zadok Hakohen (of Lublin). *Dover Zedek*. Piotrkow, 1911.

———. *Likkutei Ma'amarim*. Appended to *Divrei Sofrim*. Lublin 1913.

———. *Mahshevot Haruts*. Piotrkow, 1912.

———. *'Or Zaru'a la-Zaddik*. Lublin, 1929.

———. *Peri Zaddik*. 5 vols. Lublin, 1901-1934.

———. *Poked 'Akarim*. Piotrkow, 1922.

———. *Resisei Laylah*. Lublin, 1903.

———. *Takkanat ha-Shavin*. Piotrkow, 1926. Reprinted Beit El, 1988.

———. *Zidkat ha-Zaddik*. Lublin, 1902.

Rakeffet-Rothkoff, Aaron. *The Rav*. 2 vols. n.p., 1999.

Raphael, Yitzhak, ed. *Zikhron Rayah*. Jerusalem, 1986.

Rawidowicz, Simon. "Israel's Two Beginnings: The First and Second 'Houses.'" In Simon Rawidowicz, *Studies in Jewish Thought*, ed. N. Glatzer. Philadelphia, 1974.

Raz, Simha. *Mal'akhim ki-B'nei Adam*. Jerusalem, 2002.

Rivlin, Hillel (of Shklov). *Kol ha-Tor*, ed. Yosef Rivlin. Jerusalem, 1994.

Rosenak, Avinoam. *The Prophetic Halakhah: Rabbi A.I.H. Kook's Philosophy of Halakhah* (Hebrew). Jerusalem, 2007.

Rossi, Azariah dei-. *Me'or 'Eynayim*. Mantua, 1574.

Rotenberg, Shelomo Hakohen. *Toldot 'Am 'Olam*. Vol. 2. Brooklyn, NY, 1972.

Sa'adyah Gaon. *Beliefs and Opinions* (Judeo-Arabic). Hebrew translation by Yosef Kafah. Jerusalem, 1993.

Sartre, Jean-Paul. *Nausea*. Paris, 1938.

Schäfer, Peter. *Jesus in the Talmud*. Princeton, 2007.

Schatz-Uffenheimer, Rivkah. "The Contribution of Rav Kook's Philosophy to Modern Jewish Thought" (Hebrew) in *Yovel Orot*, ed. Benjamin Ish-Shalom. Jerusalem, 1985.

Schick, Isaac (of Karlin). *Keren Orah*. Warsaw, 1884. Reprinted Jerusalem, 2003.

Schiffman, Lawrence H. "At the Crossroads: Tannaitic Perspectives on the JewishChristian Schism." In *Jewish and Christian SelfDefinition*, ed. Sanders, Baumgarten and Mendelson. Vol. 2. Philadelphia, 1981. Reprinted in *Essential Papers on Judaism and Christianity in Conflict, From Late Antiquity to the Reformation*, ed. J. Cohen. New York and London, 1991.

Schirmann, Hayyim. *Yehudah Halevi: Shirim Nivharim*. Jerusalem, 1963.

Schneersohn, Shalom Dov Baer. *Ha-Ketav ve-ha-Mikhtav*. New York, 1917.

———. *Kuntress u-Ma'ayan mi-Beit Hashem*. Brooklyn, NY, 1958.

Schwarz, Hayyim Avihu, ed. *Mi-Tokh ha-Torah ha-Go'elet: Lectures of Rabbi Zevi Yehudah Hakohen Kook*. 4 vols. Jerusalem, 1989-1991.

Sefer ha-Yovel li-Mekhon Harry Fischel. Jerusalem, 1935.

Shishkes, Shaul. *Shevil ha-Yashar*. Vilna, 1839.

Shmidman, Michael A. "The 'Abot commentary' of R. Shem Tob ben Joseph ibn Shem Tob." In Reverence, Righteousness, and "Rahamanut": Essays in Memory of Rabbi Dr. Leo Jung. Ed. by Jacob J. Schacter. Northvale, NJ, 1992.

Shulman, Shmuel Baruch. *Ha-Rayah Kook*. Jerusalem, 1976.

Sklar, Aryeh. "'Lovers of Humanity': Rav Kook, Christianity, and the Ongoing Censorship of His Writings." *Kol Hamevaser: The Jewish Thought Magazine of the Yeshiva University Student Body*, March 22, 2015.

Sklare, David. *Samuel ben Hofni Gaon and His Cultural World: Texts and Studies*. Leiden, 1996.

Soloveitchik, Haym. "Interview with Professor Haym Soloveitchik by Rabbi Yair Hoffman," *Five Towns Jewish Times*, Wednesday, January 8, 2014.

———. "Religious Law and Change: The Medieval Ashkenazic Example," *AJS Review* 12:2 (Fall 1987).

Sonne, Isaiah. "*Tiyyulim be-historiyah u-bibliografia*," in *Sefer ha-Yovel li-Khevod Alexander Marx*. Philadelphia, 1950.

Sperber, Daniel. *Greek in Talmudic Palestine*. Ramat Gan, 2012.

Spinoza, Benedictus. *Tractatus Theologico-Politicus*. Amsterdam, 1670.

Starelitz, Shim'on. *Me-ha-Makor*. Jerusalem, 1969.

Sternhartz, Nathan. *Hayyei Moharan*. Lemberg, 1874.

Ta-Shema, Israel Moshe. "Halakha and Reality: The Tosafist Experience," in *Rashi et la culture juive en France du Nord au moyen age*, ed. Dahan, Nahon and Nicolas. Paris, 1997.

———. *Rabbi Zerahiah Halevi Ba'al ha-Ma'or u-B'nei Hugo: Le-Toledot ha-Sifrut ha-Rabbanit be-Provence*. Jerusalem, 1992.

Tchernowitz, Chaim (pseudonym "Rav Tsa'ir"). *Pirkei Hayyim: Autobiografia*. New York, 1954.

Toledot Yeshu: The Life Story of Jesus. Anonymous work edited by Meerson and Schäfer. 2 vols. (Tübingen, 2014).

Tropper, Amram. *Wisdom, Politics, and Historiography: Tractate Avot in the Context of the Graeco-Roman Near East*. Oxford and New York, 2004.

Twersky, Isadore. "Law and Spirituality in the Seventeenth Century: A Case Study in Rabbi Yair Hayyim Bacharach," in *Jewish Thought in the Seventeenth Century*, ed. Isadore Twersky and Bernard Septimus. Cambridge, Mass, 1987.

———. *Rabad of Posquières*. Cambridge, Mass, 1962.

———. "The *Shulhan 'Aruk*: Enduring Code of Jewish Law," in *The Jewish Expression*, ed. Judah Goldin. New Haven, 1976.

Urbach, E.E. *The Tosaphists: Their History, Writings and Methods (Ba'alei ha-Tosafot)*. 5th Enlarged Edition. Jerusalem, 1986.

Vital, Hayyim. *'Ets Hayyim*. Warsaw, 1891.

———. *Sha'ar ha-Mitsvot*, ed. Ze'ev Wolf Ashkenazi and Menahem Menchin Heilperin. Jerusalem, 1905.

Waxman, Meyer. *A History of Jewish Literature*. Vol. 1. New York, 1938.

Weiss, Isaac Hirsch. *Dor Dor ve-Doreshav*. Vienna, 1891.

Ya'avets, Joseph. *Yesod ha-Emunah*. Piotrkow, 1911.

Yuval, Israel Jacob. *Scholars in Their Time: The Religious Leadership of German Jewry in the Late Middle Ages*. Jerusalem, 1988.

Zimmels, H.J. *Ashkenazim and Sephardim*. London, 1958.

Zuriel, Moshe Yehiel. *Otserot ha-Rayah*. 1st edition. 4 vols. Tel-Aviv, 1988-Ashdod, 1993. 2nd edition. 7 vols. Rishon LeZion, 2002-2016.

Index of Primary Sources

Bible

Genesis
1:31   104n209, 158n305, 159n306
15:15   87n166
18:19   92n177
25:25   40n60
28:17   35n27
32:26   200n205
45:5   40n53
45:7   40n53
46:28   177n58
50:20   40n53

Exodus
19:4   104n207
19:6   120n243
32:16   116n238

Leviticus
19:17   25n16
26:12   102n202

Numbers
23:9   39n51

Deuteronomy
4:6   93n178
6:5   114n229
7:26   81n149
10:20   71n128
32:9   43n70
32:12   39n50
32:6   116n239

Joshua
7:9   179n103

Judges
2:10   87n166

1 Samuel
16:12   40n60

2 Samuel
7:23   138n279
14:14   87n165
23:1   95n185

1 Kings
11:28   41n64
14:9   41n65
22:35   46n79

2 Kings
22:20   87n166
23:25   46n82
23:29-30 46n83

Isaiah
2:3   139n282, 145n292
2:6   149n297

2:17-18	107n216	31:20	98n192	**Zechariah**	
3:8	42n68	50:19	99n196	8:22-23	66n119
11:10	41n63			9:14	79n146
16:3	49n96	**Ezekiel**		12:10	44n76, 59n113
24:20	91n174	37:15-19	48n85	12:11	38n43
24:21	91n174	37:19	41n61		
24:23	160	37:25	39n48	**Malachi**	
30:26	160			1:5	108n218
32:18	145n291	**Hosea**			
33:17	147n295	2:4	97n188	**Psalms**	
35:10	110n221	2:18-22	97n189	14:7	98n193
40:2	109n219	4:1	91n173	27:1	76n137,
43:21	107n215	5:5	42n67		105n211
44:23	99n196	7:8	41n66, 48n87	33:11	122n246
46:13	48n90	7:11	48n89	47:4-5	41n62
49:13	99n196	10:1	96n186	78:60	40n59
52:9	99n196	11:4	52n101	89:15	66n120
53:5	36			89:52	44n74
54:1	115n234	**Amos**		90:17	111n225
60:4	141n286	2:11	201n217	102:19	112n226
60:5	141n286			108:9	46n80
62:2	75n135	**Micah**		114:2	40n58
62:3	48n91	7:15	56n110	119:126	79n145
				119:165	142n287
Jeremiah		**Habakkuk**		122:5	95n185
2:13	48n88,	2:3	77n140	141:7	43n71
	150n298	2:4	77n141		
2:21	98n191	2:19	92n176	**Proverbs**	
16:19	119			7:26	115n236
17:12	99n194	**Zephaniah**		11:10	162n307
30:18	147n295	3:9	59n112, p. 118	27:8	94n181
31:8	110n220				
31:11	74n134,	**Haggai**		**Song of Songs**	
	77n139	1:8	114n231	7:14	102n201

INDEX OF PRIMARY SOURCES

Lamentations
1:7   34n25
2:9   72n129
3:6   114n233

Daniel
8:14   79n147
9:24   49n93
11:14   156n303

Ezra
6:21   101n198

Nehemiah
10:29   101n198

1 Chronicles
17:21   138n279
29:23   95n185

2 Chronicles
34:28   87n166
35:20-25 46n83

Rabbinic Literature

Megillat Ta'anit
140   143n290

MISHNAH
Berakhot
4:2   143n288

Ketubot
7:6   110n222

Sanhedrin
10:1   87n169

Avot
1:12   52n99
1:6   182n127
1:16   182n127
4:22   122n245
5:17   73n133
5:19   75n136
6:2   116n238

Yadayim
3:5   95n183

TOSEFTA
Shabbat
12:9   199n205

Hullin
2:6   229n301

TALMUD YERUSHALMI
Berakhot
1:1   56n109
7:3   228n30

Shabbat
12:4   199n205
14:4   229n301

Ta'anit
2:6   53n103
4:5   62n115

TALMUD BAVLI
Berakhot
10a   115n235
12a   33n23
12b   116n239
17b   183n127
27b   185n128
28b   34n24, 183n127
30b   35n28
33a   35n28
54a   114n230, 203n235
61b   185n128
64a   146n293

Shabbat
104b   199n205, 105n212, 155n301

'Eruvin
21b   185n128, 102n201

Pesahim
49   104n208
22b   71n128
87a   97n187

253

Yoma
9b   71n126
21b   85n161,
     114n231, n232
54a   99n195
69b   114n228

Sukkah
52a   36n33, 39n47,
       44n75, 59n113

Megillah
3a   38n45, n46
14a   199n205

Mo'ed Katan
28b   38n45, 46n79

Yevamot
45b   155n302

Nazir
23b   52n102

Sotah
22b   106n214
36b   40n54, n55
47a   184n127

Gittin
56b   35n29
57a   71n127,
       191n143, n144
58a   98n190
60b   79n145

Kiddushin
20b   53n105

Bava Kama
41b   71n128

Bava Batra
4a   49n95

Sanhedrin
21b-22a   70n122
39b   40n57
43b   229n301
64a   114n228
67a   155n301,
           229n301
98b   49n92
99b   149n296
102a   42n69, 56n108
102b   46n78, n81
104b   46n80
107b   184n127

'Avodah Zarah
3b   55n107
9a   196n11
19b   115n236,
       200n206, 205n241
27b   230n301

Horayot
14a   146n293

Menahot
29b   185n128
110a   195n170

Hullin
60b   94n180,
       101n199
124a   55n106

'Arakhin
16b   25n17
29a   113n227

EXTRA-TALMUDIC TRACTATES
Avot de-Rabbi Nathan
Ch. 5   193n162

Semahot
2:10   166n4

Soferim
1:7   228n290

HALAKHIC MIDRASHIM
Sifré
'Ekev   98n192

AGGADIC MIDRASHIM
Midrash Rabbah
Genesis Rabbah
48:7   40n52
58:5   182n125

INDEX OF PRIMARY SOURCES

63:8   40n60
73:7   40n56

Leviticus Rabbah
32:5   186n128

Ecclesiastes Rabbah
1:8   230n301

Midrash Tanhuma
Lekh Lekha 9   40n52

Yalkut Shim'oni
Joshua 7:9   53n103

Sefer Yetsirah
1:5   63n118

Kuzari
    84n157, 85n158
II, 48   202n223
III, 7   202n223

Maimonides
Commentary to Mishnah
Avot
1:3   193, 194n162

Mishneh Torah
Talmud Torah
3:13   55n107

Teshuvah
3:11   166, 167n4
8:3   194n167
9:1   198n204

Tefillah
2:1   183n127

Evel
1:10   166n4

Melakhim
11:2   185n128
11:4   119n241, 230n303

Zohar
Volume I
4a   50n97, 53n104

Volume II
9b   193n159
20a   95n184
85a   95n182
216a   111n224

Volume III
37b   95n184
107a   201n209
135b   196n171
221a   193n159
276b   36n34

Tikkunei Zohar
Introduction   94n181
tikkun 8   161
tikkun 22   105n212
tikkun 25   95n184
tikkun 26   95n184

SHULHAN 'ARUKH
Yoreh De'ah
340:5   167n4
345:5   21n4

Index of Subjects

Ashkenazic Jewry, 13, 125, 126, 127, 128, 130, 133, 134, 136, 137, 138, 207n248, 209n249, 211n254, 213n259, 214n259, 215n260, 219n263, 223n271; codification, 125, 126, 210n253; philosophy, 223n271. *See also* Dialectic Form

Bible criticism, 153, 154
Buddhism, 105; evil and, 162; Rav Kook on, 157-162

Central Yeshivah (Yeshivat Merkaz Harav), 140, 144, 150, 227n284. *See also* Yeshivot
Christianity, 11, 12, 71, 113, 183n127, 184n127, 191n148; Abraham Abulafia on, 204-205n240; blame for Spinozism, 113, 116; lie about Rav Kook's positive feelings toward, 62, 164-165; Maimonides on the origin of, 155-156, 205n241; Rabbi Akiva as a nemesis of, 185-186n128; view of Rabbi Isaac Haver, 200n205; view of Rabbi Menahem Mendel of Shklov, 191n143; view of Rabbi Zevi Yehudah Kook, 118, 119, 120, 121, 122, 123; view of Rav Kook, 164, 198n205, 199n205, 205n241, 230n311, 230n312; views of Rabbi Joshua ben Perahia and Rabban Gamliel, 183n127
Commandments, 21, 27, 29, 31, 34, 45, 49, 68, 73, 84, 99, 101, 110, 111, 119, 122, 150, 151, 156, 166n4, 167n4; non-rational, 110, 193n157; practical observance of, 83, 86, 187n132, 230n312. *See also* Ten Commandments.

INDEX OF SUBJECTS

Critical Form (*tsurah bikoratit*), 134, 135, 136, 137, 138, 207n248

Degel Yerushalayim, 37, 175n41
Dialectic Form (*tsurah pilpulit*), 125, 134, 135, 136, 137, 138, 207n248, 209n249, 213n257, 217n262
Divine idea (*ha-idea ha-elohit*), 83, 85, 88, 94, 95, 96, 97, 98, 99, 100, 101, 102, 103, 104, 105, 106, 157, 158, 197n200; mankind and the, 89-92; in Israel, 92-94. *See also* National idea, Religious idea

Evil, 25, 26, 29, 32, 50, 53, 59, 64, 70, 75, 96, 100, 160, 161, 182n124, 203n237; Buddhism and, 162
Exile, 28, 33, 43, 44, 45, 49, 61, 65, 70, 73, 74, 76, 84, 108, 109, 110, 112, 114, 122, 141, 163, 165, 192n153, 217n262; situation in, 98-100

False messiahs, 61, 62, 72
First Temple Period (First Commonwealth), 69, 85, 86, 88, 95, 100, 101, 103, 109, 185n127, 193n159, 194n163, 202n231

Ger toshav (resident alien), 117

Ha-Peless (anti-Zionist journal), 33, 52, 179n100. *See also* Zionism (Jewish nationalism)

Hasidism, 25, 61, 62, 72, 73, 187n132, 188n133, 189n138
Hebrew University, 18, 227n284; letter to Prof. Abraham Fraenkel concerning faculty appointment, 151; poster (in Volkovisk) comparing opening to Third Temple, 146-148; Rav Kook's address at the opening of the Mount Scopus campus, 24, 139-145, 149-150
Histadrut Yerushalayim (Jerusalem Organization), 37

Idolatry, 14n4, 41, 70, 78, 79, 82, 114, 115, 179n105, 201n206, 205n241, 227n284
Individuality, 85, 86, 87, 101, 102, 103, 193n162, 194n163
Islam, 11, 12, 131, 174n34, 191n143, 205n241, 224n272

K'nesset Israel (Ecclesia Israel), 58, 65, 67, 72, 73, 76, 93, 96, 99, 104, 108-109, 111-112, 115, 157, 182n124, 193n162, 200n206, 205n241

Mishneh Torah, 126, 127, 128, 131, 210n253, 211n255, 214n259
Mitnagdim, 73, 189n138

National Idea (*ha-idea ha-le'umit*), 83, 85, 95, 96, 97, 98, 99, 100, 105, 106, 107, 109, 110; in Israel, 92-94; mankind and, 89-92. *See also* Divine idea, Religious idea

National Religious Party (NRP), 88

National renascence, 33, 47, 108, 109, 132, 133, 134, 138, 227n284

Nes Ziyonah (secret Zionist society in Volozhin Yeshivah), 170-171n31

Paganism, 12, 14n4, 46, 64, 70, 71, 81, 92, 94, 95, 98, 100, 104, 105, 115, 116, 117, 119, 121, 158, 159, 182n125, 205n241

Particularism, 47, 180n113

Peshat (Simple meaning of text), 128, 217n262

Philosophy, 17, 18, 25, 63, 66, 116, 130, 145, 166n1, 192n153

Pilpul (dialectic), 136, 138, 206n247, 208n249, 217n262, 218n262, 220n265, 222n269, 223n270

Prophecy, 12, 65, 69, 70, 74, 76, 121, 156, 181n121, 191n143, 200n205, 218n262

Psyche: Ba'al Shem Tov, 73; collective, 63; cosmic, 67, 68; divine, 67, 68; existential, 64; Gaon Rabbi Elijah, 73; general, 63, 64; *K'nesset Israel*, 65; national, 69, 74; of existence, 64; personal, 71; spiritual, 64; strange, 70; unrefined, 68

Religious idea (*ha-idea ha-datit*), 83, 85, 100, 101, 104, 105, 107, 109. *See also* Divine idea, National idea

Scientific culture, 64, 100, 123, 143, 145

Second Temple Period (Second Commonwealth), 71, 85, 86, 87, 88, 100, 101, 109, 114, 116, 181n121, 182n126, 185n127, 193n159, 193n162, 194n163, 197n201, 202n231, 202n235

Sephardic Jewry, 13, 125, 126, 127, 128, 129, 130, 134, 137, 207n248, 208n249, 209n250, 216n261, 222n269; codification, 125, 127, 131, 210n253; encyclopedists, 129, 130, 222n269; *Hiddushim*, 127, 128, 137, 212n257; philosophy, 130; summarists (*ha-me'assefim ha-Sefaradim*), 129, 223n270. *See also* Critical Form.

Shekhinah (divine indwelling or divine presence), 85, 94, 103, 111, 114, 161 YES, 202n231

Shulhan 'Arukh, 126, 127, 129, 210n252, 214n259

Sinai and Golgotha, 62, 81-82

Spinozism, 113, 116, 203n237, 204n237, 204n238

INDEX OF SUBJECTS

Spirituality, 39, 41, 43, 63, 64, 65, 66, 68, 69, 70, 74, 75, 76, 102, 104, 120, 122, 157

Ten Commandments, 33-34. *See also* Commandments
Teshuvah (return), 48, 55, 152
Third Temple, 93n159
Tikkun (fixing), 54, 55, 79
Torah, 12, 28, 29, 30, 31, 39, 49, 52, 53, 54, 55, 56, 61, 68, 73, 76, 79, 84, 87, 88, 100, 102, 119, 122, 139, 140, 142, 143, 145, 146, 147, 149, 150, 151, 156, 163, 167n9, 169n12, 171n31, 172n31, 174n32, 177n58, 187n132, 189n138, 192n153, 198n205, 199n205, 208n249, 212n256, 215n260, 217n262, 218n262, 221n267, 227n284, 228n293; commandments of, 84, 110, 119; denial of, 32; destruction of, 32; deviation from, 21, 27, 29; ethics of, 104; hatred of, 48; light of, 49, 53, 227n284; mysteries of, 76, 88, 112; negation of, 29, 32-33, 34, 45; observance of, 27, 28, 31, 33, 43, 56, 98, 99, 101; sages of, 47; tents of, 144; translation to Greek, 143
Tosafists, 126, 128, 214n259, 215n260
Tsaddikim, 18, 72, 75, 152, 169n12, 189n138
Tunisian Jewry, 128

Tur (*Arba'ah Turim*), 127, 210n252, 210n253, 211n254, 211n255, 212n256, 213n259
Two Houses of Israel. *See* Ashkenazic Jewry, Sephardic Jewry

Universalism, 42, 43, 45, 47, 57, 59, 120, 180n113, 181n113

Yeshivot, 140, 142, 144-145, 150, 171n31; 'Ets Hayyim, Jerusalem, 171n31; Slabodka, 171n31; Volozhin, 170n31, 191n150, 208n249. *See also* Central Yeshivah

Zionism (Jewish nationalism), 17, 18, 21, 22, 23, 47, 52, 53, 54, 57, 84, 146, 168n9, 170n31, 171n31, 172n31, 191n150, 192n156; anti-, 30, 35, 165, 168n9, 168n10, 170n31, 172n31; debate between Rabbi Shalom Dov Baer (RaShaB) Schneersohn and Rabbi Solomon Aronsohn regarding, 168n10; Hebrew University and, 139; position of Rav Kook on, 27-35, 61, 84, 86, 111, 165, 170n31, 171n31; 172n31, 175n41; religious, 31, 32, 171n31, 191n150; secular, 83, 140, 192n153; Shalom Dov Baer Schneersohn on, 23. *See also* Ha-Peless

Index of Names

Aaron, 52
'Abd al-Rahman III, 130
Abraham, 182n125
Abraham of Preil and Sebezh (great-grandfather of Rav Kook), 172, 173n32
Abulafia, Abraham, 175n38, 204n240
Adler, Menashe, 197n195
Adret, Solomon ben Abraham ibn (Rashba), 128, 213n257
Ahab, 35, 39, 45-46
Ahad ha-'Am (Asher Ginsberg), 194n163
Akiva, 25, 62, 71, 72, 185n128, 186n128, 229n301
Albo, Joseph, 186n128
Aleksandrov, Samuel, 86, 161, 171, 172n31
Alfasi, Isaac, 127, 128, 129, 211n256, 232

Alfonso X, 130
Alkalay, Judah Hai, 192n156
Allenby, Edmund, 139, 142
Al-Sevilli, Yom Tov ben Abraham (Ritba), 128, 213n257
Aristotle, 130
Aronsohn, Solomon, 168n10
Asher ben Yehiel (ROSh), 210n254, 211n254, 211n256, 219n263, 220n263
Aviner, Shelomo Hayyim Hakohen, 159, 199n205
Azulai, Hayyim Yosef David (HIDA), 214n260

Ba'al Shem Tov, Israel, 62, 73, 188n138, 232
Bacharach, Moses Samson, 219n263
Bacharach, Ya'ir Hayyim, 219n263, 220n263
Balfour, James, 139, 142, 147

INDEX OF NAMES

Baruch, Joshua Boaz, 209n252, 210n252
Batlan, Zechariah, 169n12
Begin, Dov Ze'ev, 22
Begin, Menachem 22
Benayahu, Meir, 210n253
Ben Hadad (King of Aram), 46
Ben Koziba (Bar Kokhba), 185n128
Ben Stada, 199n205, 229n301
Berlin (Bar Ilan), Meir, 83, 191n150
Berlin, Naphtali Zevi Yehudah ("Neziv" of Volozhin), 129, 177n59, 191n150, 192n150, 208n249, 218n263
Beruriah, 114, 202n235
Bibas, Judah, 192n156
Bil'am, 79, 164, 191n144, 203n237
Bismarck, Otto von, 203n237

Chajes, Zvi Hirsch, 203n235
Charlop, Zevulun, 226n281
Cohen, Abraham ("Baba Rabbi"), 215n260
Cohen, David (*Gevul Ya'abets*) 203n235
Cohen, David (the "Nazirite"), 174n35, 203n237, 204n238, 206n242
Cordovero, Moses, 125, 208n249

David, 33, 39, 40-41, 42, 85, 95, 177n57
Diskin, Isaac Jeruham, 24, 169n12, 169n13

Diskin, [Moses] Joshua [Judah] Leib ("Maharil") (Rabbi of Brisk), 169n12, 181n113
Duran, Profiat, 62

Elijah Gaon of Vilna (Kramer, Elijah) (GRA), 36, 62, 128, 129, 172n32, 173n32, 174n32, 182n124, 188n138, 215n261, 216n261, 216n262, 217n262, 218n262, 218n263, 219n263, 220n264, 220n265, 221n267, 222n267, 232
Elyashiv, Netanel, 167n4
Ephraim, 40, 41, 42, 43, 48
Epstein, Barukh Halevi, 181n114, 187n132
Epstein, Moshe Mordechai, 171n31
Epstein, Yehiel Mikhel Halevi, 181n114
Erlich, Asher, 167n4
Esau, 40, 156, 200n205
Ezra, 33, 70

Feffer, Nehemiah, 216n261
Feinstein, Elijah Halevi (of Pruzhany), 22-23, 167n6
Feinstein, Pesha, 23, 167n6, 167n7
Feldman, Tzvi, 230n311
Fisher, Aaron, 18
Fisher, Shelomo, 18
Frank, Jacob, 61, 62, 72
Fraenkel, Abraham, 151
Freimann, A. H., 210-211n254

Friedlander, Hayyim, 174n34
Friedmann, David Moses (Rebbe of Czortkow), 23-24
Friedmann, Israel (Rebbe of Sadagura), 23
Friedman, Shamma, 214n259

Gamliel I, 182-184n127
Gamliel II, 182-184n127
Gaon, Nissim, 185n128, 202n235
Gerondi, Jonah, 128
Glitzenstein, Shim'on, 218n263
Goldman, Eliezer, 194n163
Greenblatt, Matis, 167n8
Greenhaus, Nahum, 168n9
Grodzenski, Hayyim Ozer, 168n9
Groner, Tsvi, 213n257
Günzberg, Aryeh Leib (author of "Sha'agat Aryeh"), 216n262, 217n262

Hadadrimmon, 35, 38, 39
Hakohen, Shelomo (Dayyan of Vilna), 23, 167n9, 168n9
Haman, 203n237
Harlap, Jacob Moses, 15, 169n12, 172n32, 192n150, 211n256, 212n256, 218n262, 220n264, 226n281, 227n284
Harvey, Warren Zev, 224n273
Haver (Wildmann), Isaac, 200n205
Hayyim of Volozhin, 216n261, 217n262, 219n263, 222n267

Hazan, Joseph Raphael, 209n250, 216n261
Hegel, Georg F., 166n1, 194n163
Hertz, Joseph H., 139
Herzl, Theodor, 18, 21, 22, 23, 24, 26, 35, 37, 38, 52, 54, 56, 140, 169n12, 172n32, 176n42, 178n84
Heschel, Abraham Joshua, 125
Hezekiah, 33
Hirschensohn, Hayyim, 176n42
Hoffman, David Zevi, 184n127
Hoffman, Joshua, 182n125
Horowitz, Pinchas, 219n263
Hutner, Abraham Joshua, 192n152
Hutner, Isaac, 153-154, 228n300, 232

Ibn Gabirol, Solomon, 195n170
Ibn Habib, Levi, 211n254
Ibn Migash, Joseph. See Migash, Joseph ibn
Isaac, 182n125
Isaac ben Abraham of Dampierre (Ritsba), 127
Isaac ben Samuel of Dampierre (Ri), 126
Israel (Ashkenazi) of Shklov, 216n261
Isserles, Moses, 220n263, 223n271

Jacob, 40, 41, 43, 99, 100, 200n205
Jacob ben Asher (Ba'al ha-Turim), 126, 210n253, 210n254, 212n256
Jacob of Kefar Sekhanya, 229n301

INDEX OF NAMES

Jacob of Ramerupt (Rabbenu Tam), 126, 217n262, 229n301
Jaffe, Mordekhai ("Levush"), 223n271
Jawitz, Ze'ev, 167n9
Jeroboam (son of Nebat), 36, 41, 42, 43
Jesse (father of David), 41, 42, 43, 56
Jesus, 12, 18, 61, 62, 78, 118, 155, 156, 164, 183n127, 184n127, 191n144, 204n240, 229n301, 230n301
Jonathan ben Uzziel, 35, 38, 47
Joseph, 36, 40, 41, 43, 46, 57
Joseph ben Judah ibn Shim'on, 212n256, 218n263
Joshua, 33, 55
Joshua ben Perahia, 182n127, 183n127, 184n127
Josiah, 35, 39, 46
Judah, 40, 41, 42, 43, 46, 177n58
Judah Halevi, 88
Judah the Prince, 131

Kafah, Joseph, 190n143
Kalmanson, Elhanan, 62, 81-82
Kanarfogel, Ephraim, 210n253
Kaplan, Mordechai, 226n283
Karelitz, Abraham Isaiah (*Hazon Ish*), 129, 215n260
Karo, Joseph, 126, 127, 129, 210n252, 210n253, 211n254, 211n255

Klein, Menahem, 170n20
Kook, Hava Leah, 192n152
Kook, Samuel, 24, 169n12
Kook, Zevi Yehudah Hakohen, 15, 118-123, 169n12, 169n14, 172n31, 173n32, 174n32, 182n127, 183n127, 189n142, 190n142, 192n150, 192n152, 192n153, 197n200, 199n205, 204n240, 206n242, 216n261, 223n270
Kosovsky, Isaac, 146-148
Kupfer, Ephraim, 223n271, 224n271

Lampronti, Isaac, 222n269
Landau, Elijah, 173n32
Liebes, Yehuda, 191n143, 220n265
Lintop, Pinhas Hakohen, 125, 188n138, 189n138, 208n249, 209n249
Lipschutz, Yaakov Halevi, 168n9
Lobel, Diana, 193n158
Löw, Judah (MaHaRaL of Prague), 17
Luria, Isaac, 125
Luzzatto, Moses Hayyim (RaMHaL), 17, 36, 174n34, 178n73, 190n142
Luzzatto, Samuel David (ShaDaL), 201n217

Maccoby, Hyam, 155
Magnes, Judah, 226n283
Maimon (father of Maimonides), 127

Maimonides, Moses (Rambam), 11, 12, 18, 118, 126, 127, 130, 131, 155-156, 166n4, 205n241, 210n253, 211n255, 213n259, 214n259, 215n260, 218n263, 225n275
Mazuz, Meir, 215n260
Medini, Hayyim Hezekiah, 222n269
Meir, Ya'akov (Rishon le-Zion), 139
Meiri, Menahem ha-, 183n127, 184n127
Meltzer, Isser Zalman, 171n31
Menahem Mendel (Ashkenazi) of Shklov, 191n143, 216n261
Menashe of Ilya, 173n32, 217n262
Messas, Joseph, 149-150
Messiah son of David 36, 37, 39, 43, 44, 46, 57, 59
Messiah son of Joseph 18, 35, 36, 37, 39, 44, 45, 46, 47, 48, 57, 59, 172n32, 174n35
Migash, Joseph ibn, 127, 216n261
Milikowsky, Chaim, 199n205
Milstein, Dov, 62, 78-80, 164
Mohilever, Samuel, 170n26, 171n31
Moses of Coucy, 126, 210n253
Moses, 12, 33, 36, 79, 164, 165, 173n32
Muhammad, 12, 118

Naeh, Abraham Hayyim, 18
Naeh, Barukh, 18
Nahman of Braslav, 25, 206n244

Nahmanides, Moses (Ramban), 127, 128, 137, 205n204, 212n257, 213n257, 215n261
Necho (Pharaoh), 35, 39
Nehemiah, 33
Nehunyah ben Hakanah, 142, 145
Neriyah, Moshe Zevi, 153-154, 173n32, 221n267
Nietzsche, Friedrich, 118, 204n240
Nissim Gerondi (Ran), 213n257

Ovadiah, 177n57

Pandera, 229n301
Paul (Saul) of Tarsus, 86, 155, 200n206
Philo Judaeus, 227n285
Pinhas ha-Dayyan of Alexandria, 218n263 YES
Plotski, Meir Dan (Rabbi of Dvohrt, author "*Keli Hemdah*"), 193n162

Rabinowitz, Akiva Elijah, 179n100
Rabinowitz, Alexander Ziskind (AZaR), 166n4
Rabinowitz, Solomon Hakohen (Rebbe of Radomsk), 187n128
Rabinowitz-Te'omim, Elijah David ("Aderet," Rabbi of Ponevezh, Mir and Jerusalem), 25, 51-56, 179n100
Rabinowitz, Zadok Hakohen (Rebbe of Lublin), 17, 180n113, 181n121, 197n201

INDEX OF NAMES

Rachel, 40
Rakeffet-Rothkoff, Aharon, 218n263
Rakover, Baruch, 222n267
Raphael, Yitzhak, 27
Rashi (Rabbi Shelomo Yitzhaki of Troyes), 34, 183n127, 214n259, 215n260, 224n273, 229n301
Rav Yosef, 38, 49
Rawidowicz, Simon, 194n163
Reines, Jacob Isaac, 171n31
Revel, Bernard, 226n284
Rivlin, Hillel (of Shklov), 36, 174n35
Rotenberg, Shelomo Hakohen, 184n127, 185n127
Ruth, 177n57

Sa'adyah Gaon, 84
Salant, Samuel, 25
Samson of Ostropolye, 187n128
Samuel ben Hofni Gaon, 131
Samuel, Herbert, 139, 142
Sarna, Ezekiel, 152
Sartre, Jean-Paul, 196n172
Schatz-Uffenheimer, Rivka, 203n237
Schneersohn, Hannah Hishia, 168n10
Schneersohn, Israel Noah, 168n10
Schneersohn, Menahem Mendel ("*Zemah Zedek*"), 61, 181n114, 187n132
Schneersohn, Shalom Dov Baer (RaShaB), 23, 168n10, 192n153
Shabbetai Zevi, 61, 72, 174n34

Shach, El'azar Menahem Man, 192n155
Sheinkopf, Moshe Don, 220n263
Shelomit bat Divri, 186n128
Shelomo Zalman of Volozhin, 219n263
Shiskes, Shaul, 219n263
Shneur Zalman of Liozhna and Liadi, 129
Shohetman, Eliav, 210n23
Simon the Amsonite, 62, 72
Sklare, David E., 131
Solomon, 33, 41, 85, 94
Soloveichik, Ahron, 171n31, 215n260
Soloveichik, Moshe, 167n6, 171n31
Soloveichik, Yosef, 167n7, 171n31, 220n264
Soloveitchik, Haym, 128, 213n259, 214n259, 217n262
Soloveitchik, Hayyim (of Brisk), 22, 167n6, 171n31, 209n250, 212n257, 215n260, 220n264
Soloveitchik, Joseph Baer (Rabbi of Boston), 212n257, 217n262, 220n264
Sonne, Isaiah, 210n252
Sonnenfeld, Joseph Hayyim, 18, 169n12
Spinoza, Benedictus (Barukh), 113, 116, 203n237, 204n237
Starelitz, Shim'on, 17

Taïeb, Abraham, 215n260
Ta-Shema, Israel M., 211n256

Tchernowitz, Chaim ("Rav Tsa'ir"), 220n263
Tsarfati, Tsemah, 215n260
Tur-Sinai (Torczyner), Naftali Herz, 154, 228n299
Twersky, Isadore, 211n254, 220n263

Vital, Hayyim, 190n143, 208n249
Weiss, Isaac Hirsch, 206n247
Weizmann, Chaim, 139
Yohanan ben Tortha, 62
Yosef Zundel of Salant, 222n267
Zechariah, 35, 47, 49, 59

www.ingramcontent.com/pod-product-compliance
Lightning Source LLC
Chambersburg PA
CBHW030105240426
43661CB00001B/26